PHILIPS'

POCKET

ATLAS OF THE WORLD

EDITED BY
HAROLD FULLARD, M.Sc.
CARTOGRAPHIC EDITOR

GEORGE PHILIP & SON LIMITED

LONDON

PRINTED IN GREAT BRITAIN BY GEORGE PHILIP AND SON, LIMITED, LONDON

CONTENTS

M. = Millions

WORLD MAPS

1   The World: Air Routes, 1:250M.

2-3   The World, 1:175M.

EUROPE

4-5   Europe, 1:27½M.

6-7   England and Wales, 1:3½M.

8   Scotland, 1:3½M.

9   Ireland, 1:3½M.

10-11   Scandinavia & Finland, 1:9M.
    Inset: Iceland, 1:9M.

12   Denmark, 1:3½M.

13   Switzerland, 1:2½M.

14-15   France and the Low Countries, 1:6M.

16-17   Germany & Austria, 1:5M.

18-19   W. Germany, Benelux and N.E. France, 1:3½M.

20-21   E. France, Switzerland & N.W. Italy, 1:3½M.

22-23   Poland & Czechoslovakia, 1:5M.

24-25   Mediterranean Lands, 1:20M.

26   Spain & Portugal, 1:9M.

27   Greece, Turkey & Cyprus, 1:9M.

28-29   Italy, 1:6M.

30-31   Hungary & the Balkan States, 1:6M.

32-33   Russia in Europe, 1:18M.

34-35   U.S.S.R., 1:40M.

ASIA

36-37   Asia, 1:60M.

38-39   S.W. Asia & the Nile Valley, 1:25M.

40   The Levant, 1:4M.

41   Suez Canal, 1:1M.

42-43   Central Middle East Countries, 1:17½M.

44-45   India, Pakistan, Ceylon & Burma, 1:20M.

46-47   Indo-Gangetic Plain, 1:12M.

48-49 East Indies & Further India, 1:25M.

50-51 China, 1:25M.

52-53 Korea & Japan, 1:12½M.

54-55 Japan, 1:8½M.

PACIFIC OCEAN 56-57 Pacific Ocean, 1:100M.

AUSTRALASIA 58-59 Australia, 1:22½M.

60-61 South East Australia, 1:8M.
Inset Tasmania, 1:8M.

62-63 Australia: East, 1:15M.
Inset New Guinea, 1:20M.

64-65 Australia: West, 1:15M.

66-67 New Zealand: 1:7M.
Inset (a) Fiji & Tonga Is., 1:15M.
(b) Samoa, 1:15M.
(c) New Zealand & its
Antipodes

AFRICA 68-69 Africa, 1:45M.

70-71 West & North West Africa, 1:20M.

72-73 Central & East Africa, 1:18M.

74-75 South Africa, 1:12½M.

N. AMERICA 76-77 North America, 1:40M.

78-79 Canada, 1:27½M.

80 Western Canada, 1:17½M.

81 Eastern Canada, 1:17½M.

82-83 United States, 1:25M.
Insets (a) Alaska, 1:25M.
(b) Hawaiian Is., 1:10M.
(c) Aleutian Is., 1:25M.

84-85 Western United States, 1:15M.

86-87 Eastern United States, 1:15M.

88-89 North Eastern United States,
1:7½M.

90 Mexico, 1:20M.

**CENTRAL
AMERICA** 91 West Indies, 1:20M.

S. AMERICA 92-93 South America, 1:40M.

94-95 South America: Central, 1:16M.

POLAR REGIONS 96 Polar Regions 1:80M.

INDEX

THE WORLD: AIR ROUTES

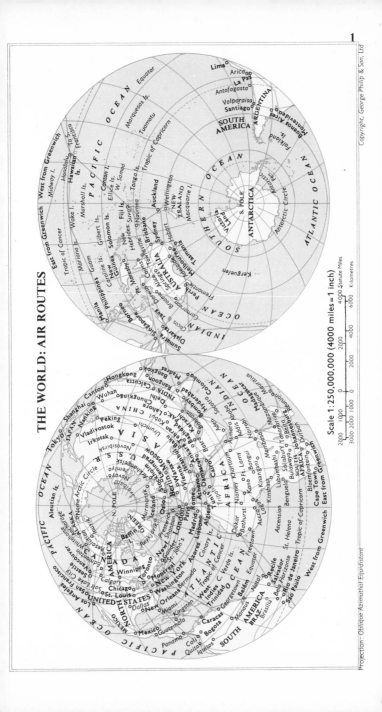

Scale 1:250,000,000 (4000 miles = 1 inch)

Projection: Oblique Azimuthal Equidistant

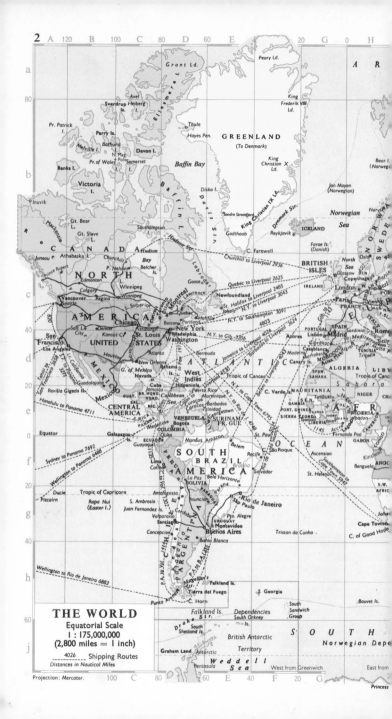

a

80

b

c

40

d

20

e

0

f

20

g

40

h

60

j

Arctic regions / Northern lands

Grant Ld.

Peary Ld.

Axel
Heiberg
Sverdrup Is.
Pr. Patrick I.
Parry Is.
Melville I.
Bathurst
N. Mag.
Pr. of Wales
Pole
Banks I.
Somerset
Victoria I.
Devon I.

King
Frederik VIII
Ld.

Thule
Hayes Pen.

GREENLAND
(To Denmark)

King
Christian X
Ld.

Baffin Bay

Ellesmere I.

Disko I.

A R

Bear I.
(Norwegian)

Inuvik
Mackenzie
Gt. Bear L.
Gt. Slave L.

Southampton I.

King Christian IX Ld.

Sondre Stromfjord

Godthaab

Reykjavik ICELAND

Denmark Str.

C. Farewell

Faroe Is.
(Danish)

Jan Mayen
(Norwegian)

Norwegian
Sea

Norwa

SWEDE

NORWA

Juneau
Athabaska L.
Prince Rupert

CANADA

Churchill
P. Nelson
Edmonton

Hudson
Bay

Belcher
Is.

Baffin I.

Davis Str.

Hudson Str.

Churchill to Liverpool 2936

North
Sea

Oslo

Copenhagen

BRITISH
ISLES

Glasgow

NORTH

Vancouver
Seattle
Salt L. City
San Francisco
Los Angeles

Calgary
Regina
Winnipeg

Superior
L. Winnipeg

Denver
Kansas City

Chicago
St. Louis

AMERICA

UNITED STATES

Atlanta

Houston

New Orleans

Toronto

Montreal

Quebec
St. Lawrence

Pittsburgh

Boston

Portland

New York
Philadelphia
Washington

Goose Bay

Newfoundland

St. John's

Halifax

Quebec to Liverpool 2625
Newfoundland to Liverpool 2485
Halifax to Liverpool 2485
N.Y. to Southampton 3091

4803

N.Y. to Gib. 3206

4026
Bordeaux to Liverpool 3614

IRELAND

London

Paris
FRANCE

Lisbon
PORTUGAL

Madrid
SPAIN

Azores

N.Y. to Liverpool 3094

Bermuda

E

Rome

Sardinia

Mediterr

Tripoli

ITAL

TUNIS
TUNISIA

Gibraltar
Casablanca
Madeira
Canary Is.

MOROCCO
ALGERIA
Sa

LIB

Tropic of Canc

Vancouver
Mexico City
Guadalajara

G. of Mexico

Havana
Cuba
Jamaica

Bahama
Is.

West
Indies

Hispaniola

Puerto Rico

Caribbean
Sea

Martinique

Barbados

Tropic of Cancer

ATLANTIC

C. Verde Is.

Dakar

MAURITANIA

SENEGAL

Timbuktu

NIGER

CHA

Tabiti to S. Francisco 3810
Tabiti to Panama 3770

Revilla Gigedo Is.

MEXICO

CENTRAL
AMERICA

GUAT.
SAL.
NIC.
C.RICA

HOND.
BR. HOND.

Honolulu to Panama 4711

Equator

Galapagos

VENEZUELA
COLOMBIA

Medellin
Bogota

Curaçao

Trinidad

SURINAM

FR. GUI.

Caracas

St. Paul

GAMBIA
PORT. GUINEA
GUINEA
SIERRA LEONE
LIBERIA
IVORY
COAST

GHANA

NIGERIA
Ibadan

Fernando Poo

A F R

Quito
ECUADOR
Guayaquil

Mandos

Amazon

Belem
São Roque

Recife

OCEAN

Ascension

GABON

Kinsh

CONGO

Sydney to Panama 7692

Wellington to Panama 6486

Lima
Callao

PERU

La Paz
BOLIVIA

SOUTH
BRAZIL
AMERICA

Brasilia

Belo Horizonte

Salvador

São Paulo

Rio de Janeiro

St. Helena

Southampton to Cape Town 5978

Benguela

ANGO

S.W.
AFRIC

Ducie
Pitcairn

Tropic of Capricorn

Rapa Nui
(Easter I.)

S. Ambrosio
Juan Fernandez Is.

Antofagasta

CHILE

Valparaiso
Santiago
Concepcion

ARGENTINA

Asuncion

Cordoba

PARAGUAY

Rio Grande
URUGUAY

Pta. Alegre

Montevideo

Buenos Aires

Bahia Blanca

Tristan da Cunha

Johan

Cape Town
C. of Good Hope

Wellington to Rio de Janeiro 6893

PATAGONIA

FALKLAND

Magellan's Str.

Tierra del Fuego

C. Horn

Punta Arenas

Falkland Is.

S Georgia

Bouvet I.

South
Sandwich
Group

THE WORLD
Equatorial Scale
1 : 175,000,000
(2,800 miles = 1 inch)

4026 ------- Shipping Routes
Distances in Nautical Miles

Falkland Is.
Dependencies
South Orkney
Is.

South
Shetland Is.

Grisham Land

Drake
Pass.

British Antarctic
Territory

Antarctic
Peninsula

Weddell
Sea

West from Greenwich

S O U T H

Norwegian Depe

East from Greenwich

Princess

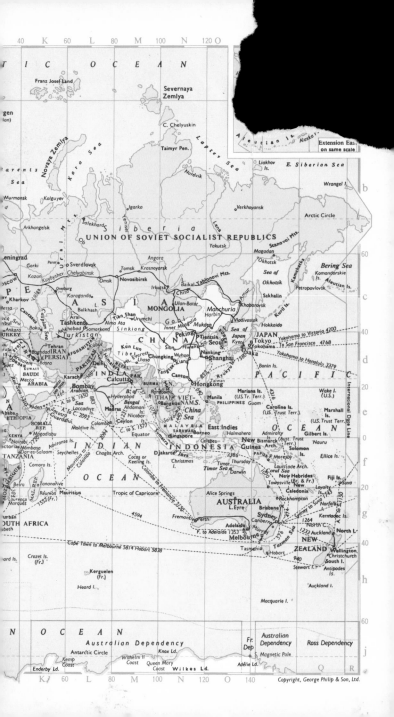

EUROPE

Scale 1 : 27,500,000 (440 miles = 1 inch)

Statute Miles
100 50 0   100   200   300   400   500

Kilometres
100 0 100 200 300 400 500 600 700 800

—— Railways   .... Canals

Projection: *Bonne*   East from Greenwich

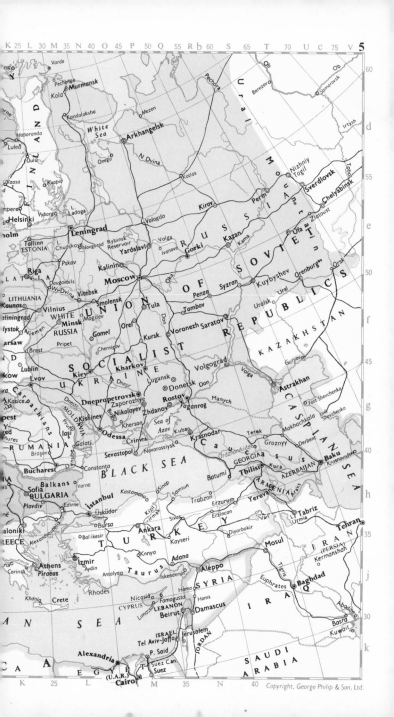

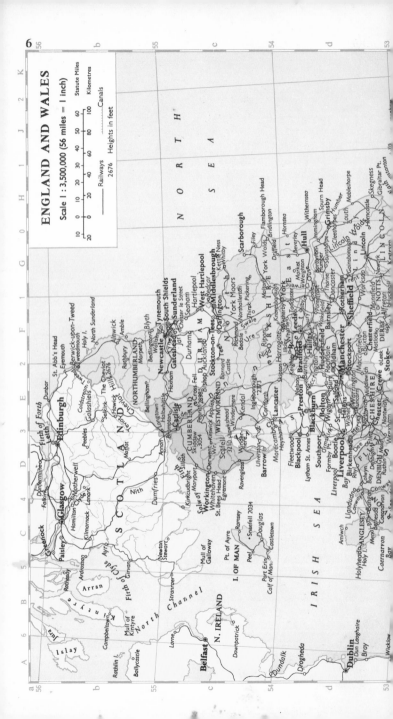

ENGLAND AND WALES

Scale 1 : 3,500,000 (56 miles = 1 inch)

Statute Miles
Kilometres

———— Railways   Canals

2676 Heights in feet

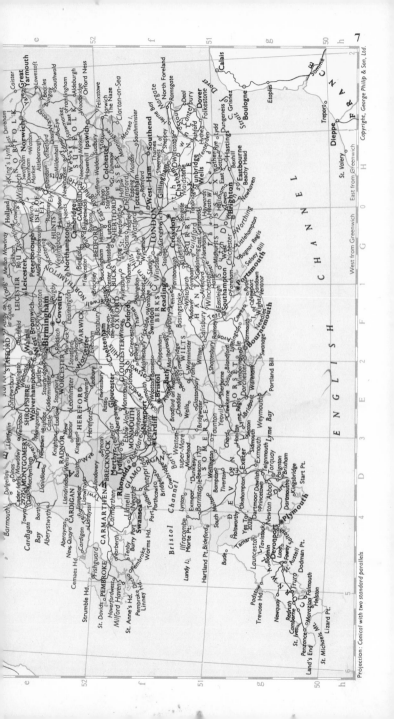

Projection : Conical with two standard parallels

SCOTLAND

Scale 1 : 3,500,000 (56 miles = 1 inch)

20 10 0 20 40 Statute Miles
20 10 0 20 40 60 Kilometres

—— Railways .... Canals 3547 Heights in feet

CL. Clackmannan
DUN. Dunbarton
E.L. East Lothian
KIN. Kinross
ML. Midlothian
REN. Renfrew
STIR. Stirling
W.L. West Lothian

Fair Isle

North Ronaldsay
Westray
Rousay
Sanday
Stronsay
ORKNEY
Stromness
Kirkwall
ORKNEY
Islands
Hoy
Burray
South Ronaldsay

Pentland Firth
John-o-Groats
Dunnet Hd.
Duncansby Hd.
Freswick
Castletown
Thurso
Halkirk
CAITHNESS
Noss Hd.
Wick
Ulbster

C. Wrath
Durness Loch Eriboll
Kinlochbervie
B. Hope
3040
Tongue
Altnaharra
Watten
Latheron
Dunbeath
Berriedale
Ord of Caithness
Helmsdale
Lothmore
Brora

Butt of Lewis
Port of Ness
Barvas
Loch Laxford
Eddrachillis Bay
Scourie
SUTHERLAND
Strathy
Forr

Carloway
Brood Bay
Stornoway
Lewis
Balallan
Enard Bay
Assynt
Inchnadamph
B. More
Loch Assynt
Loch Shin
Lairg
Bonar
Rogart
Golspie

Flannan Is.
Tarbert
Harris
North Minch
Ullapool
Inverlaxford
L. Broom
Oykell Br.
Bonar Br.
Dornoch
Dornoch Firth
Portmahomack

Sound of Harris
Stornoway
Poolewe
Melvaig
Gairloch
Loch Maree
Fannich
Achnasheen
ROSS AND CROMARTY
Dingwall
Strathpeffer
Beauly
Tain
Nigg
Cromarty
Moray Firth
Burghead
Findhorn
Forres
Rothes
Elgin
Lossiemouth
Fochabers
Buckie
Findochty
Cullen
Banff
Macduff
Fraserburgh

North Uist
Lochmaddy
Little Minch
Uig
Portree
Skye
Inner Sound
Kinlochewe
Torridon
Shieldaig
Applecross
Lochcarron
Strome Ferry
Kyle of Lochalsh
Loch Carron
Stromeferry
Contin
Conon Br.
Muir of Ord
Cannich
Drumnadrochit
Inverness
NAIRN
Nairn
MORAY
Keith
Huntly
Fyvie
New Deer
Mintlaw
Peterhead

South Uist
Kilmuir
B. More
1994
Portree
Broadford
L. Bracadale
Cuillin Hills
Cuillin Sound
Sleat
Kyleakin
Armadale
Glenelg
Glen Moriston
Fort Augustus
Invergarry
Gr. Garry
Glen Garry
Caledonian Canal
Foyers
Loch Ness
Errogie
Tomatin
Carrbridge
Grantown
Boat of Garten
Aviemore
Strathdon
Alford
Dyce
Inverurie
ABERDEEN
Aberdeen
Old Meldrum

Canna
Rhum
Eigg
Muck
Ardnamurchan Pt.
Kilchoan
Salen
Loch Shiel
Glenfinnan
Mallaig
Arisaig
Lochailort
L. Eilt
FORT WILLIAM
Ben Nevis
Spean Bridge
Kingussie
Kincraig
INVERNESS
Cairn Toul
4241
Cairn Gorm
4084
Ben Macdhui
4296
Braemar
Balmoral
Ballater
KINCARDINE
Fettercairn
Edzell
Laurencekirk
Stonehaven
Banchory
Inverbervie

Coll
Tiree
Tobermory
Dervaig
Staffa
Iona
Bunessan
Mull
Lochaline
Morven
Strontian
Loch Linnhe
Oban
Kinlochleven
Glencoe
Ballachulish
Onich
Tyndrum
Bridge of Orchy
Rannoch
Loch Rannoch
Kinloch Rannoch
Dalwhinnie
Dalnaspidal
Struan
Blair Atholl
Pitlochry
Kirkmichael
Aberfeldy
Ballinluig
Dunkeld
Blairgowrie
Alyth
Kirriemuir
Forfar
Brechin
ANGUS
Friockheim
Arbroath
Montrose

ATLANTIC
Colonsay
Scalasaig
Ardlussa
Loch Awe
Dalmally
Inveraray
Lochawe
Taynuilt
Connel
Loch Etive
Dalmally
Loch Tay
Killin
Callander
Crianlarich
Lochearnhead
B. More
3843
Ben Lawers
3984
Loch Earn
Comrie
Crieff
Aberfeldy
PERTH
Auchterarder
Perth
Scone
Coupar Angus
Newburgh
Cupar
St. Andrews
Fife Ness
Leven
Anstruther
Dundee
Carnoustie
Broughty Ferry
Monifieth
Newport

OCEAN
Port Askaig
Islay
Port Ellen
Gigha
Craighouse
Skipness
Tarbert
Lochgilphead
Crinan
Ardrishaig
Otter Ferry
Dunoon
Greenock
Helensburgh
Dumbarton
Loch Lomond
DUN.
Balloch
Drymen
STIR.
Stirling
Dunblane
Doune
3192
Ben Vorlich
Aberfoyle
Alloa
CL.
Dunfermline
KIN.
Kinross
L. Leven
Firth of Forth
Leith
Edinburgh
Cowdenbeath
Kirkcaldy
Buckhaven
Elie
Berwick

Mull of Oa
Arran
Brodick
Lamlash
Campbeltown
Mull of Kintyre
Firth of Clyde
Rothesay
BUTE
Largs
Ardrossan
Saltcoats
Irvine
Kilmarnock
Troon
Prestwick
Ayr
Maybole
Paisley
REN.
Glasgow
Barrhead
Hamilton
Motherwell
Wishaw
Airdrie
Coatbridge
Falkirk
Bathgate
W.L.
ML.
PEEBLES
Peebles
Innerleithen
Galashiels
SELKIRK
Selkirk
Melrose
Kelso
Coldstream
ROXBURGH
Hawick
Jedburgh
Newcastleton
Peel Fell
1964
Cheviot Hills

Barra
Castlebay
Barra Hd.

Rathlin
Ballycastle
N.I.
Ballymena
Larne
Carrickfergus
Belfast
Bangor
Lisburn

Ailsa Craig
Girvan
Ballantrae
Corsewall Pt.
Stranraer
Portpatrick
Luce Bay
Mull of Galloway
Whithorn
Barrhill
New Cumnock
Sanquhar
Cumnock
Mauchline
Muirkirk
Dalmellington
Moniaive
Carsphairn
Thornhill
New Galloway
Dalry
Newton Stewart
WIGTOWN
Wigtown
Castle Douglas
KIRKCUDBRIGHT
Kirkcudbright
Gatehouse
Dalbeattie
Galloway
DUMFRIES
Dumfries
Lockerbie
Moffat
Beattock
Ecclefechan
Annan
Gretna
Langholm
N. Tyne
Bewcastle
Haltwhistle
Carlisle
Bowness
Silloth
Maryport
Workington
Keswick
Penrith
ENGLAND

LANARK
Lanark
Carluke
Biggar
Carstairs
Lauder
Lammermuir Hills
Duns
Greenlaw
BERWICK
Berwick
DUMFRIES

Shetland
Islands
Unst
Yell
Fetlar
Burravoe
Hillswick
Papa Stour
ZETLAND
Scalloway
Lerwick
Bressay

Projection: Conical
with two standard parallels.

West from Greenwich

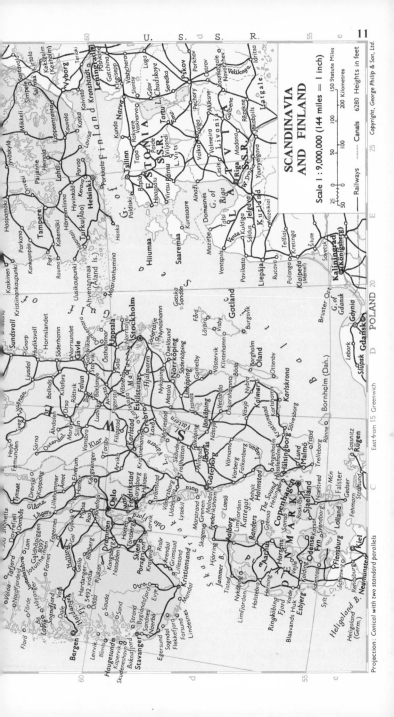

11

U. S. S. R.

POLAND

SCANDINAVIA
AND FINLAND

Scale 1 : 9,000,000 (144 miles = 1 inch)

Railways ——— Canals ----- 6280 Heights in feet

Copyright, George Philip & Son, Ltd.

East from 15 Greenwich

Projection: Conical with two standard parallels

Selected place names visible on map:

Leningrad, Kronstadt, Vyborg, Kexholm (Kexholm), Sortavala, Terioki, Helsinki, Tallinn, ESTONIA S.S.R., LATVIA S.S.R., Riga, Pskov, Tartu, Tampere, Turku (Åbo), G. of Finland, G. of Riga, Kaliningrad (Königsberg), Klaipeda (Memel), Gdynia, Gdańsk, Słupsk, Stockholm, Uppsala, Gävle, Sundsvall, Gotland, Öland, Norrköping, Linköping, Jönköping, Göteborg, Borås, Oslo, Bergen, Stavanger, Kristiansand, Copenhagen, Odense, Malmö, Helsingborg, Aalborg, Esbjerg, DENMARK, Kiel, Rügen, Bornholm (Dan.), Heligoland B., Sjælland, Fyn, Lolland, Falster

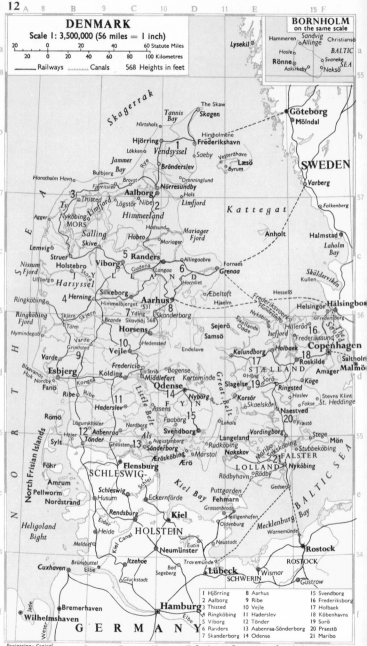

12

DENMARK
Scale 1 : 3,500,000 (56 miles = 1 inch)

20   0   20   40   60 Statute Miles
20   0   20   40   60   80   100 Kilometres

—— Railways   .... Canals   568 Heights in feet

BORNHOLM
on the same scale

Hammeren   Sandvig   Christiansö
         Allinge
Hasle   BALTIC
Rönne   SEA
   Aakirkeby   Svaneke
              Neksö

1 Hjörring	8 Aarhus	15 Svendborg
2 Aalborg	9 Ribe	16 Frederikssund
3 Thisted	10 Vejle	17 Holbaek
4 Ringköbing	11 Haderslev	18 Köbenhavns
5 Viborg	12 Tönder	19 Sorö
6 Randers	13 Aabenraa-Sönderborg	20 Praestö
7 Skanderborg	14 Odense	21 Maribo

Projection: Conical
with two standard parallels.

East from Greenwich

Copyright, George Philip & Son

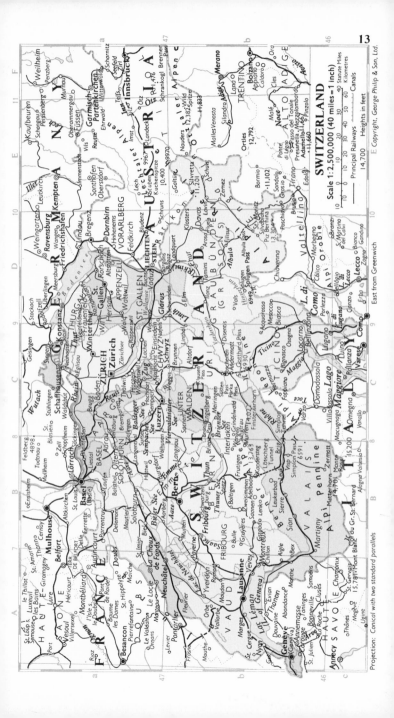

13

SWITZERLAND

Scale 1:2,500,000 (40 miles=1 inch)

Statute Miles				
10	0	10	20	30	40

Kilometres				
10	0	10	20	30	40	50

Principal Railways ——— Canals

Heights in feet

East from Greenwich

Projection: Conical with two standard parallels

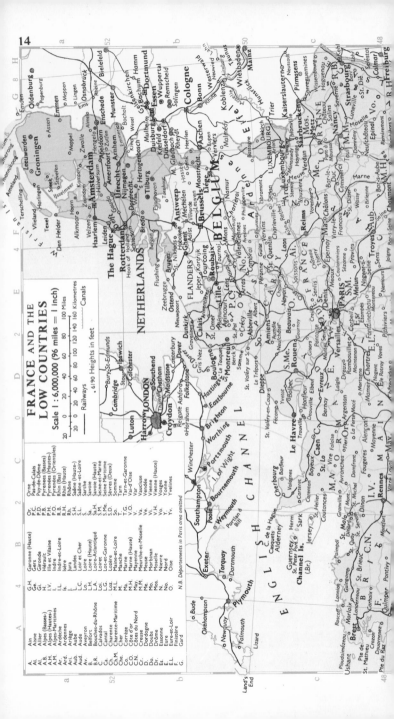

14

FRANCE AND THE LOW COUNTRIES

Scale 1 : 6,000,000 (96 miles = 1 inch)

20   0   20   40   60   80   100 Miles
20 0 20 40 60 80 100 120 140 160 Kilometres

Railways ———————
Canals

•6190 Heights in feet

N.B. Départements in Paris area omitted

A.	Ain
Al.	Aisne
Al.	Allier
A.B.	Alpes (Basses-)
A.H.	Alpes (Hautes-)
A.M.	Alpes-Maritimes
Ard.	Ardennes
Ard.	Ardèche
Ar.	Ariège
Aub.	Aube
Aud.	Aude
Av.	Aveyron
B.R.	Bouches-du-Rhône
C.	Calvados
Ca.	Cantal
Ch.M.	Charente-Maritime
Che.	Cher
Co.	Corrèze
C.O.	Côte d'or
C.N.	Côtes du Nord
Cr.	Creuse
Do.	Dordogne
Do.	Doubs
Dr.	Drôme
Eu.	Eure
E.L.	Eure-et-Loir
G.	Gard

G.H.	Garonne (Haute)
Ge.	Gers
Gi.	Gironde
H.	Hérault
I.L.	Indre-et-Loire
Is.	Isère
La.	Landes
L.C.	Loir-et-Cher
Lo.	Loire
L.A.	Loire-Atlantique
Loi.	Loiret
Lot.	Lot-et-Garonne
Loz.	Lozère
M.L.	Maine-et-Loire
Ma.	Manche
May.	Mayenne
M.H.	Marne (Haute)
M.M.	Meurthe-et-Moselle
Me.	Meuse
Mo.	Morbihan
Mos.	Moselle
N.	Nord
O.	Oise
Or.	Orne
P.C.	Pas-de-Calais
P.D.	Puy-de-Dôme
P.B.	Pyrénées (Basses)
P.H.	Pyrénées (Hautes)
P.O.	Pyrénées (Orientales)
R.B.	Rhin (Bas)
R.H.	Rhin (Haut)
Rh.	Rhône
S.H.	Saône (Haute)
S.L.	Saône-et-Loire
S.	Sarthe
Sa.H.	Savoie (Haute)
S.M.	Seine-et-Marne
S.M.	Seine-Maritime
S.D.	Sèvres (Deux)
So.	Somme
T.	Tarn
T.G.	Tarn-et-Garonne
Va.	Var
V.	Vaucluse
Ve.	Vendée
Vi.	Vienne
V.H.	Vienne (Haute)
Vo.	Vosges
Y.	Yonne
Y.V.	Yvelines

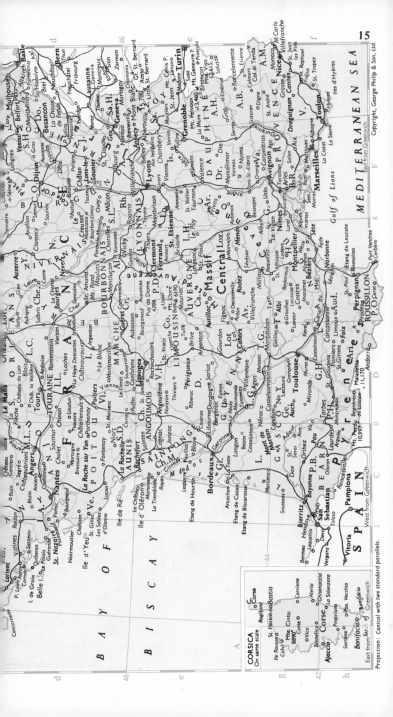

MEDITERRANEAN SEA

Gulf of Lions

BAY OF BISCAY

SPAIN

CORSICA
On same scale

CORSE

Projection: Conical with two standard parallels.

East from Str.⁰¹ of Greenwich

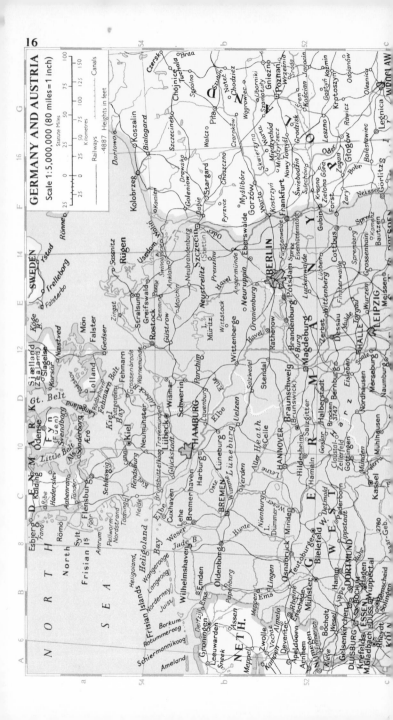

16

GERMANY AND AUSTRIA

Scale 1:5,000,000 (80 miles=1 inch)

Statute Miles

Kilometres

Railways ——— Canals

-4887 Heights in feet

C Z E C H O S L O V A K I A

PRAGUE (PRAHA)

BRNO

VIENNA (WIEN)

LOWER AUSTRIA
W. Neustadt
St. Pölten
Krems
Klosterneuburg
Bratislava

UPPER AUSTRIA
Linz
Wels
Steyr
Gmunden

SALZBURG
Salzburg
Berchtesgaden

STYRIA
GRAZ
Leoben
Bruck
Knittelfeld
Judenburg

CARINTHIA
Klagenfurt
Villach
Wolfsberg

TYROL
Innsbruck
Kufstein
Kitzbühel
Bolzano
Merano

YUGOSLAVIA
Maribor

H U N G A R Y
Sopron
Szombathely
Nagykanizsa
Zalaegerszeg

Bohemian Forest

MÜNCHEN (Munich)
Augsburg
Regensburg (Ratisbon)
NÜRNBERG (NUREMBERG)
Landshut
Ingolstadt
Freising
Passau
Straubing

Pilzen
Č. Budějovice
Pardubice
Olomouc
Jihlava
Znojmo

FRANKFURT
Mainz
Wiesbaden
Mannheim
Heidelberg
Darmstadt
Würzburg
Bamberg
Erlangen
Fürth
Bayreuth
Hof
Coburg
Schweinfurt
Fulda
Giessen
Marburg
Koblenz
Bonn
Aachen

STUTTGART
Karlsruhe
Baden
Heilbronn
Ulm
Reutlingen
Tübingen
Ludwigsburg
Esslingen
Göppingen
Schwäbisch Gmünd
Offenburg

MULHOUSE
STRASBOURG
NANCY
Metz
Saarbrücken
Kaiserslautern
Pirmasens

S W I T Z E R L A N D
ZÜRICH
BASEL (BASLE)
Bern
Luzern
Winterthur
St. Gallen
Chur
Davos
Glarus
Schaffhausen
Baden
Zug
Neuchâtel
Fribourg
Lausanne
Genève (Geneva)
Montreux
Brienz
Thun

LIECHTENSTEIN
Vaduz

Bregenz
Friedrichshafen
Kempten
Memmingen
Ravensburg
VORARLBERG

F R A N C E
St-Dié
Épinal
Belfort
Lunéville
Colmar

Copyright, George Philip & Son, Ltd.

Projection. Conical with two standard parallels.   East from Greenwich

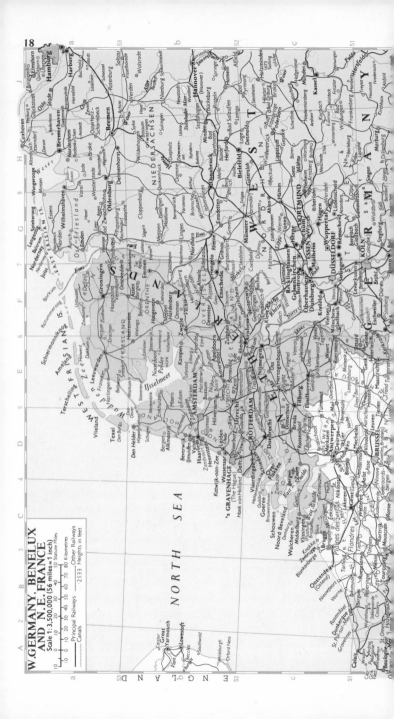

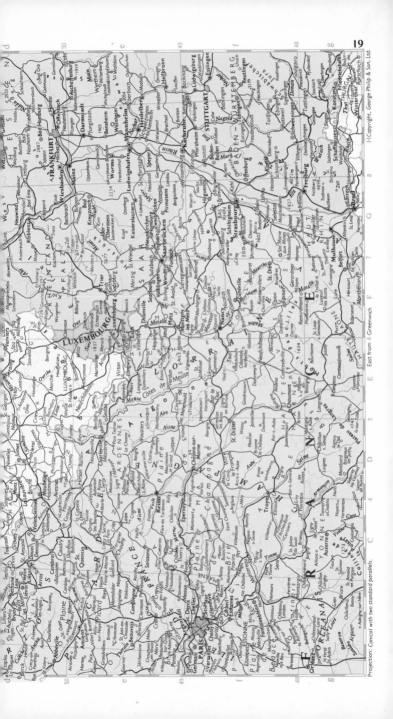

19

East from 6 Greenwich

Projection: Conical with two standard parallels.

E. FRANCE, SWITZERLAND & N.W. ITALY

Scale 1:3,500,000 (56 miles=1 inch)

Principal Railways — Other Railways
Canals — 1745 Heights in feet

J. Copyright, George Philip & Son, Ltd.

BALTIC SEA

a

Zingst • Sassnitz
Warnemünde • **Rügen** Ustka • Wejherowo
Stralsund Usedom Darlowo • Słupsk Sopot • Gdynia Noliw
Greifswald Kołobrzeg Kartuzy • **GDANSK**
Rostock Demmin Peene Koszalin • Starogard (DANZI)
Güstrow Anklam Bialogard Szczecinek Czersk Tczew

Malchin Swinoujscie Wolin Drawsko Chojnice Tuchola Grudziądz Gr
Parchim L. Neubrandenburg Odra Port Kamien Szczecin Swiecie Chełmno
Müritz Neustrelitz Szczecin Stargard Walcz o Piła Sępolno Bydgoszcz Chełmża
Wittenberge Wittstock (Stettin) Dabie Szubin (Bromberg) No
Wittenberge Angermünde Pyrzyce Choszczno Czarnków Notec Toruń Ale

b

Oranienburg Neuruppin Eberswalde Myslibórz Notec Chodzież Inowrocław Mogilno Płowce Brze
Stendal Havel Gorzów Warta Skwierzyna Wagrowiec Gniezno Strzelno Kujo
Rathenow **BERLIN** Kostrzyn Warta Oborniki Szamotuły (Gnesen) Słupca Koło
Brandenburg Fürstenwalde Frankfurt Miedzychód Wrzesnia Konin Turek Łęczy
Burg Potsdam Spree Międzyrzecz **Poznań** Środa
GERMANY Luckenwalde Nowy Tomysl Grodzisk Jarocin P O L Ozork
Zerbst Wittenberg Lübben Gubin Krosno Świebodzin Śrem Koscian Pleszew Kalisz Zduń
Dessau Mulde Finsterwalde Cottbus Zielona Góra Leszno Gostyn Koźmin Wola
HALLE Torgau Wurzen Spremberg Forst Żary Głogów Rawicz Krotoszyn Ostrów Sieradz
LEIPZIG Grossenhain Kamenz Żagan Odolanów Ostrzeszów Kepno Wieluń Rad
Zeitz Meissen Bautzen Bolesławiec Olesnica Namysłów Krz
Gera Karl-Marx-Stadt **DRESDEN** Görlitz S I L Legnica **WROCŁAW** Czestochowa
Zwickau Glauchau Lubań Jelenia **WROCŁAW** (Breslau) Oleśnica Opole Lublin
Reichenbach Geb.(Ore Mts) Podmokly Zittau Góra Krkonose (Gia Świdnica I S Tarn Gó
Plauen Teplice Liberec Snezka 5260 Wałbrzych Nysa Prudnik Zabrze Gliwice
Erz Most Mittel G. Jablonec n. Trutnov Kłodzko Opava Racibórz Chorzow
Jáchymov Žatec Chomutov Litomerice Hory Mladá Josefov Pradĕd Karviná
Karlovy Vary Kladno Hradec Králický Snĕznik 4887 Biala
Cheb Mariánské **PRAGUE** (PRAHA) Labe (Elbe) Pardubice Vysoké Sumperk Sternberk Ostrava Těšín
Lázně Beroun Kolin Chrudim Myto Svitavy Olomouc Novy Jičin Jablunka
Plzen (Pilsen) Přibram Sázava Nĕmecký Brod Morav Prostĕjov 1810 West B
Regen 4780 Domažlice Klatovy Piseck Tábor Jihlava Přerov Dolní Kt
Gr. Arber Sušice Vltava **BRNO** Kroměříž Váh Žilina
Straubing Č. Budĕjovice Třeboň Jihlava Slavkov **BRNO** Gottwaldov
Isar 4525 Blöckenstein Gmünd Znojmo White C Trenčin Bans
Passau C. Krumlov Zwettl Thaya Hodonin Kremnica Bys
UPPER Freistadt Horn Breclav Stockerau Trnava Zlaté Bans
Regen Ried Linz Urfahr Greino Melk Klosterneuburg Morovce Banská
AUSTRIA Wels Steyr St.Pölten **VIENNA** Bratislava Nitra Levice Nové
Salzburg Gmunden Enns Amstetten (WIEN) Baden Bruck Schutt Zámky Ipe
Schaf b. Ischl Mariazell Wr. Neustadt Hegyeshalom Komárno
Berchlesgaden Salzkammergut Schnee B. 6816 Sopron L. of Esztergom
Bischofshofen Dachstein 9823 Mürzzuschlag Semmering 3119 P. Neusiedl Gyor

POLAND AND CZECHOSLOVAKIA map labels:

20   F   22   G   24   H   26   J   **23**

Zelenogradsk · Baltiisk · KALININGRAD (Königsberg) · Chernyakovsk · Gusev · Kaunas (Kovno) · Vilkaviskis · Nowe Troki · Nowa Wilejka · Vilnius (Vilnyus) · Wilejka

Bagrationovsk · Pravdinsk · Braniewo · Bartoszyce · Elblag · Ilbork · Reszel · Mauer L. · Wegorzewo · Lidzbark · Giżycko · Suwałki · Druskieniki · Smorgonie · Ejszyszki · Juraciszki · Iwje · Wolozyn

Olsztyn · Spirding · Grajewo · Augustów · Grodno · Lida · Novogrudok

Ostróda · Lubawa · Stebark · Działdowo · Chorzele · Kolno · Suchowola · Sokółka · Indura · Odelsk · Knyszyn · Białystok · Zdzięciol · Molczadź · Baranovichi

Mława · Przasnysz · Ciechanów · Narew · Łomża · Ostrołęka · Łapy · Grodek · Bielsk Narew · Swisłocz · Volkovysk · Slonim · Lachowicze

Brodnica · Rypin · Sierpc · Płock · Płońsk · Ciechanów · Ostrów Mazowiecka · Brańsk · Ciechanowiec · Hajnowka · Białowieża · Kossów · Byten · Hancewicze

WARSAW (WARSZAWA) · Grodzisk · Radzymin · Wolomin · Węgrów · Kałuszyn · Siedlce · Biała · Siemiatycze · Czeremcha · Kamieniec Litewski · Orańczyce · Drohiczyn · Jasiolda · Pińsk · Janów · Telechany · Lohiszyn

Łowicz · Kutno · Łódź · Żyrardów · Skierniewice · Grójec · Mińsk Mazowiecki · Otwock · Łuków · Zelechów · Międzyrzec · Brest (Brest Litovsk) · Maloryta · Kuchecka Wola

Pabianice · Spała · Nowemiasto · Pilica · Kozianice · Radom · Zyrzyn · Puławy · Włodawa · Lubartów · Chełm (Kholm) · Pripyat · Kamen Kashirski · Lyubomi · Kovel · Antonowka · Czartorysk · Stepań

Końskie · Opoczno · Szydłowiec · Wachock · Wierzbnik · LUBLIN · Opole · Rejowiec · Krasnystaw · Zawada · Sokul · Kolki

Kielce · Małogoszcz · Ostrowiec · Świętokrzyski · Checiny · Sandomierz · Krasnik · Zawichost · Zaklikow · Janów · Zamość · Vladimir Volynski · Torczyn · Alexandriya · Lutsk · Rovno

Jędrzejów · Kliszów · Staszów · Pińczów · Nisko · Bilgoraj · Belz · Rava Russkaya · Uhnów · Stojanów · Horochow · Berestecko · Dubno · Miozcz · Zdolbuhow

Zawiercie · Miechów · Słomniki · Mielec · Dąbrowa · Kolbuszowa · Rzeszów · Lubaczów · Żółkiew · Jaworów · Kamenka Bugskaya · Dublany · Oleska · Brody · Kremenets

AKÓW (CRACOW) · Wadowice · Nowa Huta · Tarnów · Leżajsk · Przeworsk · Jarosław · Jaworów · Gródek Jagiellonski · LVOV · Zloczew · Zbarazh

Maków · Babia Góra · Nowy Targ · Limanowa · Nowy Sącz · Jasło · Krosno · Sanok · Mościska · Przemyśl · Sambor · Dniester Rozdol · Rohatyn · UKRAINE · Ternopol · Grzymałów · Skalat

High Tatra · Gerlachovka · Żomberok · Lipt. Sv. Mikulas · Bardejov · Kežmarok · Gorlice · Grybów · Dukla P. · Leśko · Turka · Drohobycz · Tustanowice · Stryi · Bereżany · Monasterzyska · Galich · Kopychintsy · Buczacz · Barysz · Chortkov · Jazlochhiki

Tatra · Brezno · Dobšiná · Levoča · Prešov · Humenné · Skole · Dolina · Ivano Frankovsk · Tysmienica · Tlumacz · Obertyn · Horodenka · Kolomiya · Sniatyn

Ore Mts · Roznava · Košice · Uzhgorod · Svalyava · Lawoczne · Nadvornaya · Delatyn · Pechenezhino · Horodenka · Chernovtsy

Rimavská Sobota · Satoraljaujhely · Saio · Latoritsa · Mukachevo · Dovge · S.P. of the Tartars

Miskolc · Eger · Tokaj · Nyiregyháza · Tisza

Gyöngyös · Hatvan · Hajdúböszörmény · Tiszafüred

POLAND AND CZECHOSLOVAKIA · Scale 1 : 5,000,000 (80 miles = 1 inch) · Railways · Canals · ·5260 Heights in feet

East from Greenwich · Copyright, George Philip & Son, Ltd.

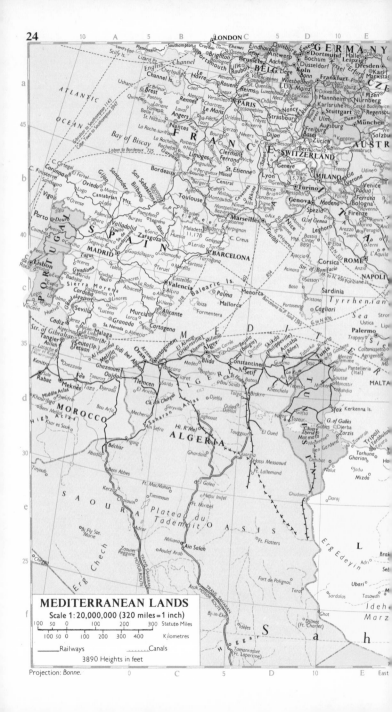

MEDITERRANEAN LANDS

Scale 1:20,000,000 (320 miles = 1 inch)

100   50   0   100   200   300   Statute Miles

100 50 0   100   200   300   400   Kilometres

──────── Railways   .... Canals

3890 Heights in feet

Projection: Bonne.

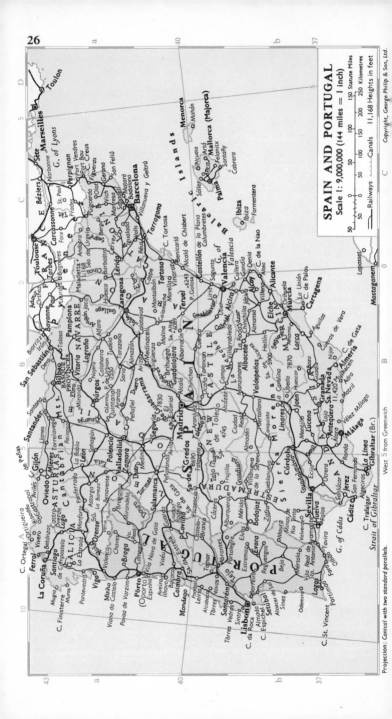

SPAIN AND PORTUGAL
Scale 1 : 9,000,000 (144 miles = 1 inch)

Railways   Canals   Heights in feet 11,168

Statute Miles 50 0 50 100 150 200

Kilometres 50 0 50 100 150 200 250

Projection: Conical with two standard parallels.

West 5 from Greenwich

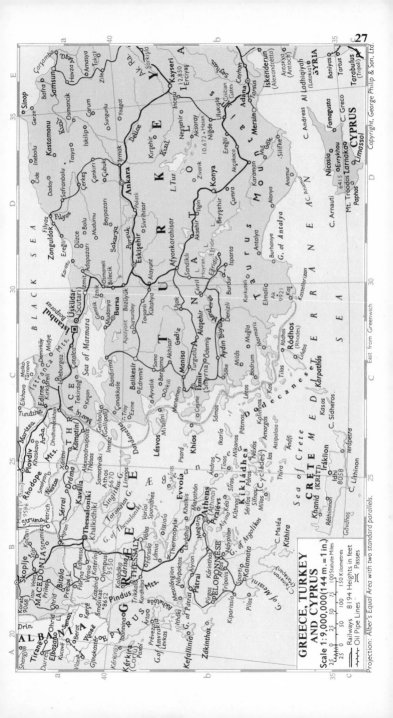

27

GREECE, TURKEY AND CYPRUS

Scale 1:9,000,000 (144 m. = 1 in.)

Miles scale			
25 0 25 50 75	100 Statute Miles
25 0 50 100	150 Kilometres

Heights in feet

—— Railways +++ Oil Pipe Lines)(Passes

Projection: Alber's Equal Area with two standard parallels.

East from Greenwich

Copyright, George Philip & Son, Ltd.

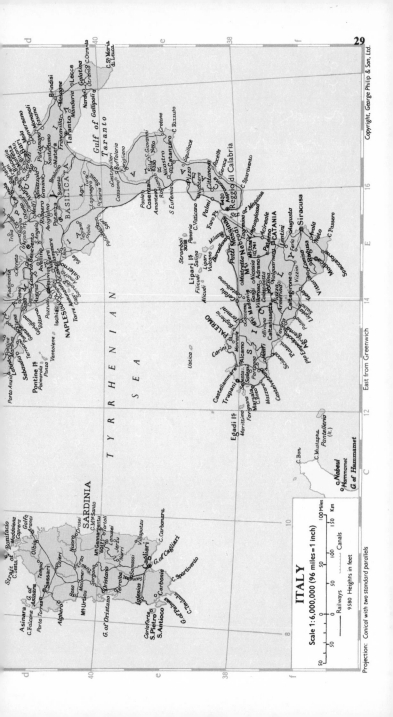

29

ITALY

Scale 1:6,000,000 (96 miles=1 inch)

Railways ——— Canals

9580 Heights in feet

Projection: Conical with two standard parallels

East from Greenwich

Copyright, George Philip & Son, Ltd.

31

HUNGARY AND THE BALKAN STATES
Scale 1:6,000,000 (96 miles = 1 inch)

Statute Miles
25 50 100 150

Kilometres
25 50 100 150

Railways
Canals
▪8300 Heights in feet

Projection: Conical with two standard parallels

East from 24 Greenwich

Copyright, George Philip & Son, Ltd.

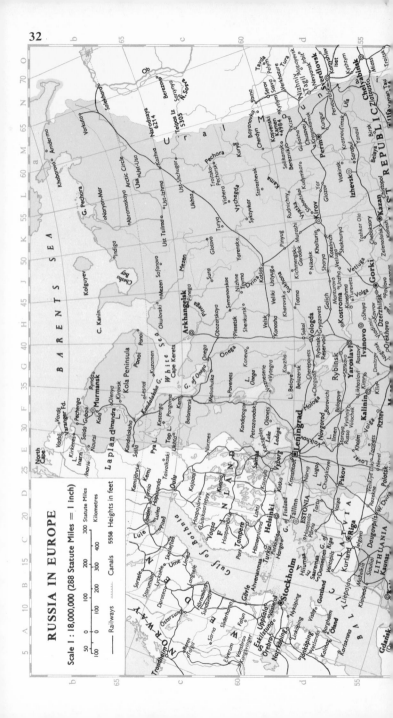

32

RUSSIA IN EUROPE

Scale 1 : 18,000,000 (288 Statute Miles = 1 inch)

Railways   ----- Canals   5558 Heights in feet

50 Copyright, George Philip & Son, Ltd.

Projection: *Conical with two standard parallels.*

East from Greenwich

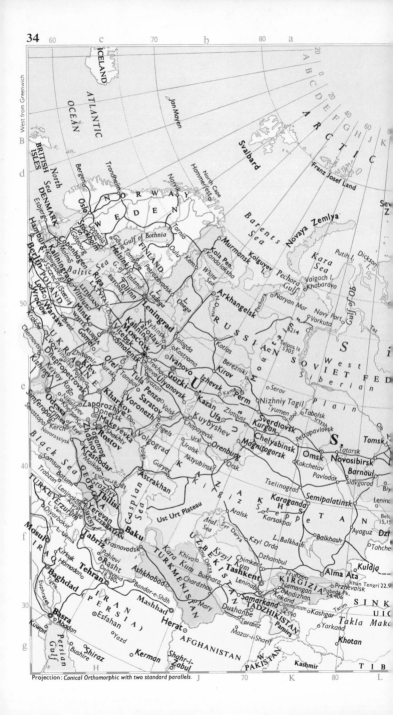

60   c   70   b   80   a

West from Greenwich

ICELAND

ATLANTIC OCEAN

Jan Mayen

A R C T I C

Svalbard

Franz Josef Land

B

d

BRITISH ISLES

North Sea

Bergen ○

Trondheim

Narvik

Hammerfest

North Cape

Barents Sea

Novaya Zemlya

Kara Sea

Putihi I.

Dickson I.

NORWAY

Oslo ○

Esbjerg ○

DENMARK

Stockholm ○

Göteborg ○

S W E D E N

Tornio

Oulu

Gulf of Bothnia

FINLAND

Gulf of Tammefors

Helsinki ○

Vaigach I.

Khabarovo

Naryan Mar

Novy Port

Vorkuta

Gulf of Ob

Taz

50

Berlin ○

Hamburg ○

Szczecin ○

Baltic Sea

Kaliningrad ○

Gdańsk ○

Klaipeda

Riga

L. Ladoga

LATVIA

Tallinn ○

ESTONIA

St. Petersburg (Leningrad) ○

L. Onega

Murmansk

Kola Pen.

Kandalaksha

White Sea

Kolguyev

Pechora Gulf

N. Dvina

Arkhangelsk ○

Kotlas

Berezniki ○

Pechora

Naryan Mar

5214

Telpos Iz 5305

R U S S I A N

S O V I E T   F E D

West Siberian

POLAND

Wrocław ○

Warsaw ○

Kraków ○

Lublin

Vilnius ○

Minsk ○

LITHUANIA

BELARUS

Vitebsk

Smolensk

Moscow ○

Kalinin ○

Yaroslavl ○

Rybinsk

Vologda

Kostroma

Ivanovo ○

Gorki ○

Izhevsk ○

Kirov

Perm ○

Serov ○

Nizhniy Tagil ○

Sverdlovsk ○

Tyumen ○

Tobolsk ○

e

Chernovtsy ○

UKRAINE

Lvov ○

Zhitomir ○

Kiev ○

Gomel ○

Orel ○

Tula ○

Ryazan

Tambov ○

Penza ○

Ulyanovsk ○

Kazan ○

Ufa ○

Zlatoust ○

Chelyabinsk ○

Kurgan ○

Petropavlovsk ○

S

Tomsk ○

Kishinev ○

MOLDOVA

Dnepropetrovsk ○

Kharkov ○

Kremenchug

Dnieper

Voronezh ○

Saratov ○

Kuybyshev ○

Chapayevsk

Engels

Volsk

Ural

Orenburg ○

Orsk ○

Magnitogorsk ○

Omsk ○

Tatarsk

Novosibirsk ○

Barnaul ○

Odessa ○

Simferopol ○

Zaporozhye ○

Makeyevka ○

Donetsk ○

Shakhty

Don

Volgograd ○

Guryev

Aktyubinsk ○

Tselinograd

Pavlodar

Slavgorod

Bi

Leninc

Sevastopol ○

Kerch

Novorossiysk ○

Rostov ○

Krasnodar ○

Maikop

Volga

Astrakhan ○

K

Black Sea

Samsun ○

Batumi ○

Sochi

Elbrus 18,481

Grozny ○

Caspian Sea

Ust Urt Plateau

Aral Sea

Syr Darya

K A Z A K H S T A N

Karaganda ○

Semipalatinsk ○

Ayaguz

Dzt

Tahche

Belu 15,15

TURKEY

Trabzon ○

Erzurum ○

Leninakan

Tbilisi ○

GEORGIA

Yerevan ○

ARMENIA

AZERBAIJAN

Baku ○

Krasnovodsk ○

TURKMENISTAN

Kara Kum

Karsakpai

Aralsk

Kzyl Orda

L. Balkhash

Balkhash ○

Dzhambul ○

Chimkent ○

UZBEKISTAN

Kokchetav

Kyzyl Kum

Kuldja ○

f

Diyarbakir ○

Mosul ○

Kirkuk ○

IRAQ

L. Urmia

L. Van

Pahlevi

Tabriz ○

Hamadan ○

Tehran ○

Rasht ○

5388

Bandar-e-Shāh

Ashkhabad ○

Mashhad ○

Chardzhou

Bukhara ○

Mary

Khiva ○

Samarkand ○

Leninabad ○

Tashkent ○

Frunze ○

KIRGIZIA

Namangan ○

Andizhan ○

Kokand

Przhevalsk

Pobeda Pk. 24,406

Khan Tengri 22,9

Communism 24,590

TADZHIKISTAN

Dushanbe ○

Termez ○

Alma Ata ○

Kashgar ○

Yarkand

SINK

UIC

Tarim

Takla Mako

Khotan ○

30

Baghdad ○

Basra ○

Kuwait ○

Abadan ○

Euphrates

Tigris

IRAN (PERSIA)

Esfahan ○

Yazd ○

Herat ○

Mazar-i-Sharif ○

Pamirs

AFGHANISTAN

Shghr-i-Zabul

W.

PAKISTAN

Kashmir

T I B

g

Persian Gulf

Bushire ○

Shiraz ○

Kerman ○

Kerman

H   70   K   80   L

Projection: Conical Orthomorphic with two standard parallels.   J

ASIA

1 : 60,000,000 (960 miles = 1 inch)

Railways — Canals ·········

ARM.	Armenia
AZER.	Azerbaijan
BHU.	Bhutan
LEB.	Lebanon
PAK.	Pakistan
SIK.	Sikkim
U.A.R.	United Arab Republic

Projection: Bonne

East from Greenwich

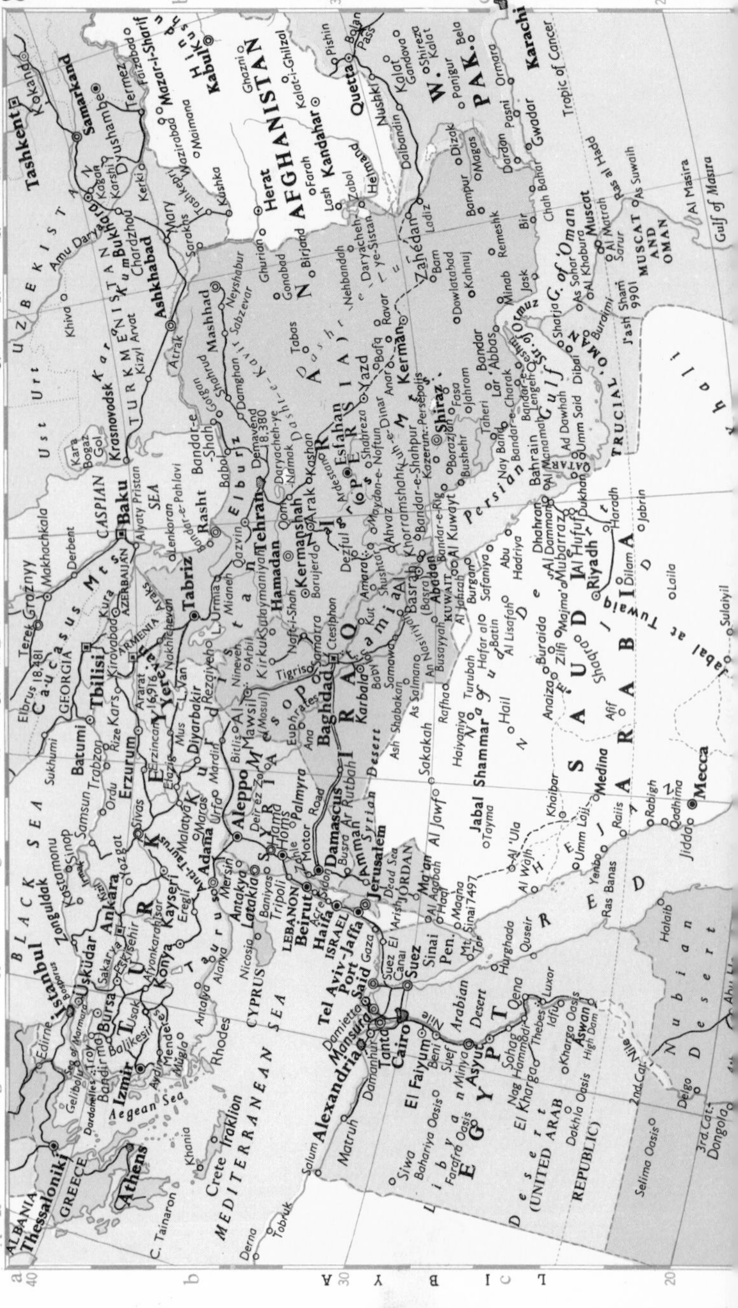

G 70 b 30 c 20

Tashkent
Kokand
Samarkand
Termez
Dyushambe
UZBEKISTAN
Khiva
Amu Darya
TURKMENISTAN
Chardzhou
Kerki
Mary
Kushka
Mazar-i-Sharif
Kunduz
Kabul
AFGHANISTAN
Herat
Kalat-i-Ghilzai
Ghazni
Kandahar
Quetta
Pishin
Bolan Pass
W. PAK.
Karachi
Tropic of Cancer

S. F. R.
Krasnovodsk
Kizyl Arvat
Ashkhabad
Meshed
Mashhad
Neyshabur
Birjand
Zabol
Zahedan
Nushki
Kalat
Panjgur
Gwadar
Ormara

E U. 60 S.
Kara Bogaz Gol
Bandar-e-Shah
N PERSIA Tehran
Qum
Esfahan
Yazd
Kerman
Bam
Bampur
Chah Bahar
Gulf of Oman

CASPIAN SEA
Baku
Baku
Rasht
Qazvin
Elburz
Hamadan
Kashan
Shiraz
Bandar Abbas
Hormuz
Bandar-e-Lengeh
MUSCAT AND OMAN
Muscat
Matrah
Sohar
Al Masira

U.S.D.S. R. 50
Makhachkala
Derbent
Grozny
Tabriz
Urmia
AZERBAIJAN
ARMENIA
Kermanshah
Khorramabad
Ahvaz
Abadan
Bushehr
Bahrain
Dhahran
Al Dammam
TRUCIAL OMAN
Abu Dhabi
Dubai
Umm Said
Buraimi

U. 40
Elbrus 18,481
Caucasus
Tbilisi
GEORGIA
Batumi
Kars
Erzurum
Ararat 16,916
Van
Mosul (Al Mawsil)
Kirkuk
IRAQ
Baghdad
Karbala
Najaf
Basra
KUWAIT
Kuwait
Hafar al Batin
Riyadh
Al Hufuf
Jabrin
QATAR

BLACK SEA
Zonguldak
Samsun
Trabzon
Sinop
Ankara
Sivas
Kayseri
Malatya
Diyarbakir
TURKEY
Aleppo
SYRIA
Deir ez Zor
Palmyra
Homs
Damascus
Syrian Desert
Rutbah
Al Jawf
Sakakah
Jabal Shammar
Hail
Buraida
Anaiza
Medina
SAUDI ARABIA
Mecca

C 30
Istanbul
Üsküdar
Bursa
Izmit
Konya
Adana
Mersin
Antakya
LEBANON
Beirut
Tripoli
Damascus
Haifa
Tel Aviv–Jaffa
ISRAEL
Jerusalem
Gaza
JORDAN
Amman
Maan
Al Aqabah
Tabuk
Al Ula
Khaibar
Yanbu
Jidda
Ras Banas

B
ALBANIA
Thessaloniki
GREECE
Athens
Crete
AEGEAN SEA
Rhodes
CYPRUS
Nicosia
MEDITERRANEAN SEA
Port Said
Damietta
Alexandria
Cairo
Suez
El Faiyum
EGYPT (UNITED ARAB REPUBLIC)
Siwa
Bahariya Oasis
Farafra Oasis
Asyut
Kharga Oasis
Luxor
Aswan
High Dam
Nubian Desert
Libyan Desert
Matruh
Solum
Tobruk
Derna

A 20
40
a
b
30
Y
B
I
L
20
Persian Gulf
Red Sea
Rub' al Khali
Ad Dawha

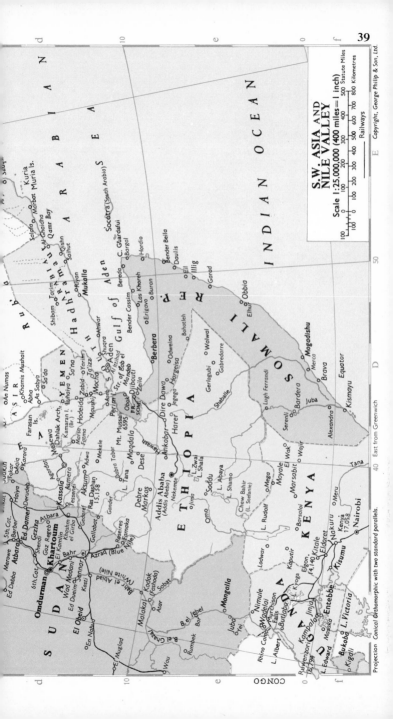

39

S.W. ASIA AND
NILE VALLEY

Scale 1:25,000,000 (400 miles = 1 inch)

Railways

Copyright, George Philip & Son, Ltd.

Projection Conical Orthomorphic with two standard parallels.

East from Greenwich

40

East from 34 Greenwich

T U R K E Y

·8005 Bucakkisla
Ermenek   ·6644 Mut   Kirobasi
Kazanci   Goksu   Elvanli
Gilindire   Silifke   Ovacik
Anamur   Gulnar

Mersin   Tarsus   **Adana**   Misis
Kozanli   Mihmandar   Erzin   Dortyol
Yumurtalik   Iskenderun   Payas   Guvenc
Gulf   Iskenderun   Yalangoz
Iskele   Belen   Kirikhan   Afrin
Arsuz   Amik   Reyhanli
Golu   Harim
Musa Dag   **Antakya**   Samandagi
4446   Bezge   Yayladagi   Idlib

CYPRUS
C. Kormakiti   C. Andreas
Kyrenia   Yialousa
Lefka   Morphou   Rizokarpaso   Ras Shamrah   Qalat   Ma'arrat
Evrykhou   Nicosia   Ayios Theodoros   Ras Ibn Hani   Sahyun   an Nu'man
Olympus   Prastio   Famagusta B.   **Al Ladhiqiyah**   Haffah
6403   Stavrovouni   Athna   Famagusta   **(Latakia)**
Khirokitia   2258   Tymbou   Dhekelia   Jablah
Larnaka   C. Greco   Baniyas   **Hamah**
Episkopi   C. Kiti   Al Quadmus   **(Hama)**
Akrotiri   **LATAKIA**   Masyaf   Kafr
Gata   Tartus   Safita   **Hims**
C. Zevghari   Hamidiyah   Shin   **(Homs)**

M E D I T E R R A N E A N

Tall Kalakh   Al
Halba   Qubayat   Al Qusayr
Riblah
Tarabulus   Al Mina   Mihniyah   Al Hatmal
(Tripoli)   Zagharta   Basharri   Al Qa
Amyun   Ba'labakk
Al Batrun   Qurtada   Alqa
Jubayl   An Nabk
Ghazir   **Ba'labakk**
Juniyah   Malula
Bayrut   Riyaq
(Beirut)   **Zahlah**   Al Qutayfah
Ba'abda   **Alayh**
Ash Shuwayfat   Zabdani
Bayt ad Din   Duma
Ba'qlin   Soghbin   **Esh Sham**
Sayda   Rashayya   **(Damascus)**
(Sidon)   Qatana   N. el Awaj
As Sarafand   **Jazzin**   Kiswah   Buraq
Marj'Uyun   Baniyas
Sur (Tyre)   Metulla   **Al Qunaytirah**   Al Mismiyah
Qana   Tibnin   Bint   Na'ran
An Naqurah   Jubayl
Nahariya   Zated   Izra   Shahba
Kefar   Carmiel   Tiberias   Nawa   **As**
Acre   L. of Galilee   Kh.   **Suwayda**
Haifa   Tiberias   Al Ghazale
Tirat Karmel   1732   **Nazareth**   Yarmuk   Dar'a
Dor (Tantura)   Mt. Carmel   Afula   Irbid   Busra ash
ISRAEL   Janin   Beit Shean   Ar Ramtha   Sham   Salkhad
Hadera   Ajlun   Al Malraq Imbron
Natanya   Burqa   Nablus   L. Ajlun   Jarash
Tul Karm   Qalqiliyah   Zarqa
Tel Aviv   Herzliyya   Jordan   Salt
Jaffa   Petah Tiqva   Az Zarqa
Holon   Lod (Lydda)   Ram Allah   Naur   **Amman**
Bat Yam   Ramle   Jericho   **JORDAN**
Yibna   Rehovot
Ashdod   Hamama   **Jerusalem**
Aguro   Bayt Lahm
Ashqelon   Faluja   (Bethlehem)
Dara   **Al Khalil**
Gaza   (Hebron)
Yatta
Khan Yunis   Dhahiriya
Rafah   Masada
Sabkhet el Bardawil   Mazra
E G Y P T (U.A.R.)   **Beersheba**
El Arish

SYRIA
Muhraddah
Jisr ash
Shughur
Ariha

THE LEVANT
Scale 1:4,000,000
(64 miles=1 inch)
Statute Miles
10 0 10 20 30 40 50
Kilometres
10 0 10 20 30 40 60 80
━━━ Railways
···· Oil Pipelines
·6644 Heights in feet

Projection: Conical with two standard parallels.

Copyright, George Philip & Son, Ltd.

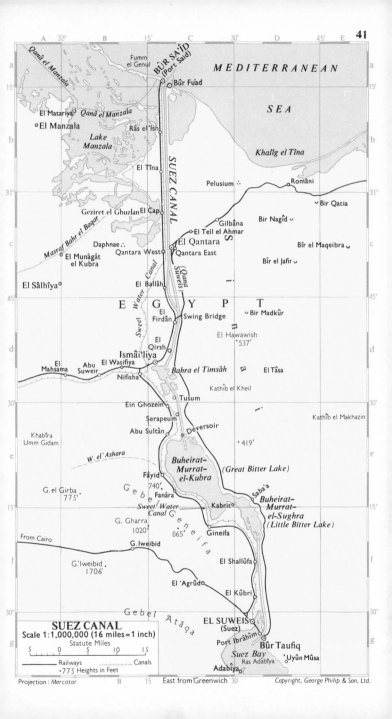

41

SUEZ CANAL
Scale 1:1,000,000 (16 miles = 1 inch)

Statute Miles

Railways ——— Canals

•775 Heights in Feet

Projection: *Mercator* B 15 East from Greenwich 30 *Copyright, George Philip & Son, Ltd.*

Map labels

- Qanâ el Manzala
- Fumm el Genul
- BÛR SAÎD (Port Saïd)
- Bûr Fuâd
- MEDITERRANEAN SEA
- El Matarîya
- Qanâ el Manzala
- El Manzala
- Râs el 'Ish
- Lake Manzala
- Khalîg el Tîna
- El Tîna
- SUEZ CANAL
- Pelusium
- Români
- Gezîret el Ghuzlan
- El Cap
- Gilbâna
- Bir Nagîd
- Bir Qatia
- Masraf Bahr el Baqar
- Daphnae
- El Tell el Ahmar
- El Qantara
- Bîr el Maqeibra
- El Munâgât el Kubra
- Qantara West
- Qantara East
- Bîr el Jafir
- El Sâlhîya
- El Ballâh
- Qanâ Suweis
- EGYPT
- Sweet Water Canal
- El Firdân
- Swing Bridge
- Bir Madkûr
- El Qirsh
- El Hawawish 537'
- Ismâ'lîya
- El Mahsama
- Abu Suweir
- El Wasifîya
- Nifisha
- Bahra el Timsâh
- El Tâsa
- Kathîb el Kheil
- Tusum
- Ein Ghozein
- Kathîb el Makhazin
- Serapeum
- Abu Sultân
- Deversoir
- 419'
- Khabîra Umm Gidam
- W. el 'Ashara
- Buheirat-Murrat-el-Kubra (Great Bitter Lake)
- Fâyid
- Gebel Geneifa
- 740'
- Fanâra
- Saba'a
- G. el Girba 775'
- Sweet Water Canal
- Kabrît
- Buheirat-Murrat-el-Sughra (Little Bitter Lake)
- G. Gharra 1020'
- 865'
- Gineifa
- From Cairo
- G. Iweibid
- El Shallûfa
- G. Iweibid 1706'
- El 'Agrûd
- El Kûbri
- Gebel 'Atâqa
- EL SUWEIS (Suez)
- Port Ibrâhîm
- Bûr Taufîq
- Suez Bay
- Ras Adabîya
- 'Uyûn Mûsa
- Adabîya

42

A 25 B 30 C 35 D 40 E

Bucharest
Pleven ○Ruse ○Constanta
BULGARIA
Turnovo ○Tolbukhin
Sofia Pazardzhik ○Sliven Varna
Plovdiv ○Sliven
Serno ○ Bramo
Edirne
Komotini Gelibolu **Istanbul** Zonguldak ○Sinop
Uskudar
İzmit Adapazarı ○Inebolu ○Samsun
Bandirma **Bursa Eskisehir Ankara** Kastamonu ○Amasya ○Ordu
Balikesir Kütahya Çankırı ○Yozgat Tokat Kelkit
Ayvalik Usak Alvonkarahisar L. Tuz **Kayseri** Sivas ○Erzincan
İzmir Manisa ○Denizli Isparta Eregli Malatya ○Elâzig ○Palu ○Muş
Aydın Milas ○Muğla Antalya Cilician Gates ○Adana Gaziantep (Euphrates) Nusaybin
○Iraklion Rhodes Alanya Silifke Mersin ○Antakya Urfa
(Candia) **CYPRUS** Nicosia Al Ladhiqiyah **Halab** **Al Mawsil**
Crete Paphos Famagusta (Latakia) **(Aleppo)** **(Mosul)**
Larnaka Baniyas **SYRIA** Deir ez Zor ○Anah
Limassol Tarabulus Hamat
○Homs Palmyra
LEBANON
Bayrut Zahlah
(Beirut) **Esh Sham**
Acre **Damascus** Ar Rutban
Tyre As Suwayda
Haifa **ISRAEL** Busra J. Unayzah ○Karbala
Tel Aviv **Jaffa** ○An Najaf
Rashid(Rosetta) Dumyat Bur Said ○El Arish **Amman**
El Iskandariya (Damietta) (Port Said) **Jerusalem** ○As Samaw
(Alexandria) El Mansura Suez Canal **JORDAN** Sakaka As Salman
Damanhur El Suweis Ma'an Rafha
El Qattara **Tanta** El Giza (Suez) ○Nekhl **Al Jawf**
Libyan Zagazig El Qantara Qal'at el Mudauwara
Cairo El Wasta Sinai ○Aqaba
Desert El Faiyum Beni Suef ○Mt. Sinai Haql Haiyaniya ○Lina
El Bahnasa Abu Zenima 7497 ○Maqna An Nafud ○Turubah
El Bawiti Er Roda ○Tor ○Al Haraiba Tayma ○Jabal Shammar ○Ajibba
El Minya ○Dhaba Hail
Manfalut Hurghada Bur
Asyut P. Safaga Anaiza ○Ar Rass
EGYPT Sohag ○Quseir Al Wajih W Hamdh Khaibar ○Hanak ○Umm Lajj **SAUDI** Adh
Nag Hammadi ○Qena **ARABIA**
El Kharga Isna (Thebes) Al'Ula Dafina
(UNITED Bulaq G. Sabahi ○Luxor 4845 ○Kôm Ombo **Medina** ○Afif
ARAB Idfu G. Hamata 6486 Ras Banas Yenbo ○Raiis
REPUBLIC) Aswan High Dam
Tropic of Cancer Halaib ○Qadhima Rabigh ○Muwaih
Kiseiba G. 7270 ○Usfan ○Ashaira
Deraheib ○Asoteriba **Mecca**
Semna Qadhima Jidda ○Bahra
Kosha Nubian Taif
Delgo **SUDAN** Desert G. Oda J. Ibrahim
Meheiza ○Abu Hamed 7412 Al Lith 852†
Dongola Nile Port Sudan

Projection: Conical Orthomorphic with two standard parallels D 40 E East from

CENTRAL
MIDDLE EAST COUNTRIES
Scale 1:17,500,000 (280 miles = 1 inch)

Statute Miles

Kilometres

	Railways	Oil-pipe Lines
	Principal Roads	•7350 Heights in feet
	Caravan Routes and Tracks	

R.

Fort Shevchenko

KAZAKHSTAN

zlyar

Makhachkala

Derbent

oznyy

Nukha Kuba

Kirovabad

ra

Sevan

AZERBAIJAN

Baku

Neftyne
Kamni

Krasnovodsk

T U R K M E N I S T A N

Bukhara

Kagan

Anu Darya

ran

Alyaty Pristan

Kara
Bogaz
Gol

Cheleken I.

Kizyl Arvat

Kara Kum

Chardzhou

Karshi

khichevan

Lenkoran

Ashkhabad

Mary

Kerki

Tabriz

Ardabil

Bander-e-
Pahlavi

Shahsavar

Bandar-e-Shah

Babol

Gorgan

Neyshabur

Sarakhs

Tashkepri

Mazar-i-Sharif

Urmia

Maraghel

Miane

Rasht

Mashhad

Kusnk

Maimana

Zanjan

Qazvin

Shahrud

Damghan

Sabzevar

Kuh-i-Dal
7350

Herat

Kohi-Sangan
2895

Bijar

Demavend
18380

Semnan

Gonabed

Ghurian

Shin Dand

AFGHANISTAN

Tehran

Daulatabad

ymaniya

(Sinneh)

Aveji

Qom

Dasht - e - Kavir

K h u r a s a n

Khuy

Birjand

Farah

Hamadan

Kermanshah

Arak

Daryacheh-ye
Namak

Tabas

Ardestan

Na'in

I R A N

Lash

bah

Borujerd

Kashan

Khash Rud

ad

Tigris

Dezful

Esfahan

Najafabad

Shahreza

Yazd

Dasht-i-Lut

Nehbandan

Daryacheh-ye-
Sistan

Zabol

Al Kut

Shushtar

Maydan-e

Bafq

Helmand

Al Amarah

Marjed

Naftun

Shir Kuh
13370

Anar

Ravar

An Nasiriyeh

Ahvaz

Kuh-e-Bol
13014

Bahramabad

Kerman

Kuh-eSeh Konj
13.103

Ladiz

Horal

Khorramshahr

Khuran

Kuh-i-Taftan
13034

ayyah

Al Basrah
(Basra)

Bandar-e-Shahpur

Hindian

Sa'idabad

Kuh-eHazaran
14,300

Zahedan

Abadan

Al Jahrah

Bandar-e-Rig

Khark I.

Shiraz

Neyriz

Rud-i-Khoran

Bam

Dizak

KUWAIT

Burgan

Kazerun

Fasa

Jahrom

Dawlatabad

Bampur

Riq'ai

Mena al
Ahmadi

Busehr

Borazjan

Kahnuj

Magos

Mashkel

Hafar al
Batin

Mishabb

Zira

Lar

Shamil

Minab

Makran

Al Lisafah

Manifa

Abu Hadriya

Taheri

Bandar Abbas

Remeshko

Bir

Dardan

Gwadar

Najma.o

Ras Tanura

Al Manamah

Bandar-e

Nay Band

Kuhran
7095

Fanuch

Al Qatif

Dhahran

Charak

Bandar-e-
Lengeh

Qeshm I.

Jask

Chah Bahar

Abqaiq

Uqayr

Ras Rakan

Gulf

Sharja

Gulf of 'Oman

Ain Darg

Bahrain I.

Dibai

D I

Al Mubarraz

Al Hufuf

Ad Dawhah

As Sohar

Arabian

ma

Ar Riyadh
(Riyadh)

Ithmaniya

Umm Said

Abu Dhabi

Mirfa

Buraimi

Al Khabura

Matrah

Muscat

Al Hair

Qatar

OMAN

Dhnk

Sarur

Sur

Ras al Hadd

Dilam

Haradh

W. Sabha

Silo

TRUCIAL

Thaih

J. asb Sham
9901

Aswat

MUSCAT

Awad

As Suwaih

Sea

nar

Qasr Umm Ramad

Jabrin

Ummaz Zamul

W. Muallim

W. Batha

Sharkh

Laila

Muqainama

W. Andam

Al Kaibah

I A

Al Faraja

R u b '   a l   K h a l i

Al Khalaf

Al Masira

Hamman

Adraj

Al Ain

Gulf of Masira

Sulayil

Ras al Madraka

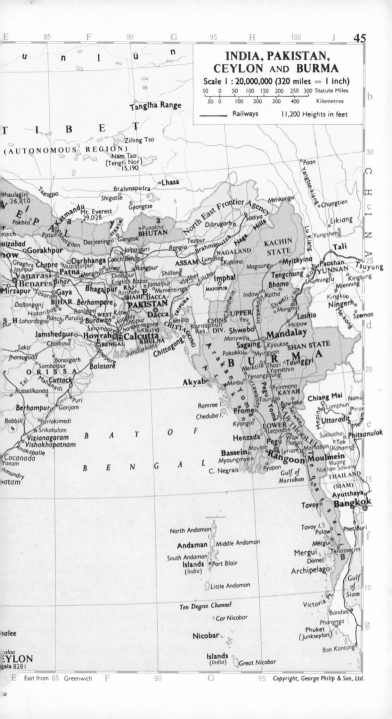

INDIA, PAKISTAN, CEYLON AND BURMA

Scale 1 : 20,000,000 (320 miles = 1 inch)

50 0 50 100 150 200 250 300 Statute Miles
50 0 100 200 300 400 Kilometres

────── Railways   11,200 Heights in feet

u   n   l   u   n

Tanglha Range

TIBET

(AUTONOMOUS REGION)   Zilling Tso

Nam Tso
(Tengri Nor)
15,190

Tsangpo   Brahmaputra   oLhasa

haulagiri   Shigatse   Gyangtse
26,810

Pokhra   Kathmandu   Mt. Everest   Paan   Yangtze-kiang   Chungtien
29,028

Pokhra   Paro   BHUTAN   a   North East Frontier Agency   Menkongo   Likiang

raich   Patan   Darjeelingo   Gangtok   Punakha   Dibrugarh   Sadiya   Lu Kiang   Yungsheng

aizabad   NEPAL   Jalpaiguri   Rangia   Tezpur   Brahmaputra   Naga   KACHIN   Tali

Gorakhpur   Cooch Behar   ASSAM   Lumding   Hills   STATE   suyung

ow   Ghaghra Chopra Muzaffarpur   Rangpur   Shillong   Kohima   Mogaung   Myitkyina   Paoshan   YUNNAN

Jaunpur   Patna   Dinajpur   Mymensingh   Silchar   NAGALAND   Tengchung   Kingtung

Vanarasi   Monghyr   Rajshahi   E.   Imphal   Indaw   Bhamo   Shurningliu   Mienning

Benares   Bhagalpur   RAJ-   DACCA   MANIPUR   Katha   Shweli   Mongmit   Kingko   Ningerh

Mirzapur   Gaya   Berhampore   SHAHI   PAKISTAN   Comilla   Karnaphuli   UPPER   Hsipaw   Lashio   Szemao

Sasaram   BIHAR   Burdwan   Hooghly   Khulna   CHITTAGONG   CHINS   DIV.   Shwebo   Kyaukse   SHAN STATE

Daltonganj   Hazaribagh   WEST   Chandernagore   Res.   Yeu   Monywa   Sagaing   Mandalay

H   Lohardaga   Ranchi Purulia   BENGAL   Serampore   Karnaphuli   Meiktila Thazi   Yamethin   Taunggyi

Jamshedpur   Howrah   Calcutta   KHULNA   Sundarbans   Chittagong   BURMA   Minbu   Pyinmana   KAYAH

Sakti   Chaibasa   Bonaigarh   Balasore   Akyab   Arakan   Toungoo   Bawlake   Chiang Mai   Nano

Jharsuguda   Sambalpur   ORISSA   Tel   Cuttack   Ramree I.   Prome   Lamphun   Phrae

Russellkonda   Mahanadi   Puri   Cheduba I.   Kyangin   Henzada   LOWER   Letpadan   Sukhothai   Uttaradit   Phitsanulok

Berhampur   Ganjam   Bassein   Maubin   Pegu   Thaton   Tak   Rahaeng

Bobbili   Parlakimedi   BAY   OF   Myaungmya   Syriam   Martaban   Muang   Moulmein

Srikakulam   Vizianagaram   Henzada   Pyapon   Rangoon   Nakhon Sawan

Vishakhapatnam   BENGAL   C. Negrais   Gulf of   THAILAND   Ayutthaya

Anakapalle   Martaban   (SIAM)   Bangkok

Cocanada   Yanam   Tavoy

hmundry   North Andaman   Tavoy I.   Palaw   Phet Buri

atam   Andaman   Middle Andaman   Mergui   Tenasserim

South Andaman   Islands   oPort Blair   Domel   Gulf

(India)   Little Andaman   Archipelago   of   Siam

Ten Degree Channel   Victoria Pt.

o Car Nicobar   Bandon

halee   Nicobar   Phangnga

caloa   Phuket   Ban Kantang

EYLON   (Junkseylon)

gala 8281   Islands   Great Nicobar

(India)

a

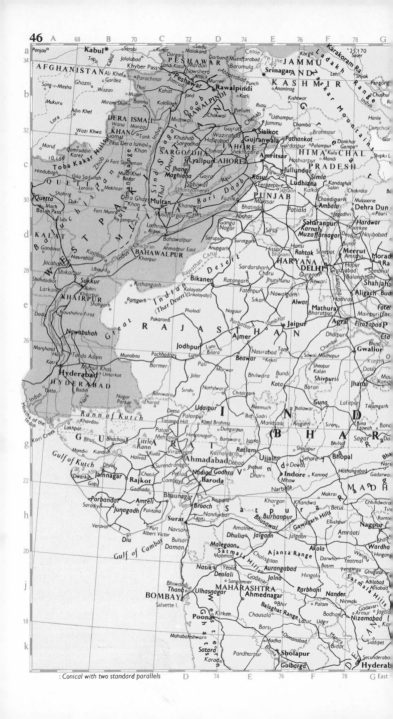

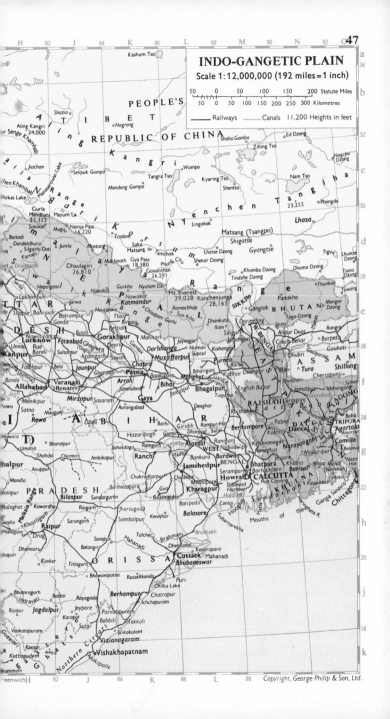

48

EAST INDIES
AND
FURTHER INDIA
Scale 1:25,000,000
(400 miles = 1 inch)

Railways
Oil Pipe Lines   Canals
9612 Heights in feet

Projection: *Conical*

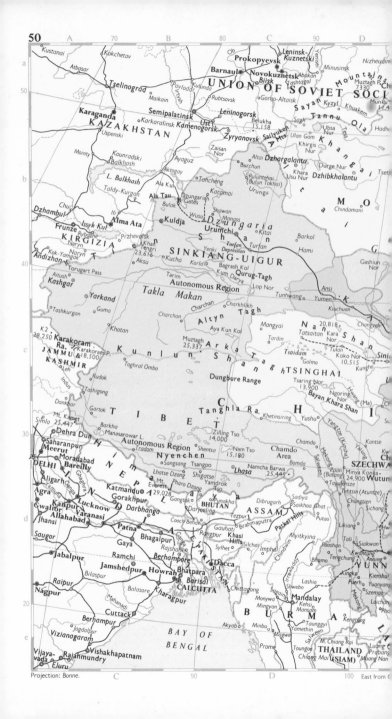

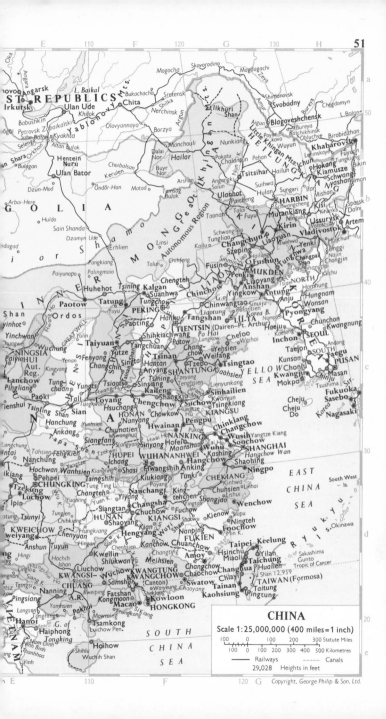

CHINA

Scale 1:25,000,000 (400 miles=1 inch)

100   0   100   200   300 Statute Miles
100   0   100 200 300 400 500 Kilometres

—— Railways   —— Canals
29,028 Heights in feet

Copyright, George Philip & Son, Ltd.

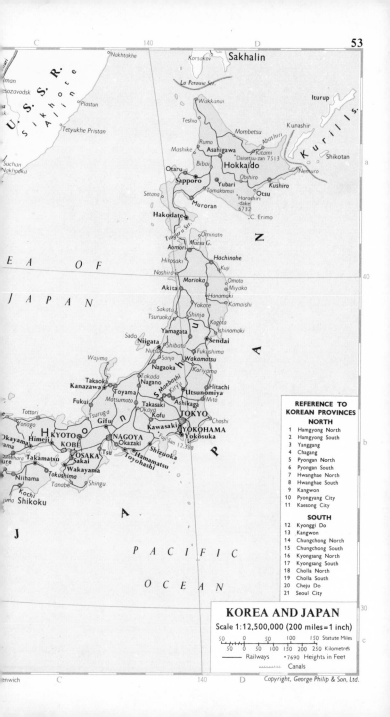

54

REFERENCE TO PREFECTURES

HOKKAIDŌ DISTRICT	KINKI DISTRICT
1 Hokkaido	24 Hyogo
	25 Kyoto
TŌHOKU DISTRICT	26 Shiga
2 Aomori	27 Osaka
3 Akita	28 Nara
4 Iwate	29 Mie
5 Yamagata	30 Wakayama
6 Miyagi	
7 Fukushima	**CHŪGOKU DISTRICT**
	31 Tottori
CHŪBU DISTRICT	32 Okayama
8 Niigata	33 Shimane
9 Ishikawa	34 Hiroshima
10 Toyama	35 Yamaguchi
11 Fukui	
12 Gifu	**SHIKOKU DISTRICT**
13 Nagano	36 Kagawa
14 Yamanashi	37 Tokushima
15 Aichi	38 Ehime
16 Shizuoka	39 Kochi
KANTŌ DISTRICT	**KYŪSHŪ DISTRICT**
17 Gumma	40 Fukuoka
18 Tochigi	41 Saga
19 Saitama	42 Nagasaki
20 Ibaraki	43 Kumamoto
21 Tokyo	44 Oita
22 Chiba	45 Miyazaki
23 Kanagawa	46 Kagoshima

Sea of Okhotsk

HOKKAIDO

Sapporo

TŌHOKU

Sendai

Sado

U. S. S. R.

Vladivostok

S E A   O F

J A P A N

Gulf of Korea

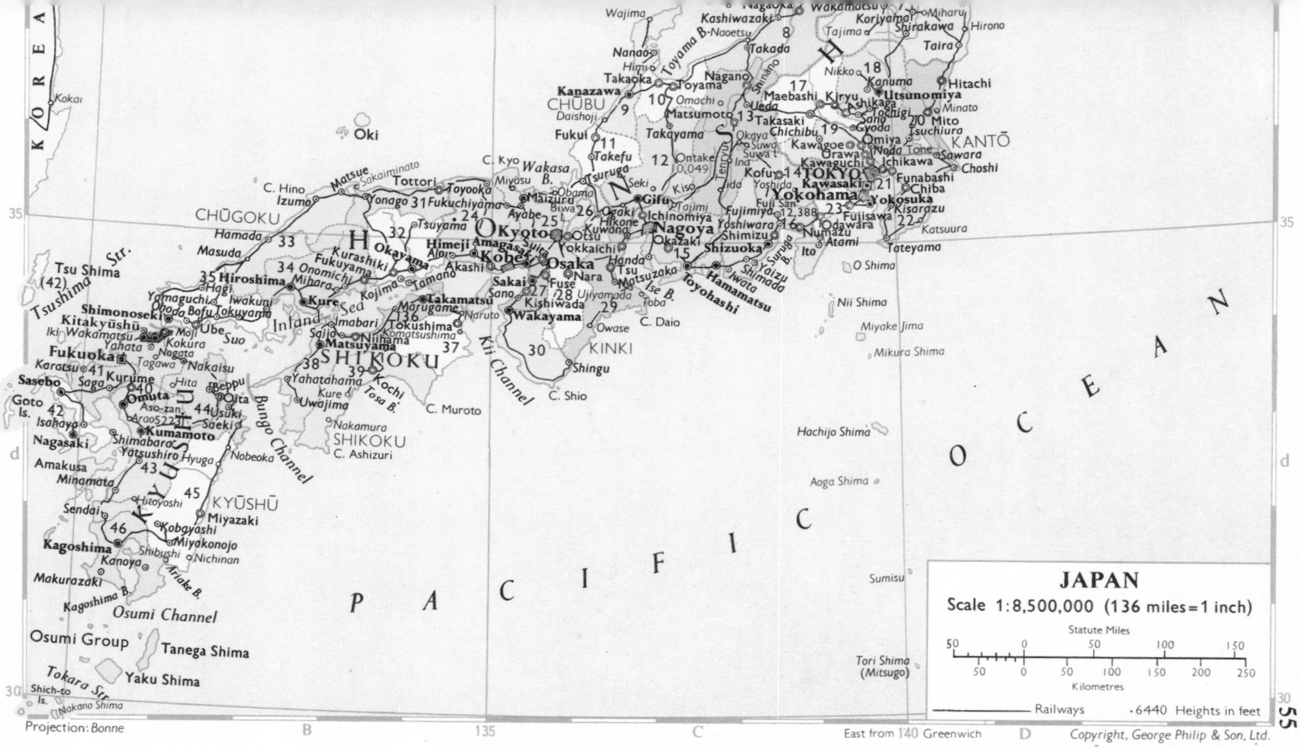

JAPAN

Scale 1:8,500,000 (136 miles = 1 inch)

Statute Miles

Kilometres

—— Railways   .6440 Heights in feet

Copyright, George Philip & Son, Ltd.

PACIFIC OCEAN

KOREA

HONSHU

CHUBU
CHUGOKU
KINKI
KANTŌ
SHIKOKU
KYŪSHŪ

TOKYO
Yokohama
Kawasaki
Chiba
Yokosuka
Funabashi
Utsunomiya
Mito
Hitachi
Chōshi
Katsuura
Tateyama
Atami
Itō
Numazu
Shizuoka
Shimizu
Hamamatsu
Toyohashi
Nagoya
Gifu
Ichinomiya
Ōkazaki
Seto
Yokkaichi
Tsu
Ise B.
Nara
Ōsaka
Kōbe
Kyōto
Sakai
Wakayama
Kishiwada
Amagasaki
Himeji
Toyooka
Tottori
Okayama
Kurashiki
Onomichi
Fukuyama
Hiroshima
Kure
Iwakuni
Hamada
Masuda
Yamaguchi
Shimonoseki
Ube
Kitakyūshū
Kokura
Fukuoka
Saga
Sasebo
Nagasaki
Isahaya
Ōmuta
Kumamoto
Sendai
Kagoshima
Miyazaki
Nobeoka
Ōita
Beppu
Nakatsu
Takamatsu
Tokushima
Matsuyama
Kōchi
Imabari
Uwajima
Nakamura
Naze
Oki
Izumo
Matsue
Kanazawa
Toyama
Takaoka
Nagano
Matsumoto
Ueda
Takada
Fukui
Tsuruga
Maizuru

Tsushima
Tsu-shima
Iki
Gotō Is.
Goto Is.
Tanega Shima
Yaku Shima
Ōsumi Group
Ōsumi Channel
Tokara Str.
Tokara Gunto

Ō Shima
Nii Shima
Miyake Jima
Mikura Shima
Hachijo Shima
Aoga Shima
Sumisu
Tori Shima (Mitsugo)

Kii Channel
Bungo Channel
Suo
C. Muroto
C. Shio
C. Dalo
Owase
Shingu
C. Ashizuri
C. Toa B.
C. Hino

Projection: Bonne

East from 140 Greenwich

D

UNION OF SOVIET SOCIALIST REPUBLICS

Lena
Kirensk

Stanovoi Range

B e r i n g

Sea

Mt. Klyuchevsk 15,912

Komandorskiye Is.

Near I. (U.S.)

Kiska I. (U.S.)

Bristol

Andreanov Is. Dutch Harbor

Aleutian Islands

Yablonovy Range

L. Baikal

Chita Shilka Sretensk

Nerchinsk

Vitim

Uda B.

Uban B.

Nikolayevsk

Sea of

Okhotsk

Ust Botsheretsk

Petropavlovsk-Kamchatski

Aleksandrovsk

Kamchatka

C. Lopatka

MONGOLIA

Gobi or Shamo

Inner Mongolia

Tsitsihar

Blagoveshchensk

Khabarovsk

Sakhalin

G. of Tartary

La Perouse Str.

Kuril Islands

Harbin

Changchun

Mukden

Peking

Tientsin

CHINESE REP.

Sinan

Sian

Tsingtao

Hwang

Kaifeng

Yenta

Lu-Ta

Seoul

Wonsan

Fusan

Korea Strait

Vladivostok

Tsugaru Strait

Sea of

Japan

Hokkaido

Hakodate

Sendai

TOKYO

Yokohama

Nagoya

Osaka

Kyoto

Manch-

Aritung

Sikhote Range

Yokohama to Honolulu 3379

Nanking

Wuhan

Yangtse-Kiang

Hangchow

Changsha

SHANGHAI

Wenchow

Foochow

East

China

Sea

Nagasaki

Kyushu

Shikoku

Ryukyu Is.

Midway I. U.S

Lisianski I. (U.S.)

Laysan I. (U.S.)

Wuchow

Amoy

Canton

Hongkong

Macao

Taipeh

Taiwan (Formosa)

Bashee Channel

Bonin Is.

Marcus I.

Hainan

C. Engano

Hue

VIETNAM

Luzon

Quezon City

Manila

PHILIPPINES

Mariana or Ladrone Is. (U.S. Trust Territory)

Wake I. (U.S.)

Yap to Yokohama 1660

P   A   C

MALAYSIA

Labuan

SABAH

Palawan

Mindoro

Panay

Negros

Samar

Mindanao

Apo Vol 9690

Yap

Palau

Guam (U.S.)

Truk I.

Ponape

Sulu Sea

Caroline Islands (U.S. Trust Territory)

Marshall Islands

Jaluit · (U.S. Trust Territory)

International Date Line

Suva to Honolulu

Baker I. (U.S.)

Canton I.

Natuna

SARAWAK

Celebes Sea

Manado

Halmahera

Dampier Strait

Equator

Schouten Is.

Admiralty (Austral. Trust Territory) Is.

Makin

Gilbert Is.

Nauru (N.Z. & Austral. Br. Trust Territory)

(Br. & U.S.)

Endurbury

Phoenix Islands

Borneo

Buru Ceram

New Guinea

Madang

New Ireland

Banggai Tanimbar

Aru

Papua

Lae

New Britain

Solomon Islands

Ellice Is.

Tokelau

Java Sea

Sumatra Bali

Makassar

Celebes

Banda Sea

Amboina

Flores Sea

Flores

Arafura Sea

Thursday Is.

Torres Strait

York

Port Moresby

Louisiade Arch.

Guadalcanal

Duff Is.

Santa Cruz

Funafuti

Rotuma

W. Samoa

Tutuila (U.S.)

Lombok

Sumbawa

Sumba

Timor

Ashmore Is.

Darwin

Arnhem

G. of Carpentaria

Coral

New Hebrides (Br. & Fr.)

Vanua Levu

Viti Levu

Suva

Fiji Is.

Palmersto

C. Levêque

Wyndham

Katherine

Newcastle Waters

Cairns

Barrier Reef

Chesterfield (Fr.)

Sea

New Caledonia

Loyalty Is.

Tongatabu

Tonga

Niue

Rai

North West Cape

Onslow

NORTHERN TERRITORY

Mt. Isa

Townsville

Rockhampton

Brisbane to Suva

Sydney to Suva 1743

Norfolk I.

Auckland to Apia

Suva to Tahiti 3299

Shark Bay

Steep Pt.

Nannine

Alice Springs

Longreach

Maryborough

Brisbane

Ipswich

QUEENSLAND

Toowoomba

C. Byron

1527

1038

1150

Sydney to Tahiti 3299

Auckland to Rarotonga 1636

Wellington to Rarotonga 1815

Geraldton

AUSTRALIA

Kalgoorlie

SOUTH AUSTRALIA

Darling

NEW SOUTH WALES

Lord Howe I.

S. to A. 1264

C. North

Fremantle

Perth

WESTERN AUSTRALIA

Eyre

Pt. Pirie

Adelaide

Murray

Newcastle

Blue Mountains

Wollongong

Canberra

Kosciusko 7316

S. to W. 1201

Auckland

North I.

Hamilton

Ruapehu 9175

Wanganui

Geographe B.

C. Leeuwin

Albany

K. George Sd.

Great Australian Bight

Fremantle to A. 1353

Encounter Bay

Geelong

VICTORIA

Bendigo

MELBOURNE

Sydney

Tasman

C. North

Nelson

South I.

Mt. Cook 12,349

NEW ZEALAND

Wellington

Palmerston N.

Christchurch

Chatham Is.

Bass Strait

TASMANIA

Launceston

Hobart

H. to W. 1293

Sea

Cook Strait

Oamaru

Dunedin

M. to Cape Town 5814

H. to C.T. 5838

H. to B. 940

Stewart I.

Invercargill

Bounty Is.

Antipodes I.

Auckland I.

Campbell I.

PACIFIC OCEAN

Equatorial Scale 1:100,000,000 (1600 miles = 1 inch)

———— Railways ---- 4570 Shipping Routes (Dist. in Naut. Miles)

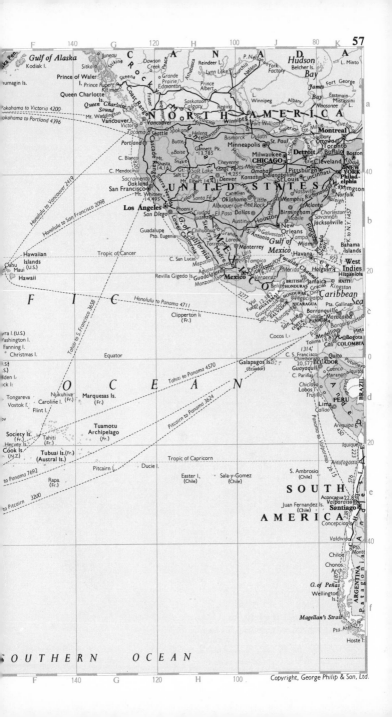

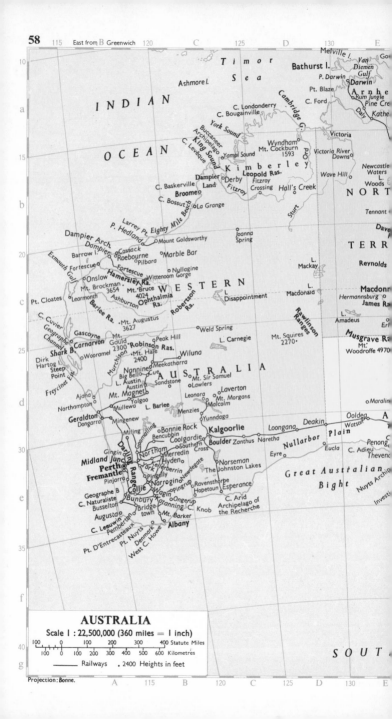

Timor

Sea

INDIAN

OCEAN

Ashmore I.

Melville I.
Van
Diemen
Gulf

Bathurst I.
P. Darwin
Pt. Blaze
Darwin
Arnhe
Rum Jungle
Pine Cre
Kathe

C. Londonderry
C. Bougainville
Cambridge G.
C. Ford

Buccaneer
Archipelago
York Sound
King Sound
C. Leveque
Yampi Sound

Wyndham
Mt. Cockburn
1593

Victoria

Victoria River
Downs

Kimberley
Leopold Ras.
Fitzroy
Fitzroy
Crossing
Hall's Creek

Newcastle
Waters
L.
Woods

N O R T

C. Baskerville
Dampier
Derby
Broome
C. Bossut
La Grange
Land

Sturt

Wave Hill

Tennant

Dave

Larrey Pt. Eighty Mile Beach
P. Hedland
Mount Goldsworthy

Joanna
Spring

T E R R

Dampier Arch.
Dampier
Barrow I.
Cossack
Roebourne
Marble Bar
Pilbara

L.
Mackay

Reynolds

Exmouth
Gulf
Fortescue
Onslow

Fortescue
Wittenoom Gorge
Nullagine

L.
Macdonald

Macdonn
Hermannsburg
James Ra

Pt. Cloates
Learmonth
Mt. Brockman
3654
Hamersley Ra.
Mt. Bruce
4024
Ashburton
Ophthalmia
Ra.

W E S T E R N

L.
Disappointment

Amadeus
Er

C. Cuvier
Barlee Ra.
Mt. Augustus
3627

Robertson
Ra.

Rawlinson
Ranges

Mt. Squires
2270

Musgrave Ra
Mt.
Woodroffe 4970

Geographe
Channel
Gascoyne
Shark B.
Carnarvon
Wooramel

Mt.
Gould
2300
Robinson Ras.
Mt. Hale
2400
Murchison

Peak Hill

Weld Spring

L. Carnegie

Dirk
Hartog I.
Steep
Point

Wiluna
Meekatharra
A U S T R A L I A

Freycinet Est.
Ajana
Northampton
Geraldton
Dongarra

Nannine
Big Bell
L. Austin
Austin
Sandstone
Cue

Mt. Sir Samuel
Lawlers

Mt. Magnet
Yalgoo
Mullewa
Mingenew

L. Barlee
Menzies

Laverton
Leonora
Mt. Morgans
Malcolm

Maralin

Milling
Goomalling
Bonnie Rock
Bencubbin
Coolgardie
Southern
Cross

Yunndaga

Kalgoorlie
Boulder Zanthus
Loongana
Deakin

Oolden
Watson

A

Gingin
Dalwallinu
Midland Junc.
Perth
Fremantle
Pinjarra

Northam
Merredin
York
Kellerberrin
Pingelly

Naretha

Nullarbor
Eyre
Eucla
C. Adieu

Penong

Thevenc

Plain

Hyden
Norseman
The Johnston Lakes

Great Australian

Darling
Range

Geographe B
Collie
Bunbury

Wogin
Narrogin
Pingrup
Ongerup
Katanning

Ravensthorpe
Hopetoun
Esperance

Bight

Nuyts Archi

Investi

C. Naturaliste
Busselton
Augusta
C. Leeuwin
Pemberton

Bridge-
town
Albany
Mt. Barker
Denmark

C. Arid
Archipelago of
the Recherche

Pt. D'Entrecasteaux
Pt. Nuyts
West C. Howe

S O U T

AUSTRALIA
Scale 1 : 22,500,000 (360 miles = 1 inch)
100   0   100   200   300   400 Statute Miles
100   0   100   200   300   400   500   600 Kilometres
———— Railways   . 2400 Heights in feet

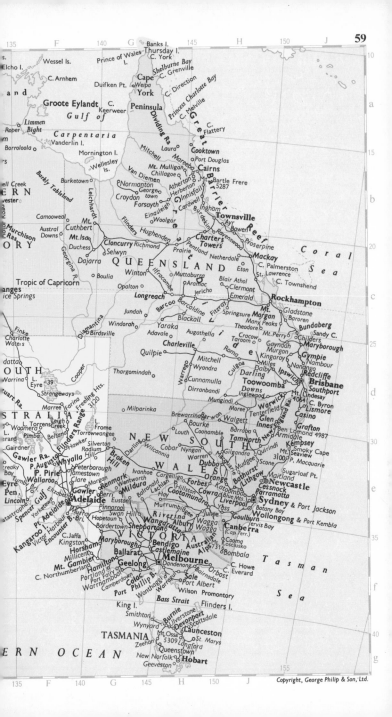

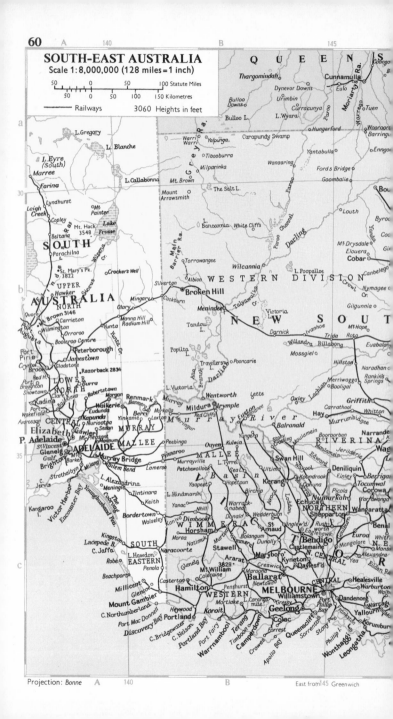

SOUTH-EAST AUSTRALIA
Scale 1:8,000,000 (128 miles=1 inch)

50   0   100 Statute Miles
50   0   50   100   150 Kilometres
——— Railways   3060 Heights in feet

Q U E E N S
Ciongo
Thargomindah   Cunnamulla
Dynevor Downs   Eulo   Tuen
Bulloo   Urimbin   Curracunya
Downs   Bulloo L.   L.Wyara   Paroo   Hungerford   Wooroore
Barringu
L.Gregory   Warri   Yalpunga   Carapundy Swamp   Yantabulla   Enngo
L. Blanche   Warri
L.Eyre   Tiboooburra   Wanaaring   Fords Bridge
(South)   L.Callabonna   Milparinka   Goombalie
Marree
Mt. Brown   The Salt L.   Louth   Bou
Farina   Mount   Byro
Leigh   Lyndhurst   Arrowsmith   L. Bancannia   White Cliffs   Coc
Creek   Mt   Mt.Drysdale   Gi
Copley   Painter   Lake   Wilcannia   Elouera   Cobar
Beltana   Frome   Torrowangee   Canbelego
Parachilna   Mt. Hack   Crocker's Well   W E S T E R N   D I V I S I O N
S O U T H   3548   Main   L. Poopallo   Nymagee
Hawker   St Mary's Pk.   Barrier Ra.   Silverton   Albion   Crowl   Gilgunnia
A U S T R A L I A   3822   Mingary   Broken Hill   Victoria   Mt Hope
NORTH   Olary   Cockburn   Meninee   Talyawalka Cr.   Ivanhoe   N E W   S O U T
Quorn   Brown 3146   Manna Hill   Tandou   Darnick   Trida   Roto   Euabalon
Carrieton   Radium Hill   L.   Willandra Billabong
Wilmington   Yunta   Popilta   Mossgiel   Hillston   Naradhan   Rankins
Augusta   Orroroo   Booleroo Centre   L.   Merriwagga   Springs
Port   Peterborough   Travellers   Pooncarie   Oxley   Lachlan   Griffith
Pirie   Jamestown   Anabranch   Booligal   Carrathool   Whitton
Crysta   Gladstone   L.Victoria   Wentworth   Lette   Hay   Murrumbidgee   Le
Red H.   Razorback 2834   Murray   Mildura   Buronga   Balranald   Boorborban   Narrande
Port   Broughton   Burra   Renmark   Morkalla   Drymple   Stony   Moulamein   Jerilderie   Wag
Snowtown   Clare   Barmera   Red Cliffs   Crossing   Edward   Deniliquin
Kadina   Riverton   Waikerie   Berri   Loxton   M u r r a y   River   Kakool   Finley   Berriga
Ardrossan   CENTRAL   Kapunda   Yinkanie   Echuca   Picola   Tocumwal
Wakefield   Nuriootpa   MURRAY   Yungera   NUMURKAH   Corowa
Elizabeth   Gawler   Sedan   MALLEE   Swan Hill   NORTHERN   Yarrawonga
P. Adelaide   St Vincent   Peebinga   Ouyen   Kulwin   Ultima   Koondrook   Shepparton   Wangaratta
ADELAIDE   Pinnaroo   Kerang   Cohuna
Glenelg   Gulf   Murray Bridge   MALLEE   L. Tyrrell   Rushw   Benal
Brighton   Barker   Murrayville   Patchewollock   Birchip   Loddon   Echawk   Euroa   Whitt
Strathalbyn   Milang   Tailem Bend   Lameroo   Hopetoun   Wedderburn   Bendigo   Mangalore   N.E.
Jervis   L. Alexandrina   Yaapeet   Donald   Ingle'w'd   Castlemaine   Yea   Alexandra
Kangaroo   Meningie   Tintinara   Yanac   Warrack-   St Arnaud   Maryboro'   Kyneton   Eildon Re
I.   Keith   nabeel   Daylesf'd
Victor Harbor   Bordertown   Nhill   Dimboola   Donald   Bolangum   Dunolly   CENTRAL   Healesville
Wolseley   Kaniva   Horsham   Murt   Stawell   Creswick   Warburton
Kingsto   SOUTH   Morea   Natimuk   Glenelg   Ararat   Mt William   BALLART   MELBOURNE   Walh
Lacepede B.   Naracoorte   Coleraine   3829   Maroona   Newtown   Williamstown   Dandenong
C. Jaffa   EASTERN   L. Hawdon   Casterton   Mt.William   Penshurst   WESTERN   Port   Narragi
Robe   Penola   Hamilton   Mortlake   Coranga-   CENTRAL   Phillip Bay   Yallourn
Beachport   Mount   Glenco   mite   Geelong   Wonthaggi   Korumbu
Millicent   Gambier   Heywood   Portland   Koroit   Colac   Queenscliff   Phillip I.
C.Northumberland   Port Mac Donnell   Port Fairy   Terang   Forrest   Sorrento   Leongatha
Discovery Bay   C.Bridgewater   Warrnambool   Timboon   Campden   Crowes   Apollo Bay   Stony

C · 150 · **D**

A N D

Oakey
Bendena   Binda   Bindle   Moonie   Toowoomba   Toowong   **BRISBANE**
Bollon   St George   Flinton   Pittsworth   Gatton   Laidley   Rosewood   Wynnum   Stradbroke I.
Mungallala Cr.   Nindigully   Millmerran   Clifton   Hendon   Ipswich   Southport
Mt. Domville   Warwick   Beaudesert   Pt. Danger
Noise R.   Hebel   Dirranbandi   Thallon   Yelarbon   Amiens   Killarney   Wilson   South Coast   Coolangatta
Dareel   Weir   Goondiwindi   Stanthorpe   Texas   Beaudesert   Murwillumbah
Hungerford   Angledool   Munindi   Boggabilla   Deepwater   Mullumbimby
Boodooga   Goondublui   Yetman   Tenterfield   Drake   Kyogle   C. Byron
Collarenebri   Boomi   Emmaville   England Ra.   Casino   Byron Bay
Brewarrina   Camurra   Glen Innes   Lismore   Ballina
Terewah L.   Pokataroo   Moree   Wariabda   4955   Rappville   Evans Head
Walgett   Bellata   Inverell   NORTHERN   Grafton   Maclean
Darling or Barwon   Pian Cr.   Wee Waa   Tingha   B. Lomond   Mt   Ulmarra
Gongolgon   Burren Junc.   Narrabri   Bundarra   4987   Hyland   Glenreagh
Pilliga   Namoi   Guyra   Dorrigo   Coff's Harbour
Nyngan   Coonamble   Baradine   Boggabri   TABLELAND   Urunga   Nambucca Heads
Quambone   Coonabarabran   N. WEST.   Armidale   Uralla   Bellingen   Macksville
CENTRAL   Warren   Gunnedah   SLOPE   Macleay   Smoky C.   Smithton & Gladstone
Nevertire   Gilgandra   Liverpool   Manilla   Walcha   Kempsey
PLAIN   Trangie   Plains   Peel   Tamworth   Hastings   Port Macquarie & Hastings R.
Tottenham   Narromine   Dubbo   Merriwa   Werris Cr.   Ra.   Comboyne
Tullamore   Peak Hill   Wellington   Dundedoo   Nundle   Wingham
Condobolin   Bogan Gate   Gulgong   Murrurundi   Taree   Manning
Trundle   Mudgee   Scone   Gloucester   Tuncurry   C. Hawke
Parkes   Molong   Rylstone   Hunter Ra.   Muswellbrook   Forster   Sugarloaf Pt
Forbes   Eugowra   CENTRAL   Newnes   Singleton   Greta   Port Stephens
Grenfell   Orange   Bathurst   TABLE   Lithgow   Kurri Kurri   Maitland   NEWCASTLE & Port Hunter
Canowindra   Portland   Cessnock   Wallsend
Cowra   Katoomba   Penrith   Gosford   Toronto
Young   Koorawatha   LAND   Windsor   Broken Bay & Hawkesbury R.
Temora   Grenfell   Tarana   Liverpool   Hornsby   Manly   SYDNEY   M-METROPOLITAN
SOUTH   Boorowa   3678   Parramatta   & Port Jackson
Cootamundra   Murrumburrah   Camden   Campbelltown   Cronulla & Botany B.
Ganmain   Junee   Burrinjuck   Pictton   Woilongong
WESTERN   Yass   Goulburn   Moss Vale   Shellharbour
Gundagai   Cullarin   Kiama
SLOPE   CANBERRA   Queanbeyan   Berry   (COMMONWEALTH TERR.)
Tumut   CAP. TER.   Nowra   Jervis Bay
Tumbarumba   Baldwood   Ulladulla
Hume Res.   Cooma   Batemans
Bogong 6508   Nimmitabel   Moruya
Kosciusko 7316   Narooma
Australian Alps   Bega
Hotham   Bombala   Eden   Twofold Bay
Omeo   Delegate   Green C.
Bright   Mt Ellery   Disaster B.
Brathen   4255   C. Howe
Maffra   Orbost   Gabo I.
Bairnsdale   Mallacoota Inlet
Sale   Wellington   Lakes Entrance
Woodside
Albert Inlet

C · 150 · **D**

TASMANIA
On the same scale

B · 145 · **C**

Narracoopa   Flinders I.
King I.   Bass Strait   Furneaux
Currie   Three Hummock   Group
Stokes Pt.   C. Barren I.   White Mark
Hunter I.   Robbins I.
Smithton   Stanley   Wynyard   Penguin
Arthur   N.W. Ulverstone   Latrobe   Bridport
Trowutta   Burnie   Devonport   Scottsdale
Waratah   Shef. d   Mole Cr.   Westbury   Launceston   Herrick
Cradle Mt.   Deloraine   Longford   Ben Lomond   5160
Zeehan   5114   L.   Great   St Marys
Queenstown   Westbury   L.   Campbell Tn   Avoca
C. Sorell   Torralea   MID.   Oatlands
Macquarie Harb.   Bothwell   Apsley
Pt Hibbs   New Norfolk   Glenorchy   Swansea   Maria I.
Huonville   HOBART
Geeveston   Storm Bay   C. Pillar
Port Davey   Dover   Bruny I.
S.E. Cape

a

b

c

d

30

35

40

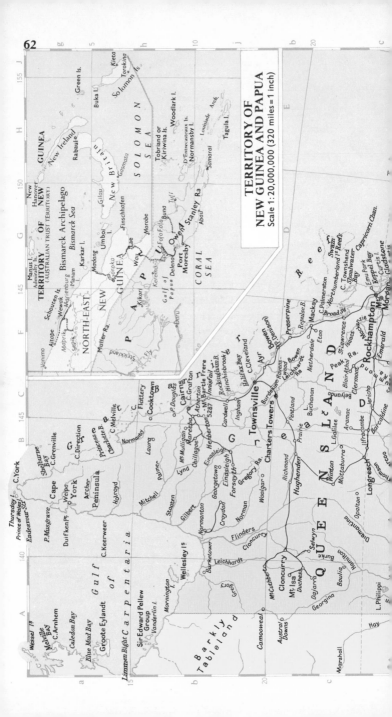

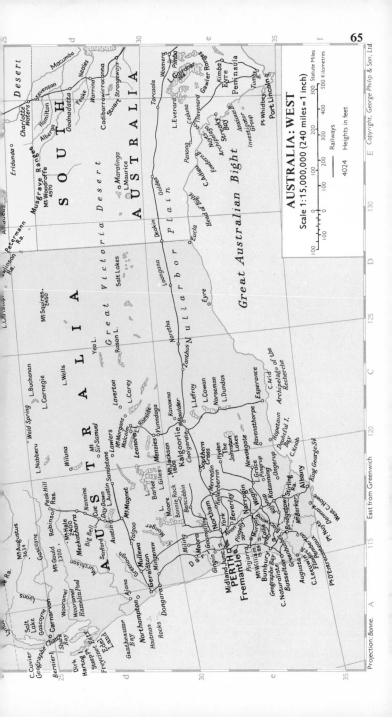

65

Charlotte Waters
Macumba
Stevenson
Neales
Hamilton
Oodnadatta
Alberga
Peake
Warrina
Cadibarrawirrachna
Stuart Strangways

SOUTH

Musgrave Range
Mt Woodroffe 4970

AUSTRALIA

Maralinga
L. Maurice

Womera
L. Gairdner
C. Pirbon
Tarcoola
Kimba
Gawler Ranges
Eyre Peninsula
Tumby
Ceduna
C. du Couedic
Streaky B.
Smoky B.
Nuyts Arch
Thevenard
Penong
Investigator Group
Pt Whidbey
Pt Lincoln

Great Victoria Desert

Salt Lakes

Deakin
Eucla
Nullarbor Plain
Loongana
Ooldea

Great Australian Bight

AUSTRALIA: WEST

Scale 1:15,000,000 (240 miles = 1 inch)

— Railways
4024 Heights in feet

E Copyright, George Philip & Son. Ltd

Wilsop
Erldunda
Petermann Ra.
Wilkinson Ra.
Mt Squires 2450

A U S T R A L I A

Yeo L.
Raeson L.
L. Wells
L. Carnegie
L. Buchanan
L. Nabberu
Weld Spring
Wiluna

Noretha
Eyre
Zanthus
Loongana

Mt Sir Samuel
Laverton
L. Carey
Leonora
Mt Morgans
Malcolm
Menzies
Yunndaga
Kanowna
Kalgoorlie
Coolgardie
L. Cowan
L. Lefroy
Norseman
L. Dundas
Esperance
C. Arid
Archipelago of the Recherche
Cape Le Grand
Doubtful I.

Mt Jackson
Southern Cross
The Johnston Lakes
Hyden
Lake Grace
Newdegate
Ravensthorpe
Hopetoun

Mt Magnet
Sandstone
Austin
L. Barlee
L. Giles
Bonnie Rock
Mullewa
Mingenew
Moore L.
Bencubbin
Mukinbudin
Merredin
Kellerberrin
Bruce Rock
Corrigin
Kulin
Lake King
C. Knob

Mt Hale 2400
Meekatharra
Nannine
Cue
Day Dawn
Big Bell
Sanford
Tuckanarra
Yalgoo
Tardun
Dalwallinu
Miling
Moora
Gingin
Wongan Hills
Goomalling
Toodyay
Northam
York
Beverley
Pingelly
Narrogin
Wagin
Katanning
Broomehill
Tambellup
Gnowangerup
Ongerup

Peak Hill Ras.
Robinson Ras.

Mt Gould 2300
Murchison

Gascoyne
Mt Augustus 3634
Lyons

C. Cuvier
Geographe Chan.
Shark Bay
Bernier I.
Dirk Hartog I.
Steep Pt
Freycinet Estuary
Edel Land
Gantheaume BAY
Zuytdorp Cliffs
Kalbarri
Hawks Head
Houtman Rocks
Ajana
Northampton
Dongara
Greenough
Geraldton
Port Gregory

PERTH
Fremantle
Midland Junction
Armadale
Pinjarra
Mandurah
Bunbury
Busselton
C. Naturaliste
Augusta
C. Leeuwin
Flinders B.
Pt D'Entrecasteaux
Donnybrook
Boyup Brook
Bridgetown
Greenbushes
Manjimup
Collie
Darkan
Williams
Narembeen
Wickepin
Kojonup
Cranbrook
Mt Barker
Denmark
Albany
King George Sd
West C. Howe
Stirling Ra.
Porongurup

Projection: Bonne.   A   115   East from Greenwich   B   120   C   125   D   130   E

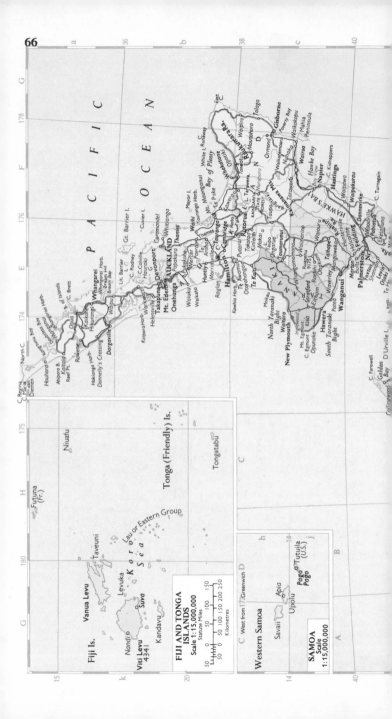

a 36 b 38 c 40

G
178

P A C I F I C

F
176

O C E A N

E

174

175

H 180

G

15

k

20

PACIFIC OCEAN

East C.

North C.
C. Regina
C. Maria
Diemen

Houhora
Red Nound Bay
Ahpara B.
Ronga a
Kaitaia o
Hokianga Harb.
Donnelly's Crossing
Rawene

Bay of Islands
Kerikeri
Kawakawa
Opua
Kaikohe
Kaeo
Hikurangi
Whangarei
Whangarei Harb.
Bream Hd.
Bream Bay

Dargaville
Waipu

Warkworth

Kaipara Harb.
Helensville

Maungaturoto

Lit. Barrier
C. Rodney
Gt. Barrier I.
Cuvier I.

C. Colville
C. Brett

Coromandel

Whitianga
Whangapoua
Waihi
Mayor I.
White I. Runaway
Maketu
Mt. Maunganui
Tauranga Harb.
Bay of Plenty

Te Araroa

Gisborne
Ormond
Waipiro
Tokomaru
Tolaga

Mahia Peninsula
Waikokopu

Takapuna
Devonport
AUCKLAND
Mt. Eden
Onehunga
Papakura

Thames
Te Aroha
Morrinsville
Paeroa
Putaruru
Cambridge
Mercer
Ngaruawahia
Hamilton
Huntly
Raglan
Waiuku
Pukekohe
Waikato

Kawhia Harb.

Te Kuiti

New Plymouth
North Taranaki
Bight
Waitara
Opunake
South Taranaki
Bight

Hawera

C. Egmont
Mt. Egmont
8260
Eltham
Stratford
Inglewood
Okato

Patea
Waverley
Waitotara
Wanganui

Marton
Bulls
Foxton Nr.
Levin
Otaki

C. Farewell
Golden
Bay
D'Urville I.
Collingwood
Bay

Rotorua
Te Puke
Rotorua
L. Rotorua
L. Tarawera
Kawerau
Murupara

Te Puke
Matata
Whakatane
Opotiki

RUAKUMARA

Waioeka
Wairoa
Frasertown

Napier
Hastings

HAWKE'S BAY
C. Kidnappers
Waipawa
Waipukurau
C. Turnagain

Taupo
L. Taupo
Turangi
Tokaanu
Mokai
Wairakei
Taumarunui
Ongarue
Taihape
Ohakune
Raetihi
Waiouru
Mangaweka

Morere
Tuai

PIRONGIA
Waimiha
Mt. Moungamui
Ongarue
Kinleith
STATE FOREST

Dannevirke
Woodville
Pahiatua
Eketahuna

RUAHINE MTS.

Ruapehu
9175
Hunterville
Ohingaiti
Mangamahu
Mangaweka

Feilding
Palmerston Nr.
Shannon

Ruatahuna
Kaingaroa

**FIJI AND TONGA
ISLANDS**
Scale 1:15,000,000
Statute Miles
50   0   50 100 150 200 250
50   0   50 100 150
Kilometres

Futuna
(Fr.)

Niuafu

Tonga (Friendly) Is.

Tongatabu

Lau or Eastern Group

K o r o
S e a

Fiji Is.

Vanua Levu

Taveuni

Levuka

Suva
Viti Levu
4341

Nandjo

Kandavu

C West from 17 Greenwich D h 174 j

B
40

Western Samoa

Savaii

Upolu
Apia

Pago
Pago Tutuila (U.S.)

SAMOA
Scale
1:15,000,000

A
14

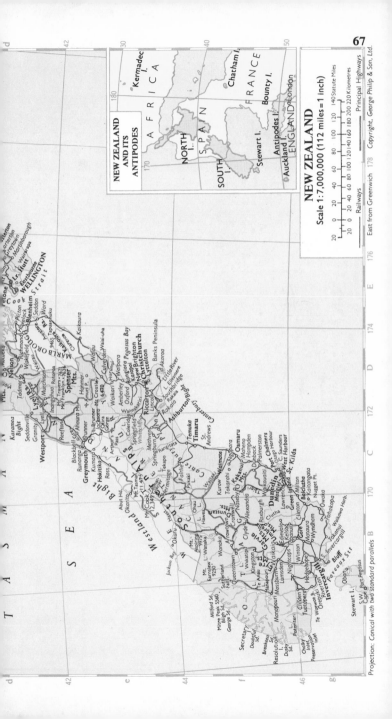

67

NEW ZEALAND

Scale 1:7,000,000 (112 miles = 1 inch)

20   0   20   40   60   80   100   120   140 Statute Miles

20   0   20   40   60   80   100   120 140 160 180 200 220 Kilometres

Railways ━━━   Principal Highways

East from Greenwich   176   178   Copyright, George Philip & Son, Ltd.

NEW ZEALAND AND ITS ANTIPODES

Kermadec I.
Chatham I.
Bounty I.
Stewart I.
Antipodes I.
Auckland I.
London
ENGLAND
FRANCE
SPAIN
NORTH
SOUTH
AFRICA

Projection: Conical with two standard parallels

T A S M A N   S E A

Karamea Bight

Westport

Greymouth
Hokitika
Ross

Mt. Cook
12,349

WESTLAND

SOUTHERN   ALPS

Mt. Tasman 11,475

Abut Hd.
Okarito

Jordan Bay

Mt. Earnslaw
9250

Milford Sd.
Mitre Peak 5560
Bligh Sd.
George Sd.

Secretary I.
Sutherland Falls
Douglas
Breaksea Sd.
Resolution I.
Dusky Sd.
Choky Inlet
Preservation Inlet

Mt. Aspiring
9975

Te Wae Wae B.
Riverton

Oban

Stewart I.
S.W. Cape
Cape Regius   Port Pegasus

Foveaux Str.

Bluff
Invercargill
Winton
Lumsden
Mossburn
Nightcaps
Nelson
Mt. Murchison
Tadmor
Granity
Seddonville

Spenser
Mts.

Reefton
Blackball
Runanga
Brunner
Mt. Brunner

Inangahua
Murchison

Lewis P.
Mt. Travers 7620
Mt. Franklin
Mt. Crossley
Kumara

L. Brunner

Otira
Arthur's Pass
Bealey

Ngatimoti

Hanmer
Waikari
Amberley
Oxford
Rangiora

Culverden Waiau-uha
Waipara
Pegasus Bay

Springfield
Whitecliffs
Coleridge

Methven

L. Coleridge
L. Heron

Hakatere
Mt. Peel

Mt. Somers

Sheffield
Darfield

New Brighton
CHRISTCHURCH
Riccarton
Lyttelton
Lincoln

Banks Peninsula
Akaroa

L. Ellesmere
L. Forsyth
Southbridge
Rakaia
Little River

Ashburton

Rakaia

(Canterbury)

Rangitata

Mayfield

Geraldine

Temuka
TIMARU

St. Andrews

Pleasant Pt.
Fairlie

Mt. Cook
Hermitage
Pukaki
L. Pukaki
Tekapo
L. Tekapo

Burke's Pass

Ohau
L. Ohau

Omarama

Kurow
Waitaki
Hawea
L. Hawea
L. Wanaka
Wanaka

Cromwell
Tarras
Clyde
Alexandra
Earnscleugh

Arrowtown
Queenstown
L. Wakatipu
Kingston

Garston
Athol

Gore

Mataura
Edendale
Wyndham

Clinton
Balclutha
Owaka
Nugget Pt.

Milton
Kaitangata

Green Island
St. Kilda
West Harbour
DUNEDIN
Port Chalmers
Otago Harbour
Cape Saunders

Lawrence
Roxburgh
Clutha
Roxburgh
L. Roxburgh
Ettrick

Palmerston
Moeraki
Hampden
Dunback
Waikouaiti

Oamaru
Maheno

Kakanui

Naseby
Ranfurly

Dunstan
Mts.

Raggedy
Mts.

Middlemarch
Outram
Mosgiel
Clarksville

Winton

Riverton

FIORDLAND

L. Te Anau
L. Manapouri
Monowai

L. Hauroko

Tuatapere
Clifden
Otautau
Waianiwa
Wairio

Waikaia
Riversdale
Balfour

Wakatipu

Waimate

Makarora

Mt. Aspiring

Doubtful Sd.

Ngapara

KAIKOURA

Kaikoura

Ward
Seddon
Wairau
Blenheim
Renwick
Picton

MARLBOROUGH

Spring Creek
Tua Marina
Havelock
Canvastown

Nelson

Richmond
Wakefield
Motueka
Takaka
Collingwood
Riwaka

Cloudy Bay

Cook   Strait

WELLINGTON
Lower Hutt
Petone
Eastbourne

Upper Hutt
Featherston
Greytown
Carterton
Masterton
Wairarapa

Paekakariki
Otaki

Ohau

Porirua

Cape Palliser

174

172

170

d

42

e

44

f

46

g

42

44

46

180   170

30   40   50

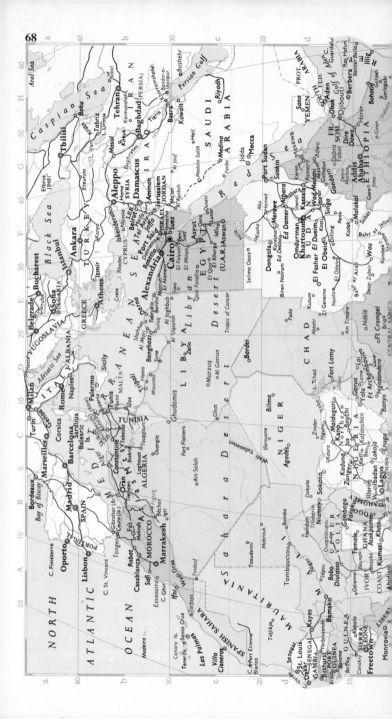

69

AFRICA

Scale 1 : 45,000,000 (720 miles = 1 inch)

200   0   200   400   600   800 Stat. Miles
200   0 200 400 600 800 1000 1200 Kilometres

—— Principal Railways   ------- Canals

17,058 Heights in feet

Copyright, George Philip & Son, Ltd.

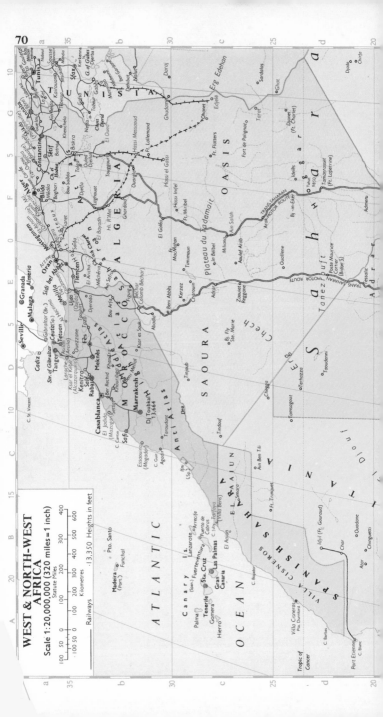

70

WEST & NORTH-WEST AFRICA
Scale 1:20,000,000 (320 miles=1 inch)

Statute Miles
100 50 0 100 200 300 400

Kilometres
100 50 0 100 200 300 400 500 600

Railways — -13,350 Heights in feet

ATLANTIC OCEAN

TUNISIA

Tunis
Sfax
G. of Gabès
Djerba
Kerkenna
Nabeul
Sousse
Kairouan
Gabès

Constantine
Sétif
Batna
Khenchela
Biskra
El Oued

ALGERIA

Oran
Mostaganem
Sidi bel Abbès
Tlemcen
Mascara
Tiaret
Laghouat
Ghardaïa
Touggourt
Ouargla

Hassi Messaoud
Ft. Lallemand
Ft. Flatters
Fort de Polignac
Djanet (Ft. Charlet)

OASIS

Fort Flatters
In Salah
Ain Salah
Fort Miribel
Timimoun
Reggane
Aoulef Arab
Ouallène

TRANS-SAHARAN MOTOR ROUTE

Tamanrasset (Ft. Laperrine)
9850
In-Eker
Bj.-in-Eker
Poste Maurice Cortier (Bidon 5)
Admer

S a h a r a

Erg Edehan
Ghadamès
Edjelé
Ghat
Tarat
Sardalas
Djado
Chirfa

M O R O C C O

Rabat
Casablanca
Meknès
Fès
Marrakesh
Dj. Toubkal 13,664
Agadir
Taroudant
Tiznit
Ifni (Sp.)
Essaouira (Mogador)
Safi
El Jadida (Mazagan)
Settat
Khouribga
Ben Rechid
Oued Zem
Khenifra
Beni Mellal
Kasba Tadla
Ksar es Souk
Taza
Oujda
Colomb Béchar (Béchar)
Figuig
Bou Arfa

SAOURA

Tindouf
Tinjoub
Abadla
Chegga
Taoudenni

EL SAHARA AAIUN

Smara
El Aaiun
Tarfaya (Villa Bens)
Tan Tan
Ain Ben Tili
Ft. Trinquet

SPANISH SAHARA VILLA CISNEROS

C. Bojador
Villa Cisneros, Pta. Durnford

MAURITANIA

Idjil (Ft. Gouraud)
Chor
Atar
Ouadane
Chinguetti
C. Barbas
C. Blanc
Port Étienne

Canary Is. (Span.)
Lanzarote
Fuerteventura
Gran Canaria
Las Palmas
Tenerife
Sta. Cruz
Gomera
Palma
Hierro

Madeira (Port.)
Funchal
Pto. Santo

Tropic of Cancer

Séville
Cadiz
C. St. Vincent
Granada
Málaga
Almería
Gibraltar (Br.)
Str. of Gibraltar
Tanger
Tetuan
Ceuta (Sp.)
Melilla

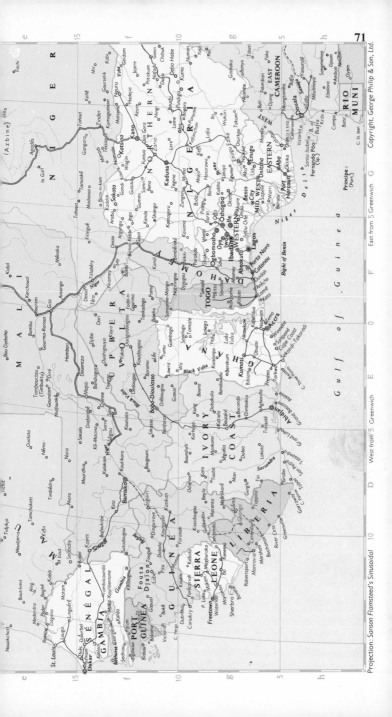

71

Projection: Sanson Flamsteed's Sinusoidal 10   D   West from 5 Greenwich   0   East from 5 Greenwich   G   Copyright, George Philip & Son, Ltd.

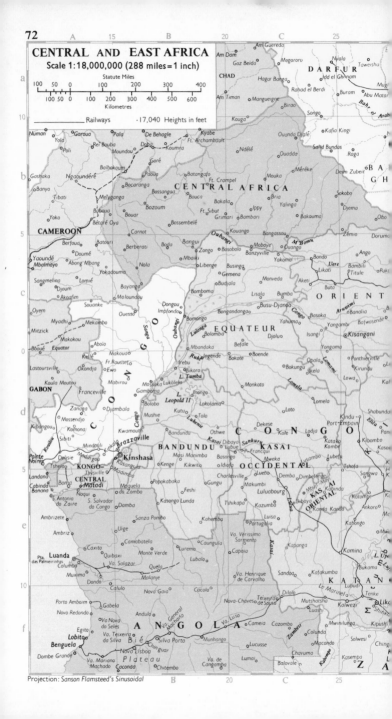

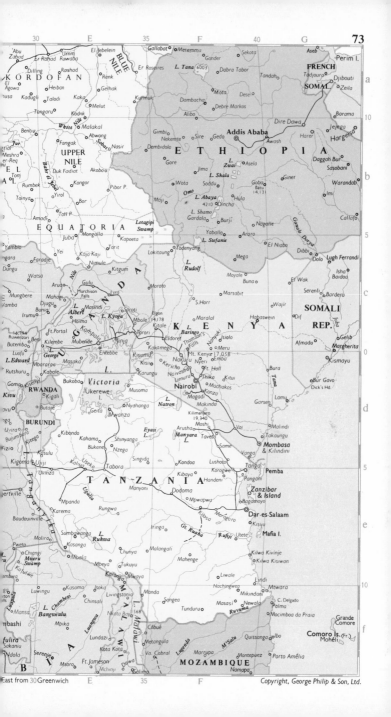

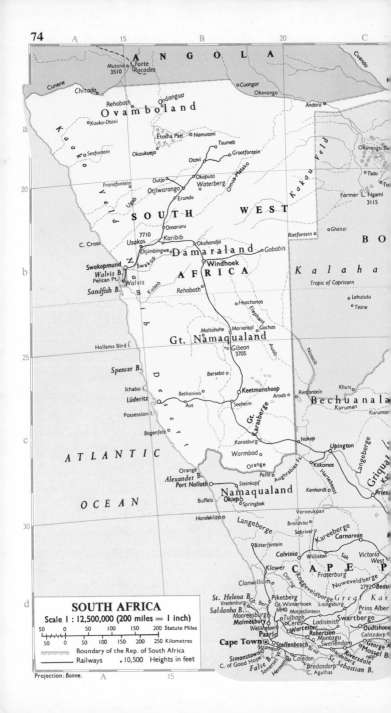

A N G O L A

Mutunda
3510
Forte
Rocades

Cunene

Chitado

Rehoboth

Ondangua

Kaoko-Otavi

O v a m b o l a n d

Sesfontein

Etosha Pan

Namutoni

Tsumeb

Okaukuejo

Grootfontein

Otavi

Okaputa

Omu-Hatako

Fransfontein

Outjo

Otjiwarongo

Waterberg

K
a
o
k
o

P
l
a
t
e
a
u

Erundu

S O U T H

W E S T

K
a
k
a
u
v
e
l
d

Rietfontein

Ghanzi

Okavango Sv

Tsu

To

Former L. Ngami
3115

B O

7710

Omaruru

Usakos

Karibib

Okahandja

Gobabis

Otjimbingwe

D a m a r a l a n d

C. Cross

Swakopmund

Walvis B.

Pelican Pt.

Windhoek

A F R I C A

K a l a h a

Walvis

Kuiseb

Rehoboth

Sandfish B.

Swakop

Hoachanas

Tropic of Capricorn

Lehututu

Tsane

Hollams Bird I.

Maltahöhe

Mariental

Gochas

Elephant

G t. N a m a q u a l a n d

Gibeon
3705

Auob

Nossob

Spencer B.

Berseba

N
a
m
i
b

Ichabo I.

Lüderitz

Bethanien

Aus

Keetmanshoop

Aroab

Rietfontein

Khuis

Kuruman

B e c h u a n a l a

Possession I.

D
e
s
e
r
t

Seeheim

G
t.

K
a
r
a
s
b
e
r
g
e

Kurumar

Bogenfels

Karasburg

Nakop

Upington

Kakamas

L
a
n
g
e
b
e
r
g
e

G r i q u a

A T L A N T I C

Warmbad

Orange

Hartebees

Pries

Orange B.

Alexander B.

Port Nolloth

Pella

Aughrabies Fs

Kenhardt

Ka

O C E A N

Steinkopf

Buffels

Okiep

N a m a q u a l a n d

Springbok

Verneukpan

Hondeklipp

L a n g e b e r g e

Brandvlei

Sakriver

Kareeberge

Carnarvon

Bitterfontein

Williston

Sak

Victoria
West

Calvinia

C A P E

Fraserburg

Nuweveldberge

2792 Beau

Klawer

Clanwilliam

Doring

Roggeveldberge

Great Kar

Prins Alber

St. Helena B.

Piketberg

Gt. Winterhoek
6840

Loxingsberg

Swartberg

Vredenburg

St. Ber

Laingsburg

Matjesfontein

Oudtshoorn

Saldanha B.

Mooreesburg

Tulbagh

Ladismith

Calitzdorp

Malmesbury

Ceres

Worcester

Montagu

George

Mossel B.

Paarl

Robertson

Riversdale

St.

Cape Town

Stellenbosch

Bree

Swellendam

Sebastian B.

Simonstown

Caledon

Heidelberg

C. of Good Hope

Somerset

Bredasdorp

False B.

Hermon

C. Agulhas

Projection: Bonne.

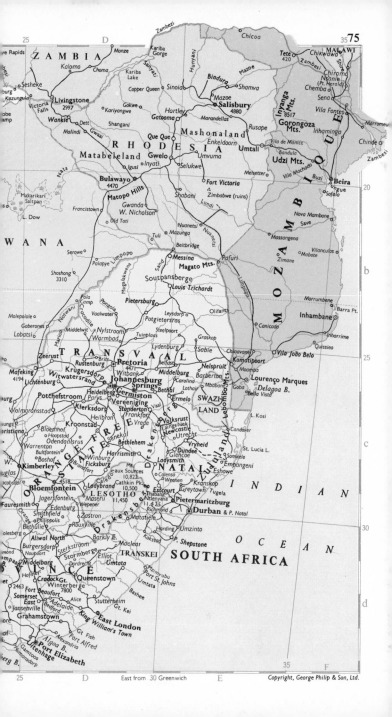

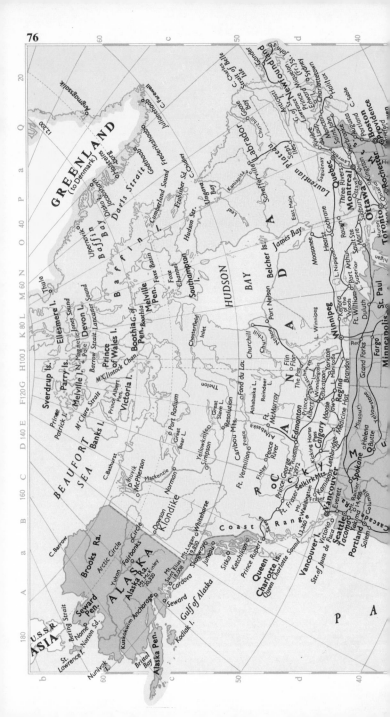

NORTH AMERICA

Scale 1 : 40,000,000 (640 miles = 1 inch)

100 0   200   400   600 Statute Miles
100 0   200   400   600   800   1000 Kilometres

—— Railways ········ Canals
14,495 Heights in feet

Projection: Bonne. F

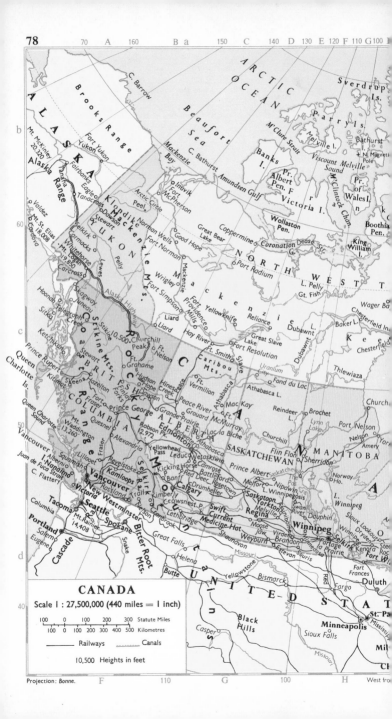

CANADA

Scale 1 : 27,500,000 (440 miles = 1 inch)

100 0   100   200   300 Statute Miles
100 0 100 200 300 400 500 Kilometres

———— Railways   Canals

10,500 Heights in feet

Projection: *Bonne.*

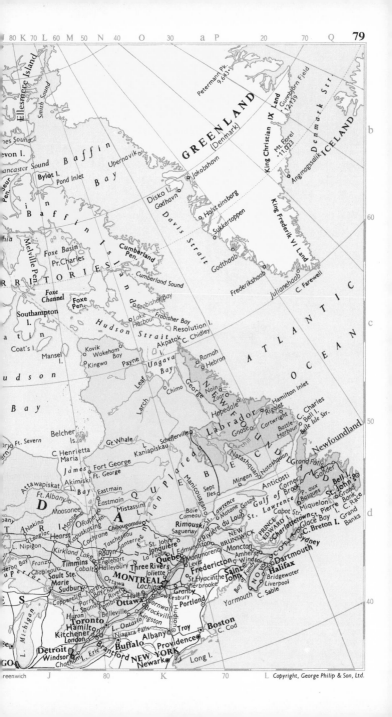

GREENLAND
(Denmark)

Petermann Pk. 9,843

Gunnbjörn Field 12,139

King Christian IX Land

Mt. Forel 11,023

ICELAND

Denmark Str.

Ellesmere Island

Smith Sound

nes Sound

evon I.

ancaster Sound

Baffin Bay

Bylot I.

Pond Inlet

Pen.

Upernavik

Jakobshavn

b

Angmagssalik

King Frederik VI Land

60

Disko I.

Godhavn

Holsteinsborg

Sukkertoppen

Davis Strait

Melville Pen.

Foxe Basin

Pr. Charles

Cumberland Pen.

Godthaab

RR TORIES

I S L A N D

Cumberland Sound

Frederikshaab

Julianehaab

C. Farewell

Foxe Channel

Foxe Pen.

Southampton

Hudson Strait

Lake Harbour

Frobisher Bay

Resolution I.

Akpatok I. C. Chidley

A T L A N T I C

c

tin

Coat's I.

Mansel I.

Kovik Wakeham Bay

Kingwa

Payne

Ungava Bay

Ramah

Hebron

O C E A N

u d s o n

Leaf

Chimo

George

Nain

Zoar

Hopedale

Rigolet

Hamilton Inlet

B a y

Larch

Scheffervile

Kaniapiskau

Belcher Is.

Gt. Whale

Churchill

Goose

Cartwright

Battle. C. Charles Harbour Bell I.

Belle Isle Str.

50

Ft. Severn

C. Henrietta Maria

L a b r a d o r P l a t e a u

Natashquan

Notashabon

Grand Falls

Newfoundland

J a m e s

Fort George

Ft. George

Eastmain

Mingan

Grand

Gander

Bell I.

B a y

Attawapiskat

Akimiski I.

Eastmain

Sept Iles

Manicouagan

Anticosti

Corner Brook

St. John's

Grand Bank

Ft. Albany

Moosonee

Mistassini

Baie Comeau

Gulf of

St. Lawrence

Gaspé

P. aux Basques

Miquelon

St. Pierre

C. Race

D

Oskelaneo

Rivière du Loup

St. Lawrence

Matane

Cabot Str.

Grand Banks

Hearst

Kapuskasing

Chibougamau

Taschereau

Rimouski

NEW

PRINCE

Glace Bay

Moose

Orupeu

La Tuque

Edmundston

BRUNSWICK

EDWARD

Charlottetown

C. Breton I.

Sydney

Cochrane

Rouyn

Senneterre

St. John

Quebec

Moncton

Windsor

T

Kirkland Lake

Englehart

Halleybury

Montmorency

Amherst

Dartmouth

Timmins

Cobalt

Three Rivers

Joliette

Lévis

Fredericton

Saint

Halifax

Sudbury

Ottawa

Lachine

MONTREAL

St. Hyacinthe

John

Liverpool

S

Sault Ste. Marie

North Bay

Pembroke

Hull

Sherbrooke

Granby

Bay

Bridgewater

Yarmouth

C. Sable

Copper Cliff

Parry Sound

Cornwall

Huron

Belleville

Kingston

Portland

Toronto

Hamilton

L. Ontario

Brockville

Troy

Boston

Kitchener

London

Niagara Falls

Albany

Providence

C. Cod

Detroit

Windsor

Chatham

L. Erie

Brantford

Buffalo

NEW YORK

Newark

Long I.

GO

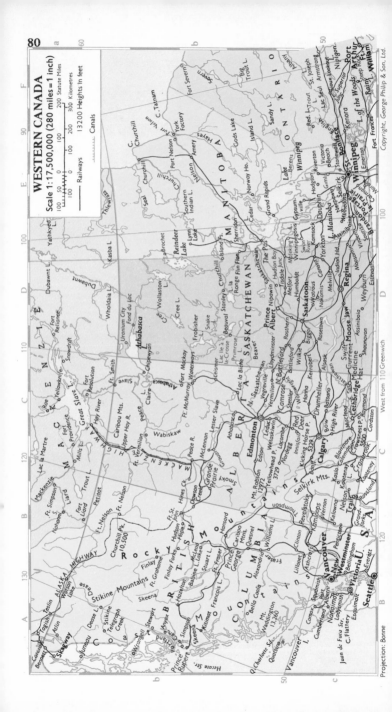

80

WESTERN CANADA
Scale 1:17,500,000 (280 miles=1 inch)

100 50 0   100   200 Statute Miles
100 50 0   100   200   300 Kilometres

13200 Heights in feet

——— Railways   .... Canals

Projection: Bonne   West from 110 Greenwich   Copyright, George Philip & Son, Ltd.

EASTERN CANADA

Scale 1:17,500,000 (280 miles=1 inch)

```
100  50   0        100       200       300 Statute Miles
100  50   0    100    200    300 Kilometres
```

—— Railways   13200 Heights in feet
—— Canals

Projection: Bonne

West from 70 Greenwich

ATLANTIC OCEAN

NEWFOUNDLAND — St. John's, Gander, Grand Falls, Corner Brook, Buchans, Bonavista, Cape Race, Placentia, St. Pierre (Fr.), Miquelon I. (Fr.), Notre Dame B., Twillingate, Bay of Islands, Port aux Basques, Belle Isle

LABRADOR — Hamilton Inlet, Grand Falls, Natashquan, Romaine, Seven Islands, Lac Joseph, Wabush

QUEBEC — Quebec, Montreal, Three Rivers, Chicoutimi, Sherbrooke, St. Hyacinthe, Sorel, Lachine, Levis, Rivière du Loup, Rimouski, Matane, Gaspé, Baie Comeau, Seven Isles, Sept Iles, Manicouagan, Peribonca, L. St. John, Senneterre, Val d'Or, Rouyn, Cabonga, Gatineau, Hull, Gouin Reservoir, Roberval

ONTARIO — Toronto, Ottawa, Hamilton, London, Windsor, Kitchener, Guelph, Kingston, Peterboro, Belleville, Cobourg, Oshawa, Owen Sound, Sudbury, Sault Ste. Marie, Timmins, Cochrane, Kapuskasing, Hearst, Kirkland Lake, Cobalt, North Bay, Pembroke, Renfrew, Georgian Bay, L. Ontario, Niagara Falls, Nipigon, Longlac, Fort Severn, Winisk, Attawapiskat, Fort Albany, Moosonee, Moose Factory

NEW BRUNSWICK — Saint John, Fredericton, Moncton, Edmundston, Campbellton, Newcastle, Woodstock, Bathurst

NOVA SCOTIA — Halifax, Dartmouth, Sydney, Truro, New Glasgow, Yarmouth, Liverpool, Shelburne, Bridgewater, Kentville, Windsor, Amherst, Glace Bay, C. Sable, C. Canso, Sable I. (Nova Scotia)

PR. EDWARD I. — Charlottetown, Summerside

Hudson Bay, James Bay, Belcher Is., C. Henrietta Maria, C. Jones, Akimiski I., Charlton I.

Gulf of St. Lawrence, Anticosti I., Cape Breton I., Cabot Str., Str. of Belle Isle, C. Gaspé, Magdalen Is.

United States cities: CHICAGO, DETROIT, Milwaukee, Grand Rapids, Toledo, Cleveland, Buffalo, Erie, BOSTON, NEW YORK, Providence, New Haven, Hartford, Springfield, Worcester, Albany, Syracuse, Rochester, Utica, Binghamton, Scranton, Elmira, Portland, Bangor, Augusta, Lewiston, Manchester, Concord, Lowell, Burlington, L. Champlain, C. Cod, Green Bay, Kenosha, Racine, Muskegon, Saginaw, Kalamazoo

Great Lakes: L. Superior, L. Michigan, L. Huron, L. Erie, L. Ontario, Georgian Bay

130 A 120 a B 110 C 100

Calgary Saskatoon C A N.
Vancouver Is. Kamloops Crow's Nest Moose Jaw Regina Manitoba
Nanaimo Selkirk Ra. Pass
Juan de Fuca Str. Bellingham Trail Lethbridge Medicine Hat Brandon
C. Flattery Victoria **Vancouver**
Everett **Seattle** Havre Glasgow Minot
Tacoma **WASHINGTON** Spokane Milk Missouri Buford N. DAKO.
Mt. Rainier Yakima Missoula Great Falls Dickinson Bismarck
14,408 Walla Walla **MONTANA** Yellowstone
Astoria Columbia Helena Red Miles Billings
Portland Grangeville Butte Bozeman City Sheridan Lead S. DAKO
Oregon Baker Yellowstone Black Rapid
Salem **OREGON** Weiser National Park Hills City Chamber
Corvallis **IDAHO** Rexburg **WYOMING** Gannett Pk. Crawford
Eugene Boise Idaho Falls 13,785 Casper
Blanco Silver Shoshone Pocatello Lead Pierre
Medford City Twin Falls Snake Rawlins Laramie **NEBRAS**
40 Klamath Falls Oakley Evanston Rock Spring Cheyenne N. Platte
Mt. Shasta Gt. Salt Lake Logan Front Ra. McCook Platte
C. Mendocino 14,162 Winnemucca Ogden **Salt Lake** Long's Pk. **Denver**
Eureka Elko **City** 14,255 Boulder
Reno **NEVADA** Denver Pikes Pk. **COLORADO** Colorado Springs KA
Golden Gate Carson City **UTAH** 14,108 **Pueblo** Dodge City
San Sacramento Tonopah Richfield Durango Blanca Pk. Dalhart
Francisco Oakland San Jose Las Vegas 14,317 Oklahoma
Fresno Death Grand Canyon Farmington Gallup **Santa Fe** Canadian
Mt. Whitney Valley Colorado Plat. Amarillo Childress Wichita Fa
Bakersfield 14,495 -276 Flagstaff Winslow Albuquerque **NEW** Llano Lubbock
Los Angeles Mojave Desert **ARIZONA** **MEXICO**
Riverside **Long Beach** Phoenix Roswell Estacado
PACIFIC **San Diego** Salton Sea Silver City Carlsbad Sweet Water Fort
OCEAN Mexicali Yuma Tucson Deming S Angelo T
120 Gila Bisbee **Ciudad** El Paso Pecos
Juarez

ALASKA
Scale 1 : 25,000,000
50 0 50 100 150 200 Miles
50 0 100 200 300 Km.

a Barrow Point Harrison 70 Inuvik
A C. Lisburne Wainwright Barrow Bay -30
Pt. Hope Colville Rio Grande Eagle
Noatak **Brooks Range** Y Peel **MEXICO**
East Cape **Baird Mts.** Chandalar Porcupine U
b of Wales Kotzebue Shungnak Arctic Circle Bettles Beaver Fort Yukon K
Seward Pen. Candle Koyukuk Hughes Yukon O 160
Shelton Council Tanana Rampart Circle Lehua Mana Kauai
Nome Solomon Mulato Ruby Chatanika Eagle N Niihau Lihue Warmea
Norton Kaltag Hot Springs **Fairbanks** Dawson Kaula Kauai Wahi
St. Kwiguk Sound Undalakleet Nenana Healy Yukon Pearl He
Lawrence Kotlik Ophir Mt. Tanana
(U.S.) Anvik McKinley 16,208
C. Romanzof Yukon 20,320 Talkeetna Mt.Blackburn
Nunivak Holy Cross Palmer Copper Wrangell
Kuskokwim Center Mts. Mt. Logan
Bethel **Anchorage** Matanuska Valdez Kennecott -19,850 Whitehorse
60 Iliamna Vol. Kendri **Whittier** Cordova Mt. St. Elias White
Nushagak 10,116 **Seward** -18,008 Pass
Kuskokwim Bay Iliamna Montague I. Yakutat Skogway **JUNEAU**
C. Newenham Lake Katmai Seldovia Mt. Fairweather Admiralty
Vol. Homer 15,320 Sitka Petersburg
Bristol Bay -7000 Afognak I. **GULF OF** Chichagof I. Wrangell
Port Mc Ugashik Kodiak Alexander Baranof I. Prince
Lakes **ALASKA** Archipelago Prince of Wales of
Unimak Peninsula Karluk Kodiak I. Dixon Entrance Rup
Alaska I. Dall I. Prince
Sanak I. Trinity Is. Graham I.
B Unimak Passage Shumagin Is. Chirikof I. Queen
Charlotte Is. Mor

Projection: Conical. 160 C West from 150 Greenwich D 140 E

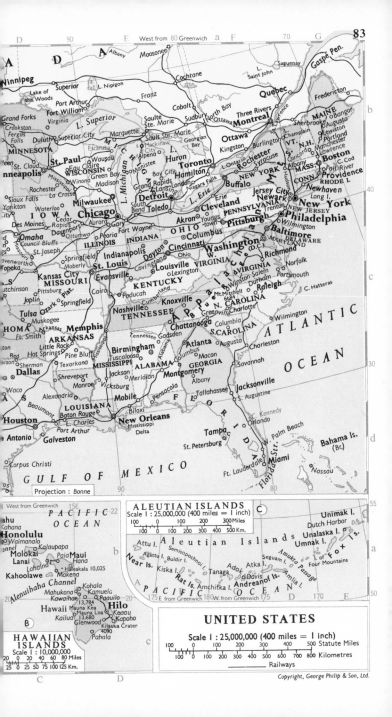

D   90   E   West from 80 Greenwich   a   F   70   G

Winnipeg
Albany
Moosonee
Cochrane
Saguenay
Gaspé Pen.

Superior
L. Nipigon
Franz
L. Saint John
Fredericton

Lake of
the Woods
Port Arthur
Fort William
Virginia
Cobalt
North Bay
Sudbury
Three Rivers
Quebec
Sherbrooke
MAINE
Bangor
Augusta

Grand Forks
Crookston
Fergus
Falls
Duluth
Superior City
Marquette
Sault
Ste. Marie
Georgian
Bay
Ottawa
Burlington
VT.
N.H.
Concord
Portland
Manchester
Lewiston

MINNESOTA
St. Cloud
Escanaba
Mackinaw
City
Champlain
Lawrence
MASS.
Boston

nneapolis
St. Paul
Eau Claire
WISCONSIN
Green Bay
Bay City
L. Huron
Kingston
L. Ontario
Syracuse
Rochester
Albany
Providence
CONN.
RHODE I.

Minneapolis
Rochester
Winona
Madison
Lansing
Grand Rapids
Toronto
Hamilton
Niagara Falls
Buffalo
NEW YORK
Jersey City
Newark
Long I.
Newhaven

Sioux Falls
Milwaukee
L. Michigan
Detroit
L. Erie
Cleveland
Erie
PENNSYLVANIA
New York

Yankton
Waterloo
Cedar
Rapids
IOWA
Chicago
South
Bend
Toledo
Akron
Youngs-
town
Trenton
NEW JERSEY
Philadelphia

City
Des Moines
Davenport
Aurora
Gary
Fort Wayne
OHIO
Columbus
Pittsburgh
Wilmington
DELAWARE
Baltimore

Omaha
Council Bluffs
Peoria
ILLINOIS
INDIANA
Dayton
Cincinnati
Washington
(D.C.)
MARYLAND

St. Joseph
Springfield
Indianapolis
Covington
Ohio
Richmond

avenworth
Moberly
St. Louis
Louisville
Lexington
VIRGINIA
Norfolk

Topeka
Kansas City
MISSOURI
Evansville
KENTUCKY
Winston Salem
Durham
Raleigh
Portsmouth

utchinson
Pittsburg
Plat.
Cairo
Paducah
Cumberland
Mt. Mitchell
6684
N. CAROLINA
C. Hatteras

Joplin
Ozark
Springfield
Nashville
Knoxville
Greenville
Charlotte

Tulsa
Muskogee
TENNESSEE
Chattanooga
Gadsden
Columbia
S. CAROLINA
Wilmington

HOMA
Ft. Smith
Arkansas
Memphis
Tennessee
ATLANTIC

Little Rock
ARKANSAS
Atlanta
Augusta
Charleston

on
Red
Hot Springs
Pine Bluff
Birmingham
Tuscaloosa
Columbus
GEORGIA
Savannah
OCEAN

ison
Sherman
Texarkana
MISSISSIPPI
ALABAMA
Macon

Dallas
Shreveport
Jackson
Meridian
Montgomery
Albany

Waco
Monroe
Vicksburg
Pensacola
Tallahassee
Jacksonville

Beaumont
Alexandria
LOUISIANA
Mobile
Biloxi
St. Augustine

Houston
Baton Rouge
New Orleans
Kennedy
Orlando

S
Port Arthur
Mississippi
Delta
FLORIDA
W. Palm Beach

Antonio
Galveston
Tampa
Bahama Is.
(Br.)

os
Corpus Christi
St. Petersburg
Miami
Nassau

GULF   OF   MEXICO
Ft. Lauderdale
Florida Str.

Projection: Bonne
90   80

West from Greenwich   156
PACIFIC
OCEAN
22

ALEUTIAN ISLANDS
Scale 1 : 25,000,000 (400 miles = 1 inch)
100   0   100   200   300 Miles
100   0   100   200   300   400   500 Km.
C

Unimak I.
Dutch Harbor
Unalaska I.

ahu
Kahana
Honolulu
Waimanalo
Kalaupapa
Molokai
Lanai
Maui
Paia
Lahaina
Hana
Kahoolawe
Haleakala 10,025

Aleutian Islands
Attu I.
Near Is.
Agattu I.
Buldir I.
Kiska I.
Rat Is.
Amchitka I.
Semisopochnoi I.
Tanaga
Adak
Atka
Andreanof Is.
Seguam I.
Amlia I.
Amukta
I. of
Four Mountains
Umnak I.
FOX IS.
Davis
Passage

Alenuihaha Channel
Kohala
Mahukona
Kawaihae
Kamuela
13,784
Mauna Kea

175 E from Greenwich   180   W. from Greenwich   175   170   E

PACIFIC
OCEAN
50

Hawaii
Kailua
Mauna Loa
13,680
Glenwood
Keaau
Kapoho
Kilauea Crater
4090
Pahala
Hilo

B
HAWAIIAN
ISLANDS
Scale 1 : 10,000,000
20   0   20   40   60   80 Miles
25   0   25   50   75   100   125 Km.

UNITED STATES
Scale 1 : 25,000,000 (400 miles = 1 inch)
100   0   100   200   300   400   500 Statute Miles
100   0   100   200   300   400   500   600   700   800 Kilometres
Railways

Copyright, George Philip & Son, Ltd.

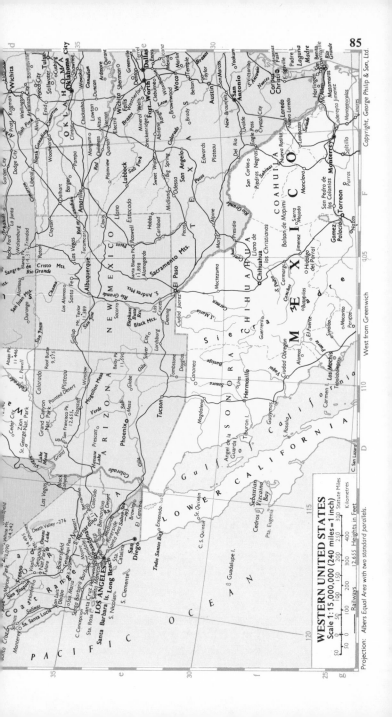

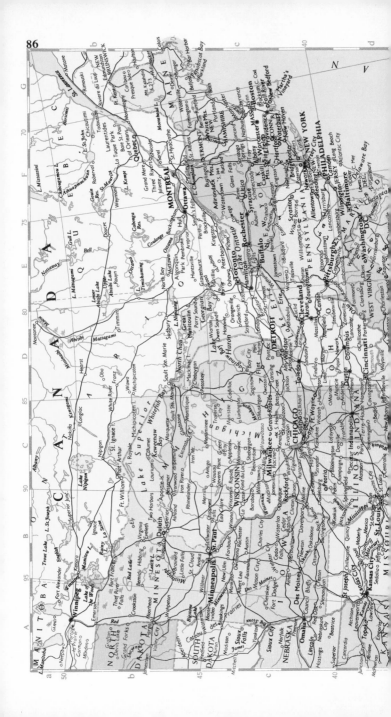

87

EASTERN UNITED STATES

Scale 1:15,000,000 (240 miles=1 inch)

Statute Miles
50 0   50 100   150   200   250
50 0   100   200   300
Kilometres

Railways ━━━━ Heights in feet 12,655

Projection: Albers Equal Area with two standard parallels

NORTH-EASTERN UNITED STATES

Scale 1:7,500,000 (120 miles=1 inch)

50   0   50   100   150   Statute Miles

50   0   50   100   150   200   Kilometres

——— Principal Railways   ········· Canals   ·5140 Heights in feet

Copyright, George Philip & Son, Ltd.

CANADA

ONTARIO

NEW YORK

PENNSYLVANIA

MARYLAND

NEW JERSEY

VIRGINIA

MASS.

ATLANTIC OCEAN

Trois Rivieres
Louiseville
Plessisville
Beauceville
St. George's
Victoriaville
Thetford Mines
Moosehead
Jackman
Sorel
Drummondville
Asbestos
Mégantic
Dover
L'Annonciation
St. Jerome
Lachute
Hawkesbury
St. Hyacinthe
Granby
MONTREAL
Lachine
Beauharnois
Valleyfield
St. Jean
Sherbrooke
Magog
Coaticook
Richardson
Lakes
Colebrook
Phillips
Rangeley
Waterville
Augusta
Lewiston
Bath
Portland
Biddeford
Saco
Kittery
Portsmouth
Dover
Concord
Manchester
Nashua
Lawrence
Lowell
Haverhill
Salem
Lynn
BOSTON
Cambridge
Quincy Bay
Brockton
Taunton
Fall River
New Bedford
Cape Cod
Nantucket Sd.
Nantucket
Martha's Vineyard
Block I.
Newport
New London
WASHINGTON D.C.
Alexandria
BALTIMORE
PHILADELPHIA
Camden
Trenton
Wilmington
Atlantic City
Cape May
Richmond
Petersburg
Norfolk
Newport News
Virginia Beach

Ottawa
Hull
Pembroke
Renfrew
Kingston
LAKE ONTARIO
Rochester
Syracuse
Utica
BUFFALO
Niagara Falls
Watertown
Oswego
Albany
Schenectady
Troy
Binghamton
Scranton
Wilkes Barre
Harrisburg
Reading
Allentown
Bethlehem
Lancaster
York
NEW YORK CITY
Newark
Elizabeth
Paterson
Yonkers
Bridgeport
New Haven
Hartford
Springfield
Worcester
Providence
Pawtucket
Raleigh
Wilson
Greenville
Henderson

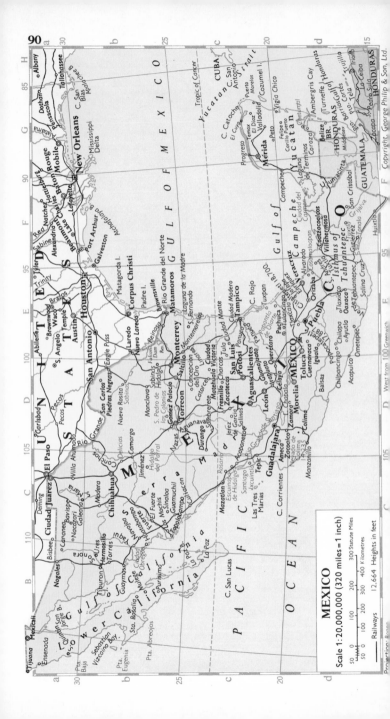

90

MEXICO

Scale 1 : 20,000,000 (320 miles = 1 inch)

50   0   100   200   300 Statute Miles
50   0   100   200   300   400 Kilometres

Railways   12,664 Heights in feet

Projection Bonne

Copyright, George Philip & Son, Ltd.

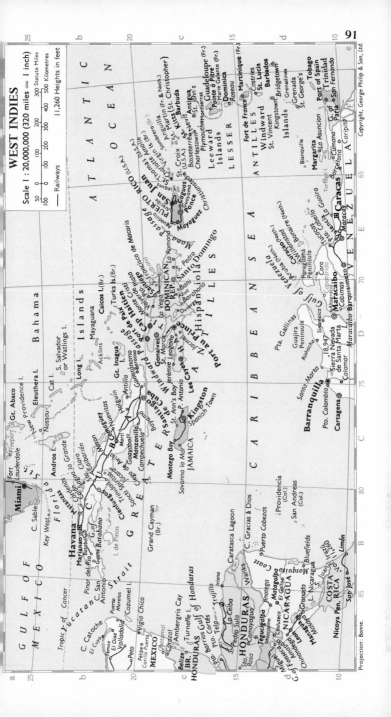

WEST INDIES

Scale 1 : 20,000,000 (320 miles = 1 inch)

50 0   100   200   300 Statute Miles
100 0 100 200 300 400 500 Kilometres

—— Railways   11,260 Heights in feet

Projection : Bonne.

ATLANTIC OCEAN

Bahama Islands

GULF OF MEXICO

MEXICO

Florida
Miami
Fort Lauderdale
C. Sable
Key West
Tropic of Cancer

Havana
CUBA
Pinar del Rio
I. de Pinos
Santiago de Cuba

JAMAICA
Kingston
Spanish Town
Montego Bay

Grand Cayman (Br.)

HONDURAS
BR. HONDURAS
Belize
NICARAGUA
Mosquito Coast
Bluefields
COSTA RICA
San José
Limón

CARIBBEAN SEA

GREATER ANTILLES

HAITI
DOMINICAN REP.
Santo Domingo
Hispaniola

PUERTO RICO (U.S.A.)
San Juan
Ponce
Mayaguez

Virgin Is.
LESSER ANTILLES

LEEWARD ISLANDS
St. Thomas (U.S.A.)
St. Croix (U.S.A.)
Anguilla
St. Martin (Fr. & Neth.)
St. Kitts (St. Christopher)
Nevis
Antigua
Barbuda
Montserrat
Guadeloupe (Fr.)
Pointe à Pitre
Marie Galante (Fr.)
Dominica
Roseau

WINDWARD ISLANDS
Martinique (Fr.)
Fort de France
St. Lucia
Castries
St. Vincent
Kingstown
Barbados
Bridgetown
Grenadines
Grenada
St. George's
Tobago
Trinidad
Port of Spain
San Fernando

VENEZUELA
Caracas
Maracaibo
L. Maracaibo
Barranquilla
Cartagena
Santa Marta
Sierra Nevada de Santa Marta 18,947
Guajira Peninsula
Margarita

a · b · 0 · c · 10 · d

30

F

40

E

50

D

60

C

70

B

80

A

10

NORTH

ATLANTIC

OCEAN

Caribbean Sea

WEST INDIES

Martinique
St. Lucia
St. Vincent · Barbados
Grenada
Margarita
Tobago I.
Trinidad
Port of Spain

Aruba · Curaçao
Sta. Marta
Barranquilla
Cartagena
Maracaibo
Coro
La Guaira · Cumaná
Barcelona

VENEZUELA

Caracas
Valencia
San Fernando
Ciudad Bolívar
Orinoco

GUYANA
Georgetown
SURINAM
Paramaribo
FRENCH GUIANA
Cayenne

CENTRAL AMERICA
GUAT.
HONDURAS
San Pedro
Tegucigalpa
NICARAGUA
Managua
COSTA RICA
San José
PANAMA
Panamá
CANAL
Colón
Gulf of Panamá

COLOMBIA
Cúcuta
Bucaramanga
Medellín
Bogotá
Cali
Popayán
Pasto

ECUADOR
Quito 9.347
Guayaquil
Cuenca
Chimborazo

Galapagos Is. (Ecuador)

PERU
Iquitos
Lima
Callao
Cuzco
Arequipa
Huancayo

BOLIVIA
La Paz
Cochabamba
Oruro
Sucre
Potosí
Santa Cruz

BRAZIL

AMAZONAS
Manaus
Amazon
PARÁ
Belém
Santarém
Marajó I.
Tocantins

RORAIMA
Boa Vista

AMAPÁ

MARANHÃO
São Luís
PIAUÍ
CEARÁ
Fortaleza
RIO GRANDE DO NORTE
Natal
João Pessoa
Recife
PERNAMBUCO
Maceió
Aracaju
Salvador
BAHIA

MATO GROSSO
Cuiabá

GOIÁS
Brasília

MINAS GERAIS

Fernando de Noronha
São Paulo
São Roque
St. Paul

Equator

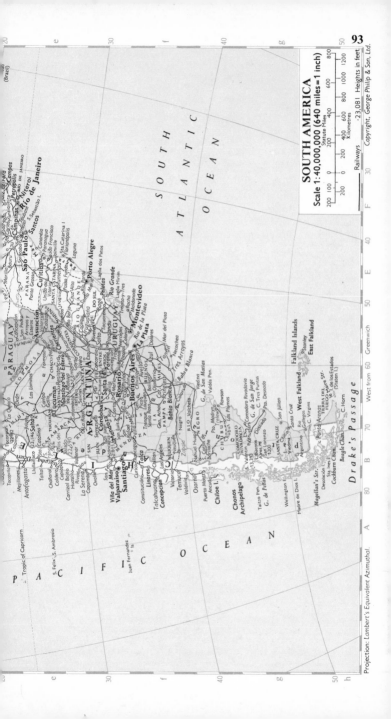

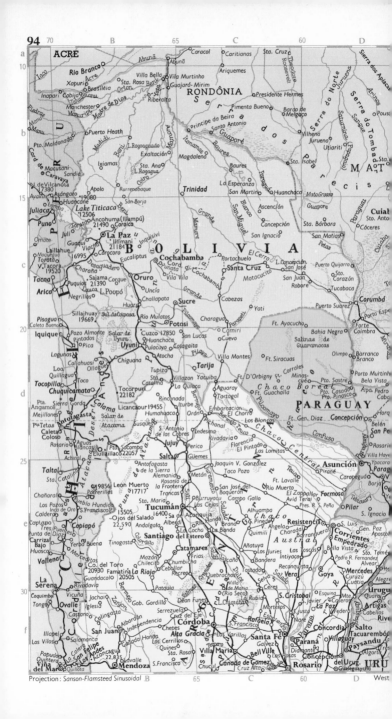

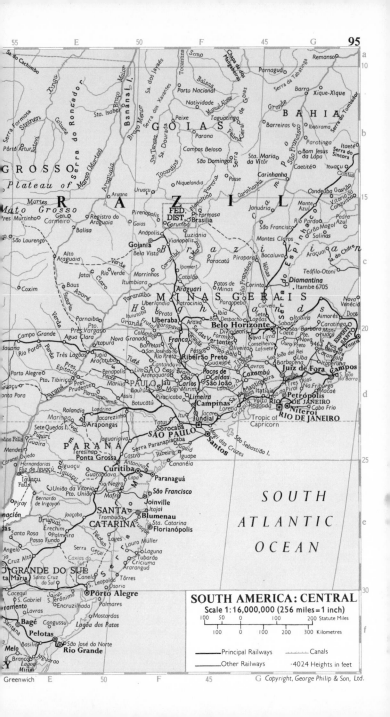

Serra do Cachimbo

Remanso

Parnaguá

Serra da Tabatinga

10

a

Xingu

Sono

Chapa dos Mangabeiros

Tocantins

Teles

Maur

Sa. dos Javaés

Porto Nacional

Natividade

Balsas

Goiás

Manuel Alves

Serra de

Barra

Xique-Xique

Serra do Tombador

Pôrto Artur

Serra Formosa

Steinen

Sta. Isabel

Braço Menor

Sa. das Xavantes

Bananal I.

GOIAS

Peixe

Taguatinga

B A H I A

Itaberaba

Steinen

Coluene

Serra do Roncador

Sta. Teresa

Sta. Dourada

Parana

Campos Beloso

Palma

Barreiras

Bom Jesus da Lapa

Paratinga

Itaeté

Serra do Sincora

b

GROSSO

Mortes

Mato Grosso

Gen.Co.

Registro do Araguaia

Goiás

São Domingos

Paranã

Sta. Maria da Vitór

Caetité

Contas

Condeúba

Gavão

Vitória da Conquista

res Murtinho

Plateau of

B R A Z I L

Carinhanha

Monte Azul

Pedra Azul

15

Araguaia

Aruana

Niquelandia

Posse

Januária

Rio Pardo

São Francisco

Salinas

Grão Mogol

c

São Lourenço

Alto Araguaia

Balisa

Pirenópolis

FED. DIST.

Brasília

Formosa

Planaltina

Luziânia

Corumbá

Vianópolis

Bocaiuva

Montes Claros

Araçuaí

Grão do Chifre

Coxim

Jataí

Rio Verde

Gojania

Bela Vista

B r a z i l i a n

Morrinhos

Catalão

Paracatú

Pirapora

Teófilo-Otoni

Nova Venécia

Itumbiara

Araguari

Patos de Minas

Corinto

Diamantina

Itambé 6705

Campo Grande

Parnaiba

Uberlândia

Patrocínio

Paraopeba

Curvelo

Itabira

Aimorés

Doce

H

MINAS GERAIS

i

g

Três Lagôas

Pres.Vargas

Agua Clara

Jupiá

Itapura

Nova Granada

Ibia

Bom Despacho

Sete Lagôas

Sabará

Aracatuba

Ituiutaba

Prata

Barretes

Colômbia

Frutal

Uberaba

Igarapava

Araxá

Divinópolis

Belo Horizonte

Nova Lima

Itabirito

Ponte Nova

9462 Pico da Bandeira

Coronel Vitória

Porto Alegre

Rio Pardo

Três Lagôas

Pres. Epitácio

Penápolis

São José do R

Franca

Pôço

Formiga

Oliveira

Conselheiro

Caratinga

20

Jauana

Porto Alegre

Pres. Tibiriçá

Mirília

Nova Granada

Rio Prêto

Ribeirão Prêto

São Carlos

Guaxupé

Lavras

Barbacena

Ouro Prêto

São João del Rei

Coronel

Ubá

Cataguases

Itaperuna

Pico da Bandeira

Campos

nta Pora

Pres. Prudente

Araraquara

Araçoara

Caxambú

Mattias

Juiz de Fora

São João da Barra

São Paulo

Bauru

Jau

Mogi Mirim

Limeira

Pôços de Caldas

Lambari

Itajuba

Na.Friburgo

PETRÓPOLIS

Macaé

Parana

Rolandia

Marília

Assis

Jacarezinho

Piracicaba

Campinas

Pouso Alegre

Volta Redonda

Três Rios

RIO

DE JANEIRO

d

Maringá

Arapongas

Botucatú

Tatu

Jundiaí

Ituverava

Lorena

Itatiaia

Niterói

RIO DE JANEIRO

Sete Quedas I.

Guaira

Londrina

SÃO PAULO

Ituú

Jacarei

Piraí

Tropic of

Cabo Frio

PARANA

Ponta Grossa

Sorocaba

 Serra Paranapiacaba

Iguapé

Santos

São Sebastião I.

Capricorn

25

Iguaçu Falls

Teresinao

Castro

Antonina

Ribeira

Cananéia

Mendes

Guaira

Guarapuava

Lapa

CURITIBA

Paranaguá

S O U T H

Piray

União da Vitória

Pto. Unido

Rio Negro

Mafra

São Francisco

A T L A N T I C

 nación

Bernardo de Irigoyen

Joaçaba

Trombuda

Joinville

Itajaí

Blumenau

O C E A N

das

Santa Rosa

Erechim

SANTA

Sta. Catarina

Florianópolis

CATARINA

e

Angelo

Passo Fundo

Palmeira

Lages

Louro Müller

Cruz Alta

Serra

Gecal

Tubarão

Criciúma

Laguna

30

GRANDE DO SUL

Caxias do Sul

Santa Cruz do Sul

Canela

Osório

Araranguá

ta Maria

Jacui

S. Jerônimo

S. Gabriel

Leopoldo

Tôrres

f

ramento

Lavras

Encruzilhada

Pôrto Alegre

Santana

Bagé

Cangussu

Lagôa dos Patos

Mostardas

Melo

Branco

São José do Norte

Rio Grande

Iaguarao

Lagôa Mirim

Greenwich E 50 F 45 G *Copyright, George Philip & Son, Ltd.*

SOUTH AMERICA: CENTRAL

Scale 1:16,000,000 (256 miles = 1 inch)

100 50 0 100 200 Statute Miles

100 0 100 200 300 Kilometres

—— Principal Railways ⋯⋯ Canals

—— Other Railways ·4024 Heights in feet

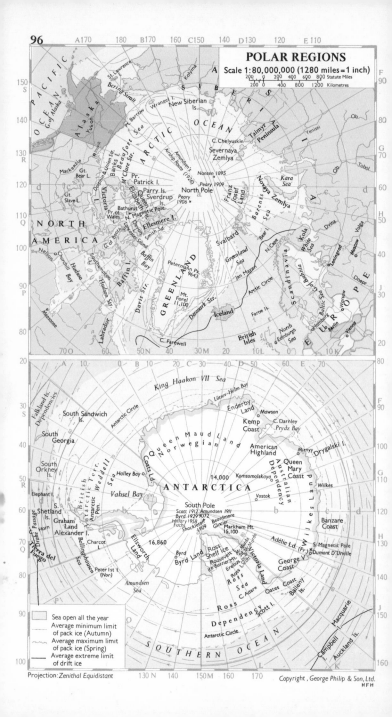

POLAR REGIONS

Scale 1:80,000,000 (1280 miles = 1 inch)

200 0   200 400 600 800 Statute Miles
200 0   400   800   1200 Kilometres

PACIFIC OCEAN

G. of Alaska
St. Lawrence I.
Bering Strait
Pt. Barrow
Wrangel I.
New Siberian Is.
Kolyma
SIBERIA
ARCTIC OCEAN
C. Chelyuskin
Taimyr Peninsula
Yenisey
Ob
Alaska
Yukon
Beaufort Sea
Amundsen's Airship Route (1926)
Severnaya Zemlya
Mackenzie
Banks I.
Dolphin & Union Str.
M'Clure Str.
Nansen 1895
Peary 1909
North Pole
Peary 1906 ×
Franz Josef Land
Novaya Zemlya
Kara Sea
Ob
Tobol
Gt. Bear L.
Pr. Patrick I.
Parry Is.
Sverdrup Is.
Barents Sea
Gt. Slave L.
Bathurst I.
N. Magnetic Pole
Pr. of Wales I.
Ellesmere I.
Svalbard
Bear I.
Kola Pen.
White Sea
N. Cape
Dvina
Leningrad
Moscow
Volga
NORTH AMERICA
G. of Boothia
Lancaster Sound
Smith Sd.
Greenland Sea
Jan Mayen
Scandinavia
Baltic Sea
Dnepr
EUROPE
Warsaw
Nelson
Churchill
Hudson Bay
Southampton I.
Baffin I.
Baffin Bay
Petermann Pk. 9643
GREENLAND
Mt. Forel 11,100
Arctic Circle
Faroe Is.
North Sea
Edinburgh
Berlin
Vienna
Hudson Str.
Chesterfield
Foxe Basin
Davis Str.
Denmark Str.
Iceland
British Isles
Labrador
C. Farewell

Projection: Zenithal Equidistant

King Haakon VII Sea
Lützow-Holm Bay
Enderby Land
Mawson
Kemp Coast
C. Darnley
Prydz Bay
Falkland Is. Dependencies
South Sandwich Is.
Antarctic Circle
Queen Maud Land
Norwegian
American Highland
South Georgia
Coats Ld.
14,000
Queen Mary Coast
Mirnyy
Drygalski I.
South Orkney Is.
Sea
Halley Bay
Weddell Sea
British Antarctic Terr.
Komsomolskaya
Australian Antarctic Dependency
Wilkes
Vahsel Bay
ANTARCTICA
Vostok
Banzare Coast
Elephant I.
S. Shetland Is.
Graham Land
Antarctic Pen.
b
South Pole
Scott 1912 Amundsen 1911
Byrd 1929-30
Hillary 1958
Fuchs
Shackleton 1909
Beardmore Glacier
Markham Mt. 15,100
Drake Passage
Horn
Alexander I.
Charcot
Bellingshausen Sea
Ellsworth Land
16,860
Byrd Land
Roosevelt I.
Ross Shelf Ice
Ice Barrier Mt.
Erebus Mt.
Ross Sea
Victoria Land
Adélie Ld. (Fr.)
S. Magnetic Pole
Dumont D'Urville
George V Coast
Terra del Fuego
Peter 1st I. (Nor.)
Amundsen Sea
C. Adare
Oates Coast
Balleny Is.
Macquarie
SOUTHERN OCEAN
Ross Dependency
Scott I.
Antarctic Circle
Campbell I.
Auckland Is.

Sea open all the year
Average minimum limit of pack ice (Autumn)
Average maximum limit of pack ice (Spring)
Average extreme limit of drift ice

Copyright, George Philip & Son, Ltd.
H F H

INDEX

ABBREVIATIONS

Afr. – Africa
Ala. – Alabama
Arch. – Archipelago
Arg. – Argentina
Aust. – Austria
Austral. – Australia
Aut. Reg. – Autonomous Region
B. – Bay, Bight
Beds. – Bedfordshire
Beig. – Belgium
Bol. – Bolivia
Braz. – Brazil
C. – Cape
Calif. – California
Can. – Canada
Cant. – Canton
Chan. – Channel
Co. – County
Col. – Colombia, Colony
Conn. – Connecticut
C. Prov. – Cape Province
cont. – Continent
Cord. – Cordillera
Dépt. – Department
Des. – Desert
Dist. – District
div. – Division
Dom. Rep. – Dominican Republic
E. – East
Eg. – Egypt
Eng. – England
Fd. – Fiord
Fla. – Florida
Fr. – France, French
G. – Gulf, Gebel
Ga. – Georgia

Gam. – Gambia
Ger. – Germany
Guin. – Guinea
Harb. – Harbour, Harbor
Hd. – Head
I.(s) – Island(s)
Ill. – Illinois
Ind. – Indiana
Ire. – Ireland
Jam. – Jamaica
Jap. – Japan
Jc., Junc. – Junction
Kan. – Kansas
King. – Kingdom
Ky. – Kentucky
L. – Lake, Lough, Loch
La. – Louisiana
Lab. – Labrador
Lancs. – Lancashire
Ld. – Land
Lib. – Liberia
Mad. P. – Madhya Pradesh
Mass. – Massachusetts
Md. – Maryland
Me. – Maine
Mex. – Mexico
Mich. – Michigan
Minn. – Minnesota
Miss. – Mississippi
Mo. – Missouri
Mor. – Morocco
Mozam. – Mozambique
Mt. – Mountain, Mount
Mts. – Mountains
Nat. – Natal
N.B. – New Brunswick
N.C. – North Carolina
Neb. – Nebraska
Neth. – Netherlands

Nev. – Nevada
Newf. – Newfoundland
N. Guin. – New Guinea
N.H. – New Hampshire
Nic. – Nicaragua
Nig. – Nigeria
N.J. – New Jersey
Nor. – Norway
N.S.W. – New South Wales
N.Y. – New York
N.Z. – New Zealand
Okla. – Oklahoma
Ont. – Ontario
Ore. – Oregon
P. – Pass, Pass
Pa. – Pennsylvania
Par. – Paraguay
Pen. – Peninsula
Pk. – Peak
Plat. – Plateau
Pol. – Poland
Port. – Portugal
Pref. – Prefecture
Prot. – Protectorate
Prov. – Province
Pt. – Point, Port
Pta. – Punta
Queens. – Queensland
R. – River
Ra. – Range
Raj. – Rajasthan
Reg. – Region
Rep. – Republic
Res. – Reservoir
Rhod. – Rhodesia
S. – Sea, South
Sa. – Sierra, Serra
S.C. – South Carolina
Scot. – Scotland

S.D. – South Dakota
Sd. – Sound
Sen. – Senegal
Somal. – Somaliland, Somali Republic
Sp., Span. – Spain, Spanish
S.S.R. – Soviet Socialist Republic
st. – state
Str. – Strait
Swed. – Sweden
Switz. – Switzerland
Tas. – Tasmania
Tenn. – Tennessee
Terr. – Territory
Tex. – Texas
Trans. – Transvaal
Tur. – Turkey
U.A.R. – United Arab Republic
Ut. P. – Utar Pradesh
U.S.A. – United States of America
U.S.S.R. – Union of Soviet Socialist Republics
Va. – Virginia
Ven. – Venezuela
Vic. – Victoria
Vol. – Volcano
Vt. – Vermont
W. – West, Wadi
Wash. – Washington
W. Austral. – Western Australia
W. Ind. – West Indies
Wis. – Wisconsin
W. Va. – West Virginia
Wyo. – Wyoming
Yorks. – Yorkshire

12 Aabenraa	Bd	
12 Aaberraa-Sonderborg, Co.	Bd	
18 Aachen	Fd	
12 Aalborg & dist.	Cb	
18 Aalsmeer	Dd	
18 Aalst	Dd	
13 Aarau	Ca	
13 Aargau, cant.	Ca	
12 Aarhus & Co.	Dc	
18 Aarschot	Dd	
71 Aba	Gg	
43 Abadan	Fc	
92 Abancay	Bd	
54 Abashiri	Db	
62 Abau	Gj	
13 Abaya, L.	Fb	
14 Abbeville	Db	
9 Abbeyleix	Dd	
71 Abeokuta	Fg	
73 Aberayron	Ce	
73 Abercorn (Mbala)	Ee	
7 Aberdare	Df	
87 Aberdeen, Miss., Co		
8 Aberdeen & Co., Scotland	Fc	
75 Aberdeen, South Africa	Cd	
84 Aberdeen, S.D.	Gb	
84 Aberdeen, Wash.	Bb	
7 Aberystwyth	Ce	
68 Abeshr	Ed	
39 Abha	Dd	
71 Abidjan	Eg	
85 Abilene, Kan.	Gd	
85 Abilene, Tex.	Ge	
7 Abingdon	Ff	
19 Abisko	Db	
46 Abohar	Ec	
92 Abong Mbang	Ac	
32 Abramoskaya	Kb	
92 Abreoos, Pta.	Bb	
28 Abruzzi, reg.	Dc	
43 Abu Dhabi	Ge	
44 Abu Kamal	Fd	
38 Abu Hamed	Cd	
39 Abu Matariq	Da	
73 Abu Zabad	Da	
90 Acaponeta	Cd	
90 Acapulco	Ed	
91 Accra	Eg	
6 Accrington	Ed	
9 Achill, Hd. & I.	Ac	
35 Achinsk	Md	
8 Achnasheen	Cd	
29 Acireale	Ef	
91 Acklins I.	Db	
94 Aconcagua, mt.	Bf	

13 Acquarossa	Cb	
21 Acqui	Ge	
40 Acre	Bc	
92 Acre, st.	Bc	
43 Ad Dawhah	Ge	
41 Adabiya	Dg	
47 Adana	Eb	
27 Adapazari	Da	
9 Adare	Cd	
63 Adavale	Bd	
60 Adelaide, South Australia	Ab	
75 Adelaide, C. Prov.	Dd	
13 Adelboden	Bb	
96 Adelie Ld.	Hb	
39 Aden & G. of	Dd	
46 Adh Dharma	Fe	
65 Adieu C.	Ee	
21 Adige, R.	Kd	
89 Adirondack Mts.	Hc	
64 Admiralty Gulf	Da	
82a Admiralty I., Alaska	Ec	
62 Admiralty Is., Terr. of N. Guin.	Gg	
46 Adoni	De	
15 Adour, R.	Cf	
29 Adrano	Ef	
70 Adrar, Algeria	Dc	
70 Adrar, Mali	Fd	
88 Adrian	Cd	
24-25 Adriatic Sea	Fb	
30 Adwa	Cd	
42 Aegean Sea	Cb	
12 Ærø, I.	De	
13 Aerösköbing	Ce	
36 Afghanistan, st.	Kf	
42 Afif	Ec	
15 Afjord	Cc	
42 Afyonkarahisar	Db	
71 Agadir	Cb	
47 Agartala	Ng	
32 Agboville	Eg	
14 Agde	Ef	
46 Agra	Fe	
26 Agrigento	Df	
95 Agua Clara	Ed	
26 Aguadas	Bb	
91 Aguadilla	Ec	
90 Aguanaval, R.	Dc	
92 Aguascalientes	Dc	
26 Aguilas	Bb	
74 Agulhas, C.	Cd	

67 Ahaura	Ce	
18 Ahlen	Gc	
46 Ahmadpur East	Cd	
46 Ahm. datad	Dg	
46 Ahmednagar	Ej	
41 Ahvenann aa Is. (Åland Is.)	Dc	
43 Ahvaz	Fc	
5 Aichi, pref.	Cc	
36 Aigoual, mt.	Be	
8 Ailsa Craig, I.	De	
70 Ain Beida	Ga	
70 Ain Salah	Fc	
71 Ain Sefra	Eb	
40 Aioi	Bd	
71 Air (Azbine), dist.	Ge	
8 Airdrie	Ee	
19 Aisne, R.	Ce	
32 Aitape	Fd	
31 Aitos	Fd	
14 Aix	Ff	
19 Aix les Bains	Dd	
14 Aix-la-Chapelle	Cd	
27 Aiyina, I.	Bb	
27 Aiyion	Bb	
15 Ajaccio	Ah	
63 Ajana	Ad	
62 Ajibba	Ed	
70 Ajlun	Bc	
46 Ajmer	Ec	
49 Ajul, Is.	Ec	
57 Ak Ra.	Ee	
88 Akaroa	De	
35 Akashi	Bd	
70 Akçakoca	Db	
72 Aketi	Cc	
33 Akhaltsikhe	Hg	
75 Akhelóos, R.	Bb	
27 Akhisar	Cb	
81 Akimiski I.	Aa	
54 Akita & pref.	Dc	
70 Akjoujt	Ce	
70 Akola	Fh	
71 Akpatok, I.	Lb	
10 Akranes	Ab	
48 Akrotiri	Ad	
48 Akron	Ed	
27 Aksaray	Eb	
27 Aksehir	Db	
56 Aksu	Cb	
59 Aksum	Cd	
10 Akureyri	Ba	
71 Akure	Gg	
10 Akureyri	Ba	
45 Akyab	Gd	
41 Al Amarah	Fc	
42 Al Aqabah	Dd	
43 Al Basrah	Fc	
40 Al Batrun	Bb	

43 Al Hair	Fe	
41 Al Haraiba	Dd	
42 Al Hoceima	Cb	
70 Al Hoceima	Cb	
39 Al Ittihad	Dd	
43 Al Jaghbub	Ec	
42 Al Jawf	Dd	
43 Al Khali	Cb	
43 Al Khalaf	He	
41 Al Khali (Hebron)	Bd	
43 Al Kut	Fc	
43 Al Kuway	Fd	
40 Al Ladhiqiyah (Lataki a)	Bb	
43 Al Lisafah	Fe	
43 Al Manamah	Gd	
43 Al Marj	Ed	
43 Al Matrah	Fe	
42 Al Mawsil	Eb	
43 Al Mubarraz	Fd	
43 Al Musira, L.	Fe	
43 Al Qatif	Fd	
68 Al Qatrun	Dc	
40 Al Qunaytirah	Bc	
39 Al Qunfidya	Dd	
40 Al Qutayfah	Cc	
42 Al'Ula	Dd	
87 Alabama, R.	Ce	
83 Alabama, st.	Bc	
70 Alagôas, st.	Fd	
92 Alagoinhas	Fd	
91 Alajuela	Bd	
26 Alamogordo	Ee	
84 Alamosa	Ed	
110 Åland (Ahvenanmaa) Is.	Dc	
27 Alanya	Db	
27 Alaşehir	Cb	
76 Alaska, st.	Cb	
82a Alaska, G. of	Dc	
78 Alaska High-way	Eb	
82a Alaska Pen.	Bc	
33 Alatyr	Je	
40 Alayah	Bc	
27 Alayunt	Db	
21 Alba	Ge	
26 Albacete	Bb	
43 Albanel, L.	Bd	
4 Albania, rep.	Jg	
92 Albano	Dd	
87 Albany, Ga.	De	
89 Albany, N.Y.	Hc	
64 Albany, Western Australia	Be	
21 Albenga	Ge	
73 Albert, L.	Ee	
78 Alberta, prov.	Fc	
73 Albertville	De	

15 Albi	Ef	
30 Albia Iulia	Db	
88 Albion, Mich.	Cc	
70 Albion N.S.W.	Bb	
13 Albula Pass	Db	
85 Albuquerque, New Mexico	Ed	
26 Alburquerque, Spain	Ab	
61 Albury	Cc	
29 Alcamo	Df	
92 Alcantara	Ed	
26 Alcázar	Bb	
70 Aicazarquivir, ex Ksar el Kebit		
26 Alcira	Bb	
26 Alcoy	Bb	
69 Aldabra, I.	Gf	
35 Aldan, & R.	Pc	
7 Alderney I.	Cg	
7 Aldershot	Gf	
35 Aleksandrovsk	Rd	
22 Aleksandrow	Eb	
33 Aleksandrow Gai	Je	
14 Alencon	Cd	
83a Alenuihaha Channel	Cb	
43 Aleppo (Halab)	Db	
20 Alès	Ce	
21 Alessandria	Ge	
14 Alesund	Bc	
83 Aleutian Is.	Cb	
82a Alexander Arch.	Cc	
74 Alexander B.	Bc	
96 Alexander I.	Cc	
67 Alexandra	Bf	
27 Alexandretta, see Iskenderun	Eb	
80 Alexandria,B,C.Bb		
38 Alexandria, Eg. Cb		
87 Alexandria, La. Be		
30 Alexandria, Rumania Ed		
89 Alexandria, Va. Ge		
27 Alexandroúpolis Ca		
26 Alfaro	Fc	
8 Alford	Fc	
71 Algeciras	Ab	
70 Alger (Algiers)	Fa	
26 Algeria, st.	Cb	
29 Alghero	Bd	
70 Algiers	Fa	
26 Algoa, B.	Dd	
26 Alhama	Bb	
85 Alhambra	Ce	
26 Alicante	Bb	
60 Alice	Dd	
72 Alice	Dd	
64 Alice Springs	Ed	
46 Aligarh	Ge	
46 Allipur	Cd	

47 Alipur Duar Me
88 Aliquippa Fd
75 Aliwal North Dd
18 Alkmaar Db
47 Allahabad Hf
85 Allegheny Mts. Ef
9 Allen, Bog of Dc
9 Allen, L. Cb
89 Allentown Hd
44 Alleppey Dg
44 Alliance, Neb. Cb
88 Alliance, Ohio Ed
20 Allier, dépt. & R. Bc
8 Alloa Ed
88 Alma Cc
35 Alma Ata Ke
76 Almada Ab
18 Almelo Eb
46 Almeria Bb
49 Alor, I. Dd
48 Alor Star Bc
88 Alpena Db
21 Alpes Maritimes, mts. & dept. Fc
20 Alpi Graie, mts. Ed
13 Alpi Lepontine, mts. Cb
13 Alpi Orobie, mts. Db
13 Alpi Pennine, mts. Bb
13 Alpi Retiche, mts. Db
85 Alpine Fc
4 Alps, mts. Gf
12 Als, dist. Cb
21 Aisace, dist. Fb
80 Alsask Db
10 Alt, R. Eb
13 Alta Cf
94 Alta Gracia Cf
50 Aitai, mts. Db
21 Altdorf Cb
20 Alto Adige, prov Kc
95 Alto Araguaia Ec
89 Altoona Ed
10 Alvarado Ed
10 Alvsby Ed
46 Alwar Fe
8 Alyth Ed
72 Am Dam Ec
68 Am Timane Ad
35 Amabarchik Tc
65 Amadeus L. Ec
55 Amagasaki Cd
12 Amager Fd
55 Amakusa, I. Bd
55 Amami O Shima Bc
28 Amandola Dc
92 Amapa, st. Db
91 Amapata Ad
55 Amarillo Fd
71 Amasya Ea
92 Amazon, R. Cc
52 Amazonas, st. Cc
46 Ambala Fc
46 Ambon Dd
71 Amban Hh
20 Amberieu Dc
20 Amberley De
20 Ambeno Dd
17 Amberg Dd
9 Amber, C. Gg
90 Ambergris Cay Gd
72 Ambizete Ae
72 Ambriz Ae
32 Amderma Mb
90 Ameca Dc
18 Ameland, I. Ea
96 American Highland Eb
18 Amersfoort Eb
80 Amery Ea
86 Ames Bc
81 Amherst Cb
14 Amiens Ec
35 Amirantes, Is. Jk
81 Amman Bd
47 Amorgos, I. Cc
51 Amoy Fd
46 Amraoti Fb
46 Amreli Ch
46 Amritsar Ec
46 Amroha Gd
18 Amsterdam, Netherlands Db
28 Amsterdam, N.Y. Hc
34 Amu Darya R. Je
78 Amundsen G. Ea
96 Amundsen Sea Qc
35 Amur, R. Pd
27 Amvrakia, G. of Bb
40 Amyun Bb
40 An Nabk Bb
42 An Nafud, des. Dd
51 An Najaf Ec
43 An Nasiriyah Fc
39 An Numas Dd
9 An Uaimh Ec
84 Anaconda Db
35 Anadyr, G. of Vc

35 Anadyr Uc
27 Anáfi, I. Cb
28 Anagni Dd
44 Anaimalai Hills Df
42 Anaiza Ed
45 Anakapalle Ee
64 Anambas Is. Bc
27 Anamur, & C. Db
44 Anantapur Df
95 Anapolis Fc
27 Anatolia, dist. Db
24 Anchorage Db
28 Ancona Dc
93 Ancud Bg
26 Andalusia, reg. Bb
45 Andaman Is. Gf
74 Andara (Libebe) Ca
10 Andenes Db
13 Andermatt Cb
88 Anderson Cd
92 Andes, mts. Bd
44 Andhra Pradesh, st. Ee
34 Andizhan Ke
52 Andong Bb
26 Andorra & st. Ca
7 Andover Ff
83 Andreanof Is. Cb
27 Andreas, C. Db
29 Andria Fd
64 Androka Gh
45 Andros Bb
91 Andros I. Cb
35 Angara, R. Nd
35 Angarsk Nd
14 Angers Cd
48 Angkor Bb
6 Anglesey, I. & Co. Cd
78 Angmagssalik Ob
72 Angola, Fort Terr., Africa Dg
15 Angoulême De
72 Angra Pequena (Lüderitz) Bc
9 Anguilla, I. Fc
5 Angus, Co. Fd
52 Anholt Ec
52 Anju Bb
51 Ankang Ec
27 Ankara Db
52 Anking Fb
42 Ankobar Ce
88 Ann Arbor Dc
70 Annaba Ga
9 Annan Ef
20 Annecy, & Lac d' Ed
22 Annemasse Ec
72 Annonay Cd
86 Anoka Bb
17 Ansbach Dd
52 Anshan Gb
52 Anshun Ed
90 Anst Db
71 Ansongo Fe
8 Anstruther Fd
27 Antakya (Antioch) Eb
27 Antalya Db
27 Antalya, Gulf of Db
96 Antarctic Pen. Qc
96 Antarctica, cont. Ra
26 Antequera Bb
70 Anti Atlas, mts. Dc
40 Anti-Lebanon, mts. Cb
81 Antigonish Cb
15 Antibes, & Cap d', C. Ff
81 Anticosti I. Cb
90 Antigo Eb
9 Antigua, I. Fc
91 Antilla Cb
91 Antilles, Greater Cc
91 Antilles, Lesser Fc
27 Antioch, see Antakya
55 Antipodes I. Df
74 Antofagasta Ad
69 Antonio Gg
9 Antrim, & Co. Eb
55 Antung Gb
18 Antwerp, see Antwerpen
18 Antwerpen & prov. Dc
45 Anupgarh Dd
45 Anuradhapura Ee
52 Anyang Fc
34 Anzhero Ld
55 Ao-ga Shima, I. Cc
54 Aomori & pref. Db
21 Aosta Fd
35 Apalachee B. Df
37 Apalachicola Cf
55 Aparri Db
90 Apatin Bc
18 Apeldoorn Eb
28 Apennines, mts. Dc
94 Apia Dh
27 Apolyont, L. Ca
86 Apostle Is. Bb

88 Appalachian Mts. Ef
21 Appennino Ligure, mts. Ge
64 Appenzell, cant. Da
18 Appleton Ab
33 Apsheronsk, C. Kg
42 Aqaba Dd
39 Aqiq Cd
59 Aquidauana Dd
28 Aquila Dc
42 Ar Ramadi Ec
42 Ar Rass Ed
43 Ar Riyadh Fe
42 Arabian Desert Cc
36 Arabian Sea Kh
72 Aracaju Af
92 Aracati Fc
95 Aracual Gc
30 Arad Cb
37 Arafura Sea Rk
26 Aragon, prov. Ba
95 Araguari Fc
70 Arak Fc
35 Arakan, Dist. Ge
45 Arakan Yoma, mts. Ge
34 Aral S. He
39 Arapawa Dd
41 Aras, R. Fd
55 Arao, prov. Bb
94 Ararat, mt. Tur. Eb
60 Ararat, Vic. Bc
55 Araxa Fc
51 Arbai-Here Eb
22 Arber, mt. Bd
8 Arbroath Fd
10 Arc Dc
20 Arc, R. Ed
87 Arcacia Dc
71 Arco Jd
96 Arctic Ocean Sb
31 Arda, R. Ee
43 Ardabil Fb
27 Ardeche, dept. & R. Ce
10 Ardennes, dept. Dc
19 Ardennes, mts. Ed
9 Ardglass Fb
9 Ardmore, Ire. De
85 Ardmore, U.S.A.Ge
Cd Ardnacrusha Cd
60 Androssan, Australia Ab
5 Ardrossan Bd
10 Åre Cc
21 Arecibo Ec
11 Arendal Bd
28 Arequipa Bd
38 Arezzo Cc
14 Argentan Cc
19 Argenteuil Bf
92 Argentina, rep. Cf
27 Argolikos, G. of Bb
19 Argonne, mts. Ed
27 Argos Bb
5 Argyll, Co. Cd
55 Ariake, B. Bd
29 Ariano Irp. Ed
76 Arica Ac
28 Arizona, st. Dc
10 Arjepiog Db
50 Arka Tagh, mts. Dc
27 Arkansas, R. Da
85 Arkansas, st. Bd
85 Arkansas City Gd
32 Arkhangelsk Hc
7 Arklow Ed
19 Arlon Cf
19 Armadale Cc
24 Armagon, R. Cb
19 Armagh, & Co. Eb
33 Armavir Hf
31 Armenia, rep. Hf
28 Armentières Bd
55 Armidale Db
80 Armstrong Bb
71 Amauti, C. Db
10 Arnes Aa
54 Arnhem C. Aa
64 Arnhem Land Ea
81 Arnprior Bb
18 Arnsberg Hc
74 Aroab Bc
13 Arosa Db
47 Arrah Kf
4 Arran, I. Cf
70 Arecife Cc
6 Arrowtown Bf
74 Artá, Greece Bb
26 Artá, Spain Cb
33 Artemovsk Gf
94 Artigas Df
19 Artois, reg. Bd
49 Aru Is. Eg

91 Aruba, I. Ed
73 Arusha Fd
72 Aruwimi, R. Dc
20 Arve, R. Ec
10 Arvidsjaur Eb
32 Arzamas Hd
35 As Salman Ec
43 As Samawah Fc
43 As Summan, reg. Fd
43 As Suwaih He
43 As Suwayda Cc
54 Asahigawa Db
94 Asansol Lg
94 Ascención Cc
69 Ascension I. Af
34 Aschaffenburg Jd
28 Ascoli Piceno Dc
39 Aseb Dd
31 Asenovgrad Ec
42 Ash Shabakah Ec
42 Ashaira Ec
67 Ashburton Ce
64 Ashburton R., Austral. Cd
7 Ashby-de-la-Zouch Fe
80 Ashcroft Bb
45 Ashdod Bd
87 Asheville Dd
7 Ashford Hj
55 Ashikaga Cc
34 Ashkhabad Hf
48 Ashland, Ky. De
88 Ashland, Ohio Dd
86 Ashland, Wis. Bb
40 Ashqelon Bd
88 Ashtabula Ed
81 Ashuanipi, L. Ca
40 Asi (Orontes) R. Cb
3 Asia, cont. Mc
49 Asia Is. Sc
87 Askham Da
54 Askja, mt. Ba
39 Asir Dd
39 Asmera Cc
55 Aso, vol. Bd
21 Asola Jd
20 Aspres De
45 Assam, st. Gc
18 Asse Cd
35 Assens Cd
80 Assiniboia Dc
95 Assis Ad
28 Assisi Dc
21 Asti Ge
47 Astipalaia, I. Cb
28 Astrakhan Jd
65 Asturias, prov. Aa
92 Asunción Ce
38 Aswan Cc
38 Asyut Cc
94 Atacama Des. Be
55 Atami Cc
39 Atbara & R. Cd
80 Athabasca Cb
80 Athabasca L. Db
80 Athabasca, R. Cb
28 Athens, Ga. De
27 Athens (Athínai), Greece Bb
88 Athens, Ohio Eb
62 Atherton Cb
27 Athínai see Athens
9 Athlone Dc
27 Athos, mt. Ba
89 Atlanta Be
28 Atlantic City He
2 Atlantic Ocean Ed
68 Atlas Mts. Bc
Kc Attleboro Kc
20 Aube, R. & dept. Ca
20 Aubenas Ce
20 Aubrac, Mts. d' Ae
89 Auburn Gc
15 Aubusson Ed
14 Auch Df
39 Auchel Bd
6 Auckland, & dist. Eb
56 Auckland I. Df
82 Auchtermuchty Ed
20 Audin ourt Eb
63 Augathella Cd
74 AughrabiesFallsBc
9 Aughrim Ja
28 Augusta, Ga. Ge
25 Augusta, Italy Ef
89 Augusta, Maine Cb
65 Augusta, Western Australia Be
23 Augustow Gb
44 Augustus Mt. Bc
46 Aurangabad Ej
18 Aurich Gc
15 Aurillac Ee
29 Aurora Cc
74 Aus Bc

86 Austin, Minn. Bc
85 Austin, Tex. Ge
65 Austin & L., W. Austral. Bd
62 Austral Downs Ac
3 Australia, st. Og
61 Australian Alps, mts. Cc
96 Australian Dependency Gb
4 Austria, rep. Hf
20 Autun Cc
20 Auvergne, dist. & mts. Bd
20 Auxerre Bb
21 Avej Fb
93 Avellaneda Df
29 Avellino Ed
29 Aversa Ed
11 Avesta Dc
20 Aveyron, R. & dept. Ae
28 Avezzano Dc
29 Avigliano Ed
20 Avignon Cf
26 Avila Ba
26 Avilés Aa
29 Avola Ef
7 Avon, R. Fg
7 Avonmouth Ef
14 Avranches Cc
2 Axel Heiberg, I. Cb
71 Axim Eg
54 Ayabe Cc
39 Ayaguz Le
26 Ayamonte Ab
27 Aydin Cb
21 Aylesbury Gf
62 Ayr, Austral. Cb
8 Ayr, & Co., Scotland De
50 Ayutla Ed
88 Ayutthaya Bb
27 Ayvalik Cb
47 Azan.garh Je
71 Azbine (Air) dist.
33 Azerbaijan Jg
2 Azores, Is. Fd
3 Azov Sea Gf
21 Azua Dc
4 Azul Cf

40 Ba'abda Bc
40 Ba'alt akk Cc
9 Bab el Mandeb, Str. of Dd
23 Babanusa Da
23 Babia Gora, mt. Ea
3 Babol Gb
49 Babuyan Is. Db
50 Bacau Fb
52 Baccarat Ea
90 Bacolod Db
20 Bacuit Cb
18 Bad Godesberg Gd
19 Bad Homtt.rg Hd
19 Bad Kreuznach Ge
46 Badajoz Ab
26 Badalona Ca
7 Baden, Aust. Gd
15 Baden, Switz. Ca
70 Baden-Baden Hf
46 Badin Bf
13 Bafatá Cf
72 Baffin Bay La
71 Baffin I. Kb
31 Bafq Hc
29 Bafra Ea
41 Bafoulabé Cf
89 Bafq Hc
15 Bafra Ea
71 Bagamoyo Gb
95 Bagé Ef
42 Baghdad Ec
29 Bagheria Be
70 Baguio Db
51 Bahama Is. Db
38 Bahariya Oasis Bc
46 Bahawalpur&st.Cd
93 Bahia Blanca Cf
72 Bahia Negra Db
83 Bahr el Abiad (White Nile) Cd
68 Bahr el Arab, R. Ea
39 Bahr el Azraq (Blue Nile), R. Cd
72 Bahr el Ghazal, prov. Cd
72 Bahr el Jebel, R. Cd
73 Bahra De
48 Bahraich He
43 Bahrain, I. Gd
45 Bahramabad Fe
52 Baia, st. Ed
50 Baia Mare Eb
81 Baie Comeau Cb
35 Baikal, L. Nd
87 Bainbridge De

61 Bainsdale Cc
30 Baitadi Hd
30 Baja Bb
90 Baja, Pta., Ab
72 Bakala Cf
72 Bakel Cf
78 Baker Cc
84 Baker, L. Hb
85 Bakersfield Cd
30 Bakony Forest Ab
72 Bakourma Cb
33 Baku Jg
9 Balabac, I. Cd
47 Balaghat Hn
60 Balaklava, South
   Australia Ab
33 Balaklava,
   U.S.S.R. Fg
71 Balama Cf
49 Balambangan,I.Cc
49 Blangir Jh
33 Balashov He
49 Balasore Lh
30 Balaton, L. Ab
9 Balbriggan Ec
53 Balchik Gd
67 Balclutha Bg
12 Baldegger See Ca
12 Balearic Is. Cb
48 Bali, I. Cd
47 Balikesir Cd
48 Balikpapan Cd
95 Balisa Ec
31 Balkan Mts. Ed
48 Balkhash, & L. Ke
9 Ballaghaderreen Cc
61 Ballarat Bc
9 Ballina,
   Australia Da
9 Ballina, Mayo Db
9 Ballina,
   Tipperary Cc
9 Ballinasloe Cc
13 Ballinluig Ed
9 Ballinrobe Cc
9 Ballinascarthy Ce
9 Ballybunion Bd
9 Ballycastle,
   Antrim Ea
9 Ballycastle,
   Mayo Cb
9 Ballyclare Eb
9 Ballymena Eb
9 Ballymoney Ea
9 Ballymote Cb
9 Ballyshannon Cb
9 Balmoral Ec
9 Balrampur Je
60 Balranald Ac
90 Balsas, R. Dd
13 Balsthal Ba
33 Baltas Ef
11 Baltic Sea Ef
9 Baltimore, Ire. Be
89 Baltimore,
   U.S.A. Ge
13 Baltrum I. Ga
44 Baluchistan,
   Dist. Bc
43 Bam Hd
71 Bamako Df
71 Bamba Ee
71 Bamberg Dd
43 Bampur Hd
72 Banalia Dc
69 Banana Df
95 Bananal I. Be
9 Banbridge Eb
9 Banbury Fe
74 Banda Atjeh Ac
46 Banda, Mad. P. Gf
9 Banda Sea Dd
9 Banda Is. Ed
55 Bandaisan, mt. Dc
43 Bandar Abbas Hd
43 Bandar-e-
   Charak Gd
43 Bandar-e-
   Lengeh Gd
43 Bandar-e-
   Pahlavi Fb
43 Bandar-e-Rig Gd
43 Bandar-e-Shah Hc
43 Bandar-e-
   Shahpur Fc
94 Bandera Ec
27 Bandirma Ca
48 Bandjarmasin Cd
9 Bandon & R. Ce
75 Bandula Ea
72 Bandundu Bd
48 Bandung Bd
87 Banff, Canada Bd
8 Banff & Co.,
   Scotland Ec
44 Bangalore Df
44 Bangalow Da
53 Bass Strait Hf
30 Bassano, Can. Cb
48 Banggi, Is. Dd
48 Banggi, I. Cc
48 Banka, I. Bd
48 Bangkok Bb
9 Bangor, Ire. Fb

6 Bangor, Wales Cd
72 Bangui Bc
8 Bangweulu, L. Ef
40 Bani Dc
28 Banjaluka Fb
48 Banjuwangi Cd
47 Bankipore Kf
78 Banks I. Ea
47 Bankura Lg
44 Bannu Cb
22 Banská Fd
22 BanskáBystricaEd
75 Barberton,
   South Africa Ec
88 Barberton,
   U.S.A. Ed
91 Barbuda, I. Fc
43 Barcaldine Cc
26 Barcelona, Italy Ee
92 Barcelona, Ven. Cb
12 Barcelos Bc
68 Bardai Dc
23 Bardejov Eb
30 Bardia Eb
18 Bardu Db
46 Bareilly Gd
34 Barents Sea Fb
14 Barfleur Cc
21 Barga Je
39 Bargal Ed
39 Bari Fd
73 Baringo, L. Fc
47 Baripada Lh
41 Barisal Ng
48 Baram Mts. Bd
48 Barito R. Cd
50 Barkha Cc
71 Barkly
   Tableland Fb
75 Barkly West Cc
93 Barkol Dd
11 Barlee L. Bd
26 Barlee Ra. Bc
25 Barletta Fd
14 Barmer Cf
7 Barmouth Ce
14 Barnaul Ld
91 Barneveld Eb
6 Barnsley Fd
7 Barnstaple Cf
73 Baro Gg
71 Baroda Gg
63 Baroren Dc
47 Barpeta Ne
95 Barquisimeto Ca
95 Barra Gb
9 Barra, I. Ad
13 Barra Hd. Cc
15 Barra Pt. Fb
61 Barraba Db
72 Barrackpore Mg
94 Barranco
   Branco
92 Barranquilla Ca
89 Barre Fb
93 Barreiras Gb
93 Barretos Fd
88 Barrie Fb
82aBarrow, Alaska Ca
6 Barrow, Eng. Dc
14 Barrow Creek Ec
7 Barry Df
32 Bartle Frere,mt.Cb
97 Bartlesville Ad
23 Bartoszyce Fa
13 Barvas Bb
60 Barwon R. Ca
13 Basel (Basle) &
   cant. Ba
29 Basilan I. Dc
29 Basilicata
   (Lucania) reg. Fd
95 Basilio Ef
9 Basingstoke Ff
13 Basle, see Basel
72 Basoko Cc
72 Basongo Cd
26 Basque Provs. Ba
41 Basra Cc
30 Bass Strait Hf
28 Bassano, Can. Cb
30 Bassano, Italy Cb
48 Bassein Ge
26 Basses-Alpes,
   dept. Ee

91 Basseterre Fc
20 Bassigny, dist. Da
47 Basti Je
15 Bastia Bg
38 Bastürshkh Ec
49 Bata Je
49 Bataan I. Db
71 Batanao & Gulf
49 Batan Is. Da
49 Batangas Db
30 Bataszek Bb
28 Batavia Fc
40 Batchelor Ea
9 Batesville Bd
7 Bath Ef
61 Bathurst,
   Australia Cb
81 Bathurst, Can. Cb
71 Bathurst, Gam. Bf
78 Bathurst I.,
   Canada Ha
49 Batna Ha
87 Baton Rouge Be
73 Battambang Bb
7 Battle Hg
78 Battle Creek Cc
79 Battle Harbour Mc
73 Batu, mt. Fh
48 Batu is. Ad
38 Batumi Hg
92 Baturité Fc
61 Baucau (Vila
   Salazar) Dd
71 Bauchi Gf
73 Baudouinville De
70 Baugie Fa
94 Bautres Cb
93 Baus Ec
31 Bautzen Fc
90 Bavispe Ca
48 Bawean, I. Cd
71 Bawku Ef
71 Baxtel Ec
88 Bay City Dc
49 Bay of Whales Lb
76 Bay Shore Jd
60 Bay View Fc
15 Bayamo Cc
14 Bayeux Cc
15 Bayonne Cf
17 Bayreuth Dd
40 Bayt ad Din Dc
40 Bayt Lahm
   (Bethlehem) Dc
7 Beachy Head Hg
96 Beardmore
   Glacier Ha
18 Beatrice Ha
61 Beaucaire Cf
61 Beaudesert Da
91 Beaufort Cc
78 Beaufort Sea Da
74 Beaufort West Cd
20 Beaujolais, dist.Cd
3 Beauly & R. Ec
8 Beaumont Be
10 Beaune Cb
74 Beauvais Ec
80 Beauval Db
96 Beaverdam Cc
95 Beawar Ec
31 Bebra Cc
3 Bechar Eb
74 Bechuanaland Cc
89 Beckley Ef
7 Bedford & Co.,
   England Ge
88 Bedford, U.S.A. Be
33 Beechworth Cc
48 Beersheba Bd
13 Bega Cc
75 Deira Cc
18 Beirut Cb
75 Beitbridge Eb
26 Beja, Port. Ab
9 Béja, Tunisia Ca
59 Bekescaba Cc
32 Bela Nc
68 Bela Crkva Cc
94 Bela Vista,
   Brazil Fc
93 Bela Vista, Par. Dd
33 Belaya F
35 Belaya R. Le
75 Belcher Is. Tb
32 Belem Ec
9 Belfast Fb
20 Belfort, & Terr. Ed
75 Belgaum Ce
4 Belgium, King. Fc
72 Belgrade Dc
46 Belitung, I. Bd
90 Belize Gd
79 Bell I., Lab. Mc

81 Bell I., Newf. Db
80 Bella Coola Bb
72 Bella Vista Ec
88 Bellaire Ed
44 Bellary Df
5 Belle I. Mc
79 Belle Isle, Str. ofMc
20 Belledonne, Chaine
   de, mts. Ed
48 Bellefontaine Dd
20 Bellegarde Dc
61 Bellerive Cd
81 Belleville, Can. Bb
26 Belleville,
   U.S.A. Gc
88 Bellingen Db
94 Bellinzona Ca
96 Bellingshausen
   Sea Qc
13 Bellinzona Cb
28 Belluno Da
64 Belly R. Da
95 Belo Horizonte Gc
35 Iselogorsk Pd
32 Belomorsk Fc
32 Beloye, L. Gc
32 Beiozersk Gd
33 Beiozerskaya Jf
60 Beitana Ab
85 Beiton Ge
9 Beiturbet Db
34 Belukha, Mt. Le
62 Belyando R. Cc
86 Bemidji Bb
61 Ben Lomond, mt.,
   N.S.W. Db
61 Ben Lomond, mt.,
   Tas. Cd
8 Ben Nevis, mt. Dd
8 Ben Wyvis, mt. Dc
60 Benalla Cc
47 Benares, see
   Varanasi
65 Bencubbin Be
84 Bend Bc
39 Bender Bella Ee
39 Bender Cassim Dd
33 Bendery Ef
49 Bendigo Bc
23 Benevento Ed
8 Bengal, B. of Fe
48 Bengal, W., st. Fd
68 Benghazi Eb
65 Benguela Af
70 Beni Abbés Eb
38 Beni Suef Cc
9 Benin,
   Bight of Fh
71 Benin City Gg
80 Bennett Ab
19 Bensheim He
73 Bentiu Db
68 Benton Harb. Cc
71 Benue, R. Gg
13 Beppu Bd
32 Berat Bd
31 Berat Ed
39 Berbera Dd
33 Berdichev Ef
35 Bereda Ed
33 Berdyansk Df
13 Berezina R. Ee
12 Berezniki Ld
27 Bergama Cb
31 Bergamo Hd
81 Bergen, Neth. Db
11 Bergen, Nor. Bc
18 Bergen-op-
   Zoom Dc
18 Bergisch
   Gladbach Gc
47 Berhampore Mf
47 Berhampur Kj
5 Bering Sea Tk
82aBering Str. Ad
84 Berkeley Bd
7 Berkshire, Co. Ff
16 Berlin Eb
13 Bern, & cant. Bb
14 Bernay Dc
16 Bernburg Dc
13 Berner Alpen,
   mts. Bb
22 Beroun Cd
60 Berri Bb
60 Berrigan Cc
61 Berry, Austral. Db
20 Berry, dist., Fr. Ab
74 Berseba Bc
35 Bering I. Tb
12 Berwick, Co. Fb
6 Berwick-upon-
   Tweed Fb
20 Besançon Eb
72 Betaré-Oya Ab
75 Bethal Cc
74 Bethanien Bc
40 Bethlehem (Bayt
   Lahm), Israel &
   Jordan Bd
75 Bethlehem, South
   Africa Dc

89 Bethlehem,
   U.S.A. Hd
75 Bethulie Dd
18 Bethune Bd
81 Betsiamites Cb
47 Bettiah Ke
65 Beverley Be
18 Beverwijk Db
7 Bexhill Hg
87 Beypazari Da
27 Beysehir, L. Db
33 Bezhitza He
15 Beziers Ef
30 Bhachau Cg
47 Bhagalpur Lf
63 Bhiano Hd
37 Bhamragarh Hh
46 Bhanuara Ge
16 Bharatpur, Raj. Fe
37 Bharatpur,
   Mad. P. Hg
46 Bhatinda Ec
47 Bhatpara Mg
46 Bhaunagar Dh
46 Bhilwara Ef
46 Bhima R. De
46 Bhiwandi Dj
46 Bhiwani Fd
46 Bhopal Fg
47 Bhubaneswar Kh
46 Bhuj Bg
46 Bhusawal Eh
45 Bhutan, st. Gc
21 Biafra, B. of Gh
22 Biala, Kraków Ed
23 Biala
   (Podlaska) Gb
22 Bialogard Cd
23 Bialowieza Gb
23 Bialystok Gb
15 Biarritz Cf
54 Bihai Db
21 Biberach Ha
71 Biblani Eg
7 Bicester Ff
70 Bida Gg
49 Bidar Fk
23 Bidford Kc
72 Bie Plateau Bf
13 Biel Bb
16 Bielefeld Hb
21 Bielia Gd
23 Bielsk Gb
48 Bien Hoa Bb
68 Big Rapids Cc
85 Big Spring Fe
32 Biggar Fb
7 Biggleswade Ge
28 Bihac Eb
44 Bihar, & st. Kf
34 Bisk Ld
14 Bijapur De
33 Bijeljina a
43 Bijar Fb
46 Bikaner Dd
31 Bikin Hb
72 Bikoro Bd
44 Bilara Dc
35 Bilaspur Jg
38 Bilauk Taung Ra.,
   mts. Ab
26 Bilbao Ba
21 Bilceik Da
28 Bilek Gc
71 Billings Db
68 Biloxi Ce
71 Bimbéréké Fg
73 Bindura Ea
89 Binh Dinh Bb
55 Bir Hd
46 Birdum & R. Eb
63 Birdsvile Ad
35 Biren Natrum Ed
43 Birjand Hc
46 Birkenhead Df
30 Bitlad Fg
7 Birmingham,
   England Fe
87 Birmingham,
   U.S.A. Dc
71 Birnin-Kebbi Ff
35 Birobidzhan Qe
23 Birr Dc
32 Birsk Ld
9 Biscay, Bay of Df
29 Biscezlie Fd
17 Bischofshofen Ee
7 Bishop's
   Stortford Hf
31 Biskra Fb
70 Biskra Fb
71 Bismarck Fb
62 Bismarck Arch. Gg
41 Bissau Bf
30 Bistra Eb
30 Bistrita Eb
30 Bitlis Eb
31 Bitola Eb
70 Bitonto Fd
75 Bitterfontein Bd
23 Bivona Dd
55 Biwa, L. Cc
70 Bizerte Ga

28 Bjelovar Fb
10 Bjornfjell Db
30 Black Crisul, R. Db
4 Black Sea Mg
71 Black Volta, R. Eg
72 Blackall Cc
67 Blackball Ce
6 Blackburn Ed
6 Blackpool Dd
9 Blackrock Ec
9 Blackwater, R. Ec
65 Blackwood R. Be
75 Blagoveschensk Pd
62 Blair Athol Cc
8 Blair Atholl Ed
8 Blairgowrie Ed
80 Blairmore Cc
70 Blanc, Mont, mt. Ed
60 Blanche L. Aa
8 Blanco, C., Afr. Ac
84 Blanco, C., U.S.A. Cc
7 Blandford Eg
18 Blankenberge Gd
91 Blanquilla, I. Fd
84 Blantyre Fg
28 Bled Ea
67 Blenheim Ed
70 Blida Fa
88 Blind River Da
22 Blöckenstein Cd
75 Bloemfontein Dc
14 Blois Dd
9 Bloody Foreland Da
55 Bloomington, Ill. Cc
88 Bloomington, Ind. Be
61 Blue Mountains, see Katoomba Db
62 Blue Mud B. Aa
39 Blue Nile, Bahr el Azraq, R. Cd
7 Blue Ridge Ef
91 Bluefields Bd
7 Bluff Bg
83 Blumenau Fe
8 Blyth Fb
95 Bö Fb
62 Boa Vista Cb
47 Bobbili Jj
71 Bobo-Dioulasso Ef
30 Bobruisk Ee
18 Bocholt Fc
18 Bochum Gc
55 Bodaibo Od
8 Boddam Gc
10 Boden Eb
13 Bodensee, L. Da
7 Bodha Fj
48 Bodjonegoro Cd
7 Bodmin Cg
10 Bodo Cb
72 Bodrum Cd
72 Boende Cd
5 Bofu Bd
74 Bogenfels Bc
22 Bogense Dd
70 Boggeragh Mts. Cd
70 Boghari Fa
7 Bognor Regis Gg
43 Bogo Bd
92 Bogota Bb
43 Bogra Mf
22 Bohemian Forest Bd
25 Bohol, I. Dc
39 Bohotleh Ee
74 Boise Cc
70 Bojador, C. Cc
11 Boknafjord Bd
72 Bokote Cd
72 Bokungu Cd
44 Bolan Pass Bc
14 Bolbec Dc
60 Boleroo Centre Ab
22 Boleslawiec Cc
25 Bolinao Bb
72 Bolivia, rep. Cd
72 Bolobo Bd
28 Bologna Cb
28 Bologne Da
32 Bologoye Fd
35 Bolshevik I. Nb
6 Bolton Ed
27 Bolu Da
28 Bolzano Cb
55 Bom Despacho Fc
72 Boma Ae
14 Bombala Cc
46 Bombay Dj
50 Bomda Dc
72 Bomili Dc
72 Bomongo Bc
70 Bon, C. Ha
91 Bonaire, I. Ed
81 Bonavista Db
72 Bondo Cc
49 Bone, G. of Dd
72 Boness Ed
72 Bongandanga Cc

15 Bonifacio & Str. Bh
56 Bonin Is. Cb
18 Bonn Gd
65 Bonnie Rock Be
51 Bonthe Cg
28 Boom Dc
61 Boonah Da
79 Boothia, G. of Ja
79 Boothia Pen. Ha
6 Bootle Dd
73 Bor Eb
73 Borama Ga
43 Borazjan Gd
15 Bordeaux Ce
60 Bordertown Bc
10 Bordeyri Aa
11 Borgholm Dd
28 Borgo S. Lorenzo Cc
21 Borgo Val di Taro He
21 Borgosesia Gd
33 Borisogiebsk He
33 Borisov Ee
52 Borja Ec
18 Borkum Fa
44 Bornec, I. Cc
12 Bornholm, I. Fa
22 Borovichi Fd
64 Bortoloola Fb
10 Borselv Fa
43 Borujerd Fc
28 Bosa Bd
28 Bosanska Gradiška Fb
28 Bosnia & Hercegovina, prov. Fb
27 Bosporus, str. Ca
7 Boston, Eng. He
73 Boston, U.S.A. Kc
11 Bothnia, G. of Dc
30 Botosani Fb
71 Botou Ff
74–75 Botswana, st. Cb
18 Bottrop Fc
95 Botucatú Fc
71 Bouaké Dg
20 Bouches du Rhone, dept. Ff
62 Bougainville Hh
64 Bougainville C. Da
65 Boulder Cc
62 Boulia Ac
14 Boulogne Db
56 Bounty Is. Df
20 Bourbonnais, dist. Ec
20 Bourbonne Ee
72 Bourem Ee
20 Bourg de Péage Dd
20 Bourg en Bresse Dc
20 Bourg St. Maurice Ed
15 Bourges Ed
20 Bourgogne, dist. Cc
60 Bourke Cc
7 Bournemouth Fg
70 Boutilimit Ce
2 Bouvet Is. Hh
22 Bovino Ed
62 Bowen Cb
88 Bowling Green Bf
9 Boyle Cc
9 Boyne, R. Ec
61 Boyne City Cb
28 Brod Cb
72 Bozeman Db
72 Bozoum Bb
27 Bozüyük Db
21 Bra Fe
28 Brac, I. Fc
62 Bracadale, & L. Bc
88 Bracebridge Fb
7 Brackley Fe
67 Bradenton Df
62 Bradford, Eng. Fd
89 Bradford, U.S.A. Fd
7 Bradford on Avon Ef
85 Brady Ge
5 Braemar Ec
52 Braes of Angus Ed
26 Braga Aa
92 Bragança, Braz. Ec
26 Bragança, Port. Aa
47 Brahmambaria Ng
47 Brahmani, R. Kh
43 Brahmaputra, R. Kh
8 Braidwood Cc
30 Braila Fc
74 Brainerd Bb
18 Brampton Fc
58 Branch Gb
76 Brandenburg Eb
77 Brandon, Eng. Hc
80 Brandon, Can. Dc
23 Braniewo Ea
23 Bransk Gb
81 Brantford Ab
95 Brasilia Fc
95 Brasov Ec
58 Brasschaat Dc
22 Bratislava Dd

16 Braunschweig (Brunswick) Db
9 Brava Ec
9 Bray Ec
92 Brazil, rep. Dd
95 Brazilian Highlands Ed
72 Brazzaville Bd
8 Brechin Fd
85 Breckenridge Ge
7 Brecknock, Co. Df
27 Brecon Df
28 Breda Dc
74 Bredasdorp Cd
21 Bregenz Hb
10 Breidafjördur Aa
16 Bremen Cb
16 Bremerhaven Cb
13 Bremgarten Ca
21 Brenner P. Kb
21 Bréscia Jd
22 Breslau (Wroclaw) Dc
28 Bressanone Ca
8 Bressay Inset
20 Bresse, Plaine de, dist. Dc
14 Brest, France Ac
73 Brest, U.S.S.R. De
30 Breteak Fd
92 Breu Branco Ec
8 Brewarrina Ca
23 Brezno Fd
72 Bria Cb
20 Briançon Ca
20 Briare Ab
20 Bricon Ca
89 Bridgeport Jd
89 Bridgeton He
65 Bridgetown, Australia Be
91 Bridgetown, West Indies Fd
81 Bridgewater Cb
7 Bridgwater Ef
19 Brie, Plaine de Cf
13 Brig Bb
84 Brigham Dc
7 Brighton, Eng. Gg
62 Brighton, South Australia Ac
26 Brihuega Ba
75 Bulawayo Db
61 Brisbane Da
7 Bristol, Eng. Ef
89 Bristol, U.S.A. Kd
7 Bristol Channel Df
96 British Antarctic Territory Rc
78 British Columbia, prov. Ec
77 British Honduras Kg
4 British Isles Ce
14 Brittany, reg. Bc
7 Brixham Dg
22 Brno Dd
46 Broach Dh
8 Broad Law Ee
62 Broad Sound Cc
6 Broadford Bc
80 Brochet Db
64 Brockman Mt. Bc
88 Brockton Kc
89 Brockville Hb
28 Brod Cb
72 Brodersley Cb
72 Brodeur Pen. Ja
28 Brodnica Eb
69 Broken Hill, Australia, Bb
69 Broken Hill, (Kabwe) Zambia Eg
22 Bromberg (Bydgoszcz) Eb
16 Brönnoysund Cb
87 Brookhaven Be
65 Brookton Ab
64 Broome Bb
86 Burley Dc
8 Broughty Ferry Fd
85 Brownsville Gf
85 Brownwood Ge
19 Bruay Bd
64 Bruce Mt. Bc
17 Bruck Fe
18 Bruges (Brugge) Cc
16 Brühl Fd
48 Brunei, st. Cc
74 Brunette Downs Fb
13 Brunig Pass Cb
67 Brunner Ce
16 Brunswick, see Braunschweig
64 Brunswick B. Cb
96 Brusque Fe
18 Brussels (Brussel, Bruxelles) Dd
61 Bruthen Cc
18 Bruxelles, see Brussels
88 Bryan, Ohio Cc
87 Bryan, Tex. Ae
33 Bryansk Fe

92 Bucaramanga Bb
64 Buccaneer Arch. Cb
71 Buchanan Cg
30 Bucharest Fc
13 Buchs Da
8 Buckhaven Ed
8 Buckie Fc
89 Buckingham, Canada Hb
7 Buckingham & Co., England Ge
88 Bucyrus Dd
30 Budapest Bb
64 Budaun Gd
7 Bude Cg
22 Budejovice Cd
33 Budennovsk Hg
10 Budir Ab
28 Budrio Cb
69 Buea Ce
92 Buenaventura Bb
93 Buenos Aires Df
93 Buenos Aires, prov. Cf
89 Buffalo, N.Y. Fc
84 Buffalo, Wyo. Ec
29 Buffaloria Fe
74 Buffels Bc
23 Bug, R., Pol. Fb
33 Bug R., U.S.S.R. Ff
49 Bugsuk, I. Cc
32 Buguima Ke
33 Bugurasalan Ke
41 Buheirat-Murrat-el Kubra (Great Bitter Lake) Ce
41 Buheirat-Murrat-el Sughra (Little Bitter Lake) Ce
73 Bujumbura Dd
62 Buka I. Hh
72 Bukama De
73 Bukavu Dd
73 Bukene Ed
34 Bukhara Jf
48 Bukittingi Bd
73 Bukoba Ed
50 Bulak Cb
49 Bulan Db
46 Bulsahahn Hf
75 Bulawayo Db
46 Bulsar Dh
30 Bulun Pb
65 Bunbury Be
9 Buncrana Da
61 Bundaberg Dc
9 Bundoran Cb
18 Bunessan Bc
44 Bungatan Is. Bc
41 Bûr Sa'id (Port Said) Ca
61 Bûr Taufiq Dg
42 Buraida Ed
43 Buraimi Hd
72 Buram Cb
39 Buran Ed
85 Burbank Ce
52 Burchun Cb
62 Burdekin R. Cb
27 Burdur Db
47 Burdwan Lg
16 Burg Db
52 Burgas Fd
75 Burgersdorp Dd
8 Burghead Ec
26 Bûrgos Ba
11 Burgsvik Dd
15 Burgundy, reg. Fd
27 Burhaniye Db
46 Burhanpur Fh
65 Burketown Ab
86 Burley Dc
88 Burlington, N.C. Ff
88 Burlington, Iowa Bc
88 Burlington, Vt. Jb
37 Burma, Union of, rep. Ng
64 Burma Road Hd
63 Burnett R. Dc
61 Burnie Cd
6 Burra Ab
61 Burren Junc. Cb
7 Burry Port Cf
27 Bursa Ca
7 Burton-on-Trent Fe
49 Buru, I. Dd
73 Burundi, st. Dd
6 Bury, Lancs. Ed
7 Bury, Suffolk He
7 Bury St. Edmunds He
43 Bushehr Gd
43 Bushire Gd

9 Bushmills Ea
42 Busra Dc
40 Bustaash Sham Cc
65 Busselton Be
18 Bussum Eb
21 Busto Arsizio Gd
72 Busu-Djanoa Cc
72 Buta Cc
73 Butare Dd
73 Bute Dd
8 Bute, co. Ce
84 Butte Db
48 Butterworth Bc
49 Butung, I. Dd
33 Buturlinovka He
6 Buxton Fd
33 Buynaksk Jg
47 Büyük, R. Cb
30 Buzâu Fc
33 Buzuluk Ke
30 Byala Dd
23 Bydgoszcz (Bromberg) Eb
33 Byelgorod Ge
11 Byglandsfjord Bd
79 Bylot I. Ka
96 Byrd Ob
96 Byrd Land Nb
60 Byrock Cb
81 Byron Bay, & C. Da
35 Byrrang Mts. Mb
22 Bytom Ec

C

94 Caazapa De
49 Cabanatuan Db
94 Cabezas Cc
69 Cabinda Df
81 Cabonga Res. Bb
81 Cabot Str. Cb
26 Cabrera, I. Cb
55 Caccamo Df
90 Cacouzal Ee
72 Cachoeira Fd
72 Caconda Bf
88 Cadillac Cb
26 Cadiz & G. Ab
14 Caen Cc
5 Caenannus Mor (Kells) Ec
6 Caernarvon, Co. & Bay Cd
7 Caerphilly Df
95 Caetité Gb
45 Cagayan Dc
28 Cagli Db
28 Cagliari Bc
21 Cagnes-sur-Mer Ff
91 Caguas Ec
15 Cahors Dc
91 Caicos I. Dc
8 Cairn Gorm Ec
8 Cairn Toul, mt. Ec
62 Cairns Ca
21 Cáiro Montenotte Ge
8 Caithness, Co. Eb
71 Calabar Gh
28 Calabria, reg. Fe
14 Calais Db
84 Calama Bd
49 Calamian Group, Is. Cb
90 Calarasi Fc
49 Calbayog Db
47 Calcutta Mg
13 Caldoro Fb
84 Caldwell Cc
74 Caledon Bd
8 Caledonian Canal Dc
94 Caleta Coloso Ad
80 Calgary Cc
90 Cali Bb
90 Californian, Gulf of Bb
82 California, st. Bc
74 Calitzdorp Cd
73 Callafo Gb
13 Callao Dd
92 Callao Bd
29 Caltagirone Ef
29 Caltanissetta Ef
26 Caluire et Cuire Cd
74 Calvinia Bd
91 Camaguey Cb
90 Camargo Cb
20 Camargue, dist. Cf
48 Camau, & pt. Bc
46 Cambay Eg
46 Camberley Dd
46 Cambay, G. of Ch
48 Cambodia, st. Bc
7 Camborne Bg
7 Cambrai Dd
7 Cambridge & I. of Ely, co. He
7 Cambridge, England Eb
89 Cambridge, Md. He
89 Cambridge, Mass. Kc
66 Cambridge, N.Z. Eb
88 Cambridge, Ohio Ed

64 Cambridge G. Da
61 Camden, Australia Db
89 Camden, U.S.A. He
72 Cameia Cf
28 Camerino Dc
71 Cameroon Pk. Gh
68 Cameroon, rep. De
92 Cameta Ec
94 Camiri Cd
29 Camocim Ec
62 Camooweal Ab
28 Campagna Dd
29 Campania, reg. Ed
56 Campbell I. Df
51 Campbell Town, Tas. Cd
44 Campbellpore Cb
81 Campbellton Cb
61 Campbelltown Ce
8 Campbeltown Ce
92 Campêche, & G. of Fd
91 Campechuela Cb
60 Camperdown Bc
30 Campina Ba
95 Campinas Fd
71 Campo Gh
94 Campo Gallo Cd
95 Campo Grande Ed
95 Campobasso Ed
95 Campos Gd
95 Campos Belos Fb
95 Campos, mts. Ed
44 Campulung Ec
30 Campulung, Pitesti Ec
80 Camrose Cb
44 Can Tho Bd
76 Canada Hc
7 Canakkale Ca
92 Canal Zone, Panama Bb
90 Cananea Ba
68 Canary Is. Ac
59 Canberra Hf
27 Cangussu Ef
75 Canicado Ef
27 Cankiri Da
8 Canna I. Bc
9 Cannanore Df
15 Cannes Gf
3 Cannich Dc
17 Cannstatt Cd
80 Canon City Ed
80 Canora Db
71 Canowindra Cb
7 Canso, C. Cb
26 Cantabrian Mts. Aa
7 Canterbury, England HJ
67 Canterbury, dist., N.Z. Ce
67 Canterbury B. Df
67 Canterbury Plains Ce
27 Canton, Miss. Ce
88 Canton, Ohio Ed
7 Canton, China Fd
56 Canton I. Ed
21 Cantù Hd
51 Cap Haitien Dc
74 Capaia Ce
61 Cape Adare Lb
81 Cape Breton, I. Cb
71 Cape Coast Eg
74 Cape Province Cd
74 Cape Town Bd
62 Cape York Pen. Ba
62 Cape Verde Is. Fe
62 Cape York Pen. Ba
24 Capraia, I. Bd
24 Capri, I. Ed
45 Capricorn Chan. Dc
24 Capua Ed
45 Car Nicobar, I. Gg
24 Caracal Ec
30 Caracas Ca
91 Caransebes Dc
91 Caratasca Lagoon Bc
95 Caratinga Gc
91 Carbonear Db
89 Carbondale Hd
28 Carbonia Bc
15 Carcassonne Ef
34 Carcross Db
91 Cardenas Db
7 Cardiff Df
7 Cardigan & co. Ce
7 Cardigan B. Ce
80 Carstorn Cc
62 Cardwell Cb
39 Carei Db
29 Caribbean Sea Dd
95 Carinhanha Gb
79 Carini De
28 Carioforte Be
9 Carlingford Eb
7 Carlisle, Eng. Ec
81 Carlisle, U.S.A. Gd
7 Carlow & co. Ed
8 Carloway Bb
85 Carlsbad Db
78 Carmacks Db

21 Carmagnola Fe
80 Carman Ec
7 Carmarthen & Co. Cf
40 Carmel, mt. Bc
74 Carnarvon, South Africa Ch
65 Carnarvon, W. Austral. Ac
9 Carndonagh Da
8 Carnoustie Fd
9 Carnsore Pt. Ed
92 Carolina Ec
56 Caroline Is. Cc
30 Carpathians Mts. Eb
62 Carpentaria, Gulf of Aa
20 Carpentras De
21 Carpi Je
9 Carrantuohill, mt. Be
28 Carrara Cc
9 Carren, L. Cc
30 Carrick-on-Suir Dd
9 Carrickfergus Fb
81 Carrick.macross Ec
60 Carrieton Ab
94 Carriza Bajo Ae
27 Carşamoa Ea
84 Carson City Cd
8 Carstairs Ee
92 Cartagena, Col. Ba
26 Cartagena, Sp. Bb
91 Cartago Be
46 Cartagoan Eh
30 Carterton Ed
20 Carthage Bd
92 Carúpano Ca
92 Casablanca De
21 Casale Monferrato Gd
21 Casalpusterlengo Hd
28 Caserta Ed
9 Cashel Dd
61 Casino Da
84 Casper Ec
2 Caspian Sea Kc
88 Cass City Dc
27 Cassino Ed
64 Castel di Sangio Ed
24 Castellammare, Campania Ed
25 Castellammare, Sicily De
26 Castellón de la Plana Bb
26 Castelo Branco Ab
20 Castelvetrano Df
60 Casterton Bc
28 Castiglione Cc
8 Castle Douglas Ed
15 Castlebar Bc
8 Castlebay Ad
9 Castleblaney Eb
15 Castleisland Bd
26 Castlemaine Bc
9 Castlerea Cc
81 Castlereagh B. Fa
15 Castletown Dd
15 Castres Ef
91 Castries Fd
24 Castro Overde Aa
26 Castropol Aa
91 Cat I. Cb
95 Cataldo Fc
27 Catalca Ca
26 Catalonia, prov. Ca
94 Catamarca Bd
49 Catanduanes, I. Db
24 Catania Ef
24 Catanzaro Fe
90 Catôche, C. Gd
74 Catorce Dc
34 Catskill Mts. Hc
33 Caucasus Mts. Hg
7 Cavan & Co. Dc
24 Cavaillon Df
94 Caxambú Gd
84 Caxias Ec
27 Caxias do Sul Ee
28 Cazin Eb
15 Ceara, st. Ec
49 Cebu, & I. Db
88 Cedar City Dd
95 Cedar Falls Bc
84 Cedar Rapids Bc
65 Ceduna Ef
29 Cefalu Ee
56 Cegléd Bb
32 Celaya Dc
42 Celebes, I. Dd
42 Celebes S. Dc
28 Celje Ea
28 Celle Db
7 Cemaes Hd. Be
72 Central America Jg
44 Central Makran Ra, mts. Db
86 Centralia, Ill. Cd
84 Centralia, Wash. Bb

49 Ceram, I. & S. Dd
49 Ceram S. Ef
21 Cerea Kd
74 Ceres, Arg. Ce
74 Ceres, C. Prov. Bd
29 Cerignola Ed
27 Cerkeş Da
28 Cerknica Eb
26 Cervera Ca
29 Cerrero Ed
24 Cesena Cc
27 Ceşme Cb
51 Cessnock Db
31 Cetinje Bd
70 Ceuta Da
29 Cevennes, mts. Be
27 Ceyhan Eb
36 Ceylon, Rep. Mj
20 Céze, R. Ce
32 Chabis Bb
92 Chachapoyas Be
44 Chacharan Cd
94 Chaco Austral Ce
94 Chaco Boreal Cd
94 Chaco Central Cd
68 Chad, L. Bd
68 Chad, rep. Dd
44 Chadron Fc
32 Chagada Gd
3 Chagos Arch. Lf
44 Chakansur Ab
47 Chakradharpur Kg
46 Chakwal Db
51 Chalantun Gb
46 Chalaigaon Eh
51 Chalôns-sur-Saône Bd
51 Chalôns Fc
44 Chaman Bb
20 Chambéry Dd
73 Chambezi, R. Ef
59 Chamonix Dd
19 Champagne, Plaine de Df
51 Champagne, reg. Fc
86 Champaign Cc
89 Champlain, L. Jh
46 Chanda Gj
46 Chandigarh Fc
51 Changchih Fc
51 Changchow, Fukien Fd
51 Changchow, Klangsu Fc
51 Changchun Gb
51 Changhua Gd
51 Changsha Fd
51 Changteh Fd
51 Changyeh Ec
14 Channel Is. Bc
51 Chanthari Bb
51 Chaochow Fd
51 Chapala, L. Dc
90 Charagua Cc
94 Charaña Bc
90 Charcas Dc
51 Charchan Cc
94 Chardzhou Jf
50 Charkhlik Cc
38 Charleroi Dd
24 Charles C. Lc
86 Charles City Bc
74 Charleston, S.C. De
86 Charleston, W. Va. Ee
91 Charlestown Cc
72 Charleville Cd
7 Charleville, Australia Cd
91 Charleville, Mich. Cc
74 Charlotte, Mich. Cc
85 Charlotte, N.C. Dd
51 Charlotte Amalie Ee
87 Charlotte Harb. Df
85 Charlotte Waters Ed
37 Charters Towers Cb
66 Chartres Cb
15 Chateaubriant Cd
15 Châteaudun Cc
11 Châteauroux Dd
15 Châtellerault Dd
81 Chatham, N.B. Cb
51 Chatham, Ont. Ab
26 Chatham Ab
20 Châtillon sur Seine Cc
51 Chattanooga Cd
20 Chaumont Dc
26 Chaves Aa
72 Chavuma Cf
22 Cheb Bc
32 Cheboksary Jd
88 Cheboygan Cb
51 Cheddar Ef
51 Chefoo Gc

52 Cheju Do Bb
51 Chekiang, prov. Fd
19 Chelles Bf
23 Chelm (Kholm) Gb
22 Chelmno Eb
7 Chelmsford Hf
22 Chelmza Eb
7 Cheltenham Ef
34 Chelyabinsk Jd
75 Chemba Éa
51 Chengchow Fc
51 Chenteh Fb
51 Chengtu Ec
51 Chenyuan Ed
29 Cher, dept. Ab
46 Cherdyn Lc
35 Cheremkhovo Nd
52 Cherepovets Gd
33 Cherkassy Ff
33 Cherkessk Hg
33 Chernigov Fe
33 Chernovtsy Ef
33 Cherokee Ac
47 Cherrapunji Nf
31 Cherven Bryag Ed
89 Chesapeake, B. Ge
6 Chester, Eng. Ed
78 Chester, U.S.A. He
6 Chesterfield, Canada Hb
6 Chesterfield, England Fd
78 Chesterfield Inlet Hb
56 Chesterfield Is. Cd
90 Chetumal Gd
80 Chevlot Hills Eb
92 Chew Bahir(L., Stefani) Fc
48 Chiang Mai Ab
90 Chiapa Fd
28 Chiavari Bb
21 Chiavenna Hc
51 Chiayi Gd
51 Chiba & pref. Dc
88 Chicago Bd
88 Chicago Heights Bd
82a Chicago? I. Ec
7 Chichester Gg
50 Chichibu Cc
85 Chickasha Gd
54 Chico Bd
75 Chicoa Bd
89 Chicopee Jc
81 Chicoutimi Bb
79 Chidley, C. Lb
73 Chiengi Dc
21 Chieri Fc
21 Chieti Ec
90 Chiguana Bd
43 Childers Dd
51 Childress Fe
93 Chile, rep. Bf
62 Chillagoe Bb
29 Chillan Bf
86 Chillicothe De
16 Chillicothe De
51 Chilloe I. Bg
90 Chilpancingo Ed
50 Chimai Ec
34 Chimkent Je
79 Chimo Kc
51 China Nf
91 Chinandega Ad
51 Chinavane Ec
26 Chinchilla Bb
51 Chinchow Gb
50 Chindamani Db
75 Chinde Fa
45 Chindwin, R. Gd
32 Chiniqui vol. Be
32 Chishmy Le
51 Chisone, R. Fd
32 Chistopol Kd
50 Chita Od
74 Chitado Ac
44 Chitaldrug Df
4 Chitral & dist. Ca
85 Chittagong Gd
44 Chittoor Df
21 Chiusi Cc
21 Chivasso Fd
75 Chobe Swamp Ca

22 Chodziez Eb
51 Choibalsan Fb
22 Cholnice Db
51 Cholet Cd
19 Choisy Bf
22 Chorzow Ec
51 Choluteca Ad
51 Chomutov Bc
52 Chongin Ba
52 Chonju Bb
93 Chonos Arch. Bg
55 Choshi Dc
51 Choszczno Cb
51 Chowkow Fc
46 Chotila Cg
67 Christchurch Ef
75 Christiana Cc
91 Christiansted Fc
57 Christmas, I. Fc
85 Chuanchow Fd
51 Chuanchow Fd
55 Chûbu, dist. Cc
93 Chubut R. & prov. Cg
51 Chuchow Fd
32 Chudskoye, L. Ed
55 Chûgoku, dist. Bc
51 Chuhsien Fd
51 Chukot Ra. Uc
35 Chukot S. Vc
31 Chumatien Fc
52 Chunchon Bb
51 Chungju Bb
51 Chungking Ed
94 Chuquicamata Bd
3 Chur Db
80 Churchill Db
80 Churchill, C. Eb
80 Churchill Falls Db
80 Churchill Pk. Bb
80 Churchill, R. Bb
46 Churu Ed
32 Chusovoi Ld
88 Cicero Bd
88 Cide Da
23 Ciechanów Fb
93 Ciego de Avila Cb
52 Cienaga Ba
51 Cienfuegos Bb
27 Cilician Gates Ca
88 Cincinnati Ce
14 Cinto, mt. Ag
7 Cirencester Ff
90 Citlaltepetl, mt. Ed
28 Città della Pieve Cc
24 Cittanova Fe
92 Ciudad Bolivar Cb
90 Ciudad del Carmen Fd
90 Ciudad Garcia Salinas Dc
90 Ciudad Juarez Ca
90 Ciudad Madero Ec
90 Ciudad Mante Ec
90 Ciudad Obregon Cb
90 Ciudad Real Bb
26 Ciudad Rodrigo Aa
90 Ciudad Victoria Ec
28 Cividale Da
8 Civitanova Dc
24 Civitavecchia Cc
27 Civril Cb
8 Clackmannan, co. Ed
6 Clacton-on-Sea Jf
20 Clairvaux Bb
20 Clamecy Bb
74 Clanwilliam Bd
9 Clara Cc
9 Clare, co. Bd
9 Clare I. Ic
89 Claremont Jc
9 Claremorris Cc
88 Clarksburg Ee
87 Clarksdale Be
88 Clarksville Bf
51 Claustal Zellerfeld
85 Clayton Fd
9 Clear, I. Be
42 Clermont Dc
20 Clermont Ferrand Bd
62 Cleveland C. Bc
9 Clifden, Ire. Ac
67 Clifden, N.Z. Ag
80 Clinton, Can. Bb
87 Clinton, N.Z. Bg
87 Clinton, U.S.A. Gd
57 Clipperton I. Hc
9 Clona Kilty Be
80 Cloncurry Bc
62 Cloncurry R. Bb
9 Clones Db
9 Clonmel Dd
9 Clontarf Ec
8 Clyde, R. Ee

8 Clydebank De
94 Coast Ra., Chile Be
44 Coast Ra., U.S.A. Bc
8 Coatbridge Ce
79 Coat's I. Jb
96 Coats Coast Ab
90 Coatzacoalcos Fd
81 Cobalt Bb
60 Cobar Cb
3 Cobh Ce
81 Cobourg Bb
17 Coburg Dc
44 Cocanada Ce
44 Cochabamba Bc
44 Cochin Dg
41 Cochrane Ab
60 Cockburn Bb
3 Cocos (Keeling) Is. Mf
89 Cod, C. Kd
61 Coff's Harbour Db
22 Cognac Ce
89 Cohoes Jc
46 Cohuna Bc
26 Coimbatore Df
26 Coimbra Aa
32 Col du Pt. St. Bernard Ed
62 Colac Bc
7 Colchester Hf
80 Coleman Cc
6 Coleraine, Australia Ea
9 Coleraine, Ire. Ea
94 Colima & mt. Dd
8 Coll, I. Bd
44 Collahuasi Bc
65 Collie Be
7 Collier B. Ca
86 Collingwood, Canada Eb
66 Collingwood, N.Z. Fg
14 Colmar Gc
32 Cologne (Köln) Gd
95 Colombia Fd
8 Colombia, rep. Bb
44 Colombo Dg
88 Colombus Dc
91 Colon, Panama Ce
91 Colón, W. Ind. Bb
14 Colonsay I. Bd
85 Colorado Desert Ce
85 Colorado Plat. Dd
85 Colorado, R. Cd
82 Colorado, st. Cc
84 Colorado Springs Fd
87 Columbia, S.C. De
87 Columbia, Tenn. Bg
83 Columbia, Dist. of Fc
84 Columbia, R. Bb
72 Columbus Ae
72 Columbus, Ga. De
85 Columbus, Ind. Ce
87 Columbus, Miss. Ce
87 Comacchio Db
71 Comayagua Ad
45 Comilla Ff
34 Commentry Ac
34 Communism Pk. Kf
21 Como Hd
71 Como, L. di Hc
93 Comodoro Rivadavia Cg
93 Comodoro Rivadavia, prov. Cg
44 Comorin, C. Dg
45 Comoro, Is. Gg
86 Comox Bc
19 Compiegne Be
71 Conakry Cf
93 Concepción, Arg. Df
94 Concepción, Bol. Cc
90 Concepción, Paraguay Dd
85 Concepcion, L. Cc
93 Conception Bf
90 Concepcion del Oro Cc
90 Conchos, R. Cb
87 Concord, N.C. Dd
87 Concord, N.H. Kc
84 Concordia, Arg. Df
84 Concordia, U.S.A. Gd
43 Condamine R. Cd
95 Condeuba Gb
11 Condobolin Cb
48 Condore Is. Bc
14 Confolens Dd
69 Congo, rep. De
69 Congo (ex. Belg.) Rep. Ef
72 Congo, R. Bc
9 Connacht, prov. Bc
88 Conneaut Ed
83 Connecticut, st. Fb
8 Connel Cd

9 Connemara Bc
88 Connersville Ce
30 Constanta Ce
44 Constantine Ga
70 Contonou Fg
71 Contonou Fg
87 Conway Br
44 Conway, R. Dd
47 Cooch Behar Ne
57 Cook Is. Ne
46 Cook, Mt. Ce
47 Cook Str. Ed
62 Cooktown Cb
9 Cookstown Eb
75 Coolagatta Da
65 Coolgardie Ce
61 Cooma Cc
61 Coonamble Cb
60 Coongoola Ca
63 Cooper Cr. Ad
44 Coorg, St. Df
85 Cootamundra Cb
75 Cootehill Db
12 Copenhagen Fd
95 Copiapó Ae
40 Copley Ab
88 Copper Cliff Ba
75 Copper Queen Da
27 Copperciff Ab
78 Coppermine Fb
30 Corabia Ed
56 Coral Sea Cd
29 Corato Fd
19 Corbeil Essonnes Bf
88 Corbin Cf
94 Córdoba, Arg. Cf
95 Córdoba, Sp. Bb
27 Córdoba, prov. Cf
82a Córdova Dd
27 Corfu, see Kérkira Ab
27 Corinth Ce
9 Cork & co. Ce
9 Cork Harbour Ce
41 Corner Brook Db
14 Cornwall Eb
7 Cornwall, co. Cg
94 Corocoro Bc
94 Corotco Bc
66 Coromandel Eb
44 Coromandel Coast Ef
59 Coronation G. Fb
72 Coronel Pringles Cf
60 Corowa Cc
90 Corozal Ad
85 Corpus Christi Gf
44 Corque Bc
62 Corrientes Cb
15 Corrientes, C. Cb
15 Corse, see Corsica Bg
13 Corsica (Corse) I. & dept. Bg
87 Corsicana Ae
28 Cortina Da
19 Cortland Gd
28 Cortona Cc
27 Corum Da
91 Corumba, Fed. Dist., Braz. Fc
94 Corumba Goias, Brazil Dc
84 Corvallis Bc
91 Cosamaloapan Ed
29 Cosenza Fe
20 Cosne Ad
64 Cossack Bc
91 Costa Rica Ad
91 Costa Rica, rep. Bd
49 Cotabato Dc
94 Cotagaita Bd
20 Côte d'Or, ridge & dept. Dc
71 Cotswold Hills Ef
86 Cottbus Fe
86 Council Bluffs Ac
20 Cours Cc
14 Coutances Cc
7 Coventry Fe
26 Covilha Ba
88 Covington Ce
65 Cowan L. Ce
8 Cowdenbeath Ed
7 Cowes Fg
61 Cowra Cb
95 Coxim Ec
11 Cozumel, I. Gd
63 Cracow Dd
61 Cradle Mt. Cd
75 Cradock Dd
86 Craiova Dc
92 Cranbrook Cc
86 Crateus Ec
95 Crato Fc
14 Crawfordsville Bd
14 Crécy Db
19 Creil Be
21 Crema Hd
21 Cremona Jd
28 Cres, I. Eb
86 Creston Ec
27 Crete (Kriti) I. Bb

27 Crete, Sea of Cb
21 Crevalcore Ke
6 Crewe Ed
7 Crewkerne Eg
95 Criciuma Ef
6 Crieff Ed
33 Crimea Ff
9 Croagh Patrick, mt.
28 Croatia, prov. Eb
87 Crockett Ae
75 Crocodile, R. Db
8 Cromarty Dc
7 Cromer Je
67 Cromwell Bf
86 Crookston Ab
74 Cross, C. Ab
29 Crotone Fd
3 Croydon, Australia Bb
7 Croydon, Eng. Gf
3 Crozet, Is. Kh
22 Cruz Alta Ee
95 Cruzeiro Ed
63 Cruzeiro do Sul Bc
10 Crystal Brook Ab
85 Crystal City Gf
9 Cuando, R. Eg
74 Cuangar Da
91 Cuba, I. & rep. Cb
27 Cubuk Da
92 Cúcuta Bb
44 Cuddalore Df
44 Cuddapah Df
63 Cue Bd
52 Cuenca Bd
82 Cuenco Ba
90 Cuernavaca Ed
26 Cuevas de Vera Bb
74 Cuevo Cd
90 Culabá Dc
8 Cuillin Hills Bc
90 Culiacan Cc
20 Culoz Dd
67 Culverden Dd
80 Cumberland, Canada Bc
89 Cumberland, U.S.A. Fc
6 Cumberland, co. Ec
79 Cumberland Pen. Lb
79 Cumberland Sd. Lb
8 Cumnock De
74 Cumra Db
66 Cunene, R. Aa
39 Cúneo Ee
60 Cunnamulla Ca
90 Curacao Ed
92 Curacao I. Ca
93 Curico Bf
95 Curitiba Fe
62 Curtis I. Dc
67 Cushing Ad
20 Cusset Bc
47 Cuttack Kh
16 Cuxhaven Cb
49 Cuyo Is. Db
91 Cuzco Bd
77 Cyclades, see Kikiadhes Bb
27 Cyprus, I. Dc
22 Czarnkow Dh
4 Czechoslovakia Jf
23 Czeremcha Gb
22 Czestochowa Dc

74 Damaraland, dist. Bb
40 Damascus (Esh Sham) Cc
73 Dambacha Fa
43 Damghan Gb
38 Damietta Cb
84 Dampier Bc
64 Dampier Arch. Bc
64 Dampier Land Cb
49 Dampier Str. Ef
71 Dan Gora Gf
39 Danbury Jd
47 Dandeldhura Hd
60 Dandenong Cc
11 Dannemora Dc
65 Dannevirke Fd
30 Danube Db
88 Danville, Ill. Bd
88 Danville, Ky. Cf
88 Danville, Va. Ff
40 Dar'a Cc
73 Dar-es-Salaam Fe
47 Darbhanga Ke
43 Dardan Jd.
27 Dardanelles, str. Ca
94 Dargaville Da
71 Darjeeling Me
63 Darling Downs Cd
63 Darling Ra. Be
60 Darling R. Bb
6 Darlington Fc
20 Darlowo Da
11 Darmstadt He
60 Darnick Bb
56 Darnley, Cape Ec
7 Dartmoor Cg
81 Dartmouth, Canada Cb
7 Dartmouth, England Dg
62 Daru Fh
44 Darwin Ea
43 Daryacheh-y-Namak L.
43 Daryacheh-ye-Sistan, L., Jc
43 Dasht-e-Kavir, reg. Gb
43 Dasht-e-Lut, reg. Hc
46 Datia Gf
32 Daugavpils Ed
20 Daulis Ee
20 Dauphin Bb
20 Dauphine, dist. Dd
20 Davao, & G. Dc
86 Davenport Bc
57 David Ab
79 Davis Str. Ma
13 Davos Db
43 Dawlatabad Hd
7 Dawlish Dg
78 Dawson Db
30 Dawson Creek Bb
62 Dawson R. Cc
65 Day Dawn Bd
86 Daylesfield Bc
54 Dayton, Can. Dc
88 Dayton, U.S.A. Ce
88 Dayton, Ohio Ce
87 Daytona Beach Df
50 De Aar Cd
20 De Behagle Bf
35 De Long is. Sb
88 De Pere Ab
87 De Soto Bd
40 Dead Sea Bd
25 Deakin De
22 Dearborn Dc
80 Dease Lake Ab
78 Dease Str. Gb
85 Death Valley Ce
71 Deba Habe Hf
72 Debica Fc
39 Debra Tabor Cd
73 Debre Markos Fa
30 Debrecen Cb
77 Decatur, Ala. Ce
87 Decatur, Ga. De
86 Decatur, Ill. Cd
88 Decatur, Ind. Cd
44 Deccan, plat. Df
22 Decin Cc
20 Decize Bc
6 Dee, R. Bd
44 Deesa Df
36 Defiance Cd
44 Dehra Dun Gc
72 Dein Zubeir Db
30 Dej Db
65 Del Rio Ff
75 Delagoa B. Ec
88 Delaware Cd
83 Delaware, st. Fc
12 Delaware, R. Je
13 Delémont Ba
62 Delena Gh
13 Delft Da
18 Delfzijl Fa
73 Delgado, L. Gf
38 Delgo Cc

46 Delhi Fd
27 Delice R. Db
50 Delicias Cb
20 Delle Fb
18 Delmenhorst Ha
6 Deloraine Cd
43 Demavend, mt. Gb
72 Demba Ce
92 Demerara Db
85 Deming Ee
12 Demirköy Ca
87 Demopolis Ce
18 Den Helder Db
6 Denbigh, & Co. Dd
62 Denham Ra. Cc
26 Denia Cb
85 Deniliquin Bc
27 Denizli Cb
65 Denmark, Australia Be
4 Denmark, King. Gd
8 Denny Ed
62 D'Entrecasteaux Is. Hh
65 D'Entrecasteaux Pt. Be
84 Denver Fd
25 Deolali Cd
12 Deoria Je
46 Dera Ghazi Khan Cc
14 Dera Ismail Khan Cc
33 Derbent Jg
44 Derby, Austral. Cb
6 Derby, co., Eng. Fd
9 Derg, L. Cd
28 Derna Eb
39 Deruebé Cd
28 Derventa Fb
6 Derwent, R., Gd
36 Des Moines Fa
21 Desenzano del Garda Jd
33 Desna R. Fe
71 Dessa Ec
16 Dessau Ec
18 Detmold Hc
34 Detroit Dc
18 Deurne, Belg. Dc
18 Deurne, Neth. Dc
32 Deva Dc
18 Deventer Fb
8 Deventry Dc
7 Devon, co. Dg
79 Devon, I. Ja
27 Devonport, Eng. Cg
81 Devonport, N.Z. Eb
61 Devonport, Tas. Cb
44 Dewas Fg
32 Dhaba Dd
43 Dhahran Gd
47 Dhamtari Hd
77 Dhangarbi Hd
33 Dhank He
47 Dhankuta Le
24 Dharwar Ce
47 Dhaulagiri, mt. Jd
40 Dhekelia Ab
68 Dhidhimótikhon Ca
36 Dholpur Fe
44 Dhrol Cg
27 Dhkili Cb
68 Dikwa Hd
43 Dilam Fe
49 Dili Dd
23 Dilolo Cf
11 Dimbokro Eg
60 Dimboola Bc
34 Dimitrovgrad Ed
31 Dimitrovo Bd
43 Dimapat I. Db
44 Dinajpur Mf
26 Dinan De
8 Dincha Fb
9 Dingle Bay Ad
71 Dinguirasye Cf
33 Dingwall Db
71 Diorbet Bf
44 Dir, Dist. Cb

73 Dire Dawa Gb
64 Dirk Hartog I. Ad
4 Disappointment
  L. Cc
79 Disko, I. Mb
46 Diu Ch
95 Divinopotis Gd
86 Dixon Cc
42 Diyarbakir Ed
43 Dizak Jd
48 Djakarta Db
70 Djanet
  (Ft. Charlet) Gd
71 Djang Hg
43 Djatinegara Bd
48 Djember Cd
71 Djerba I. Hb
70 Djerid, Chott Gb
73 Djibouti Ga
70 Djidjelli Ga
72 Djolu Cc
70 Djupivogur Cb
32 Dmitrov Gd
33 Dnepr (Dnieper),
  R. Fe
33 Dneprodzerz-
  hinsk Ff
33 Dnepropetrovsk Ff
33 Dnestr (Dniester),
  R. Ef
75 Doboj Gb
30 Dobrogea, dist. Gc
72 Dobrzyn Eb
23 Dobšiná Fb
45 Dodecanese, Is. Cb
85 Dodge City Fd
71 Dodman Pt. Cg
73 Dodoma Fe
18 Doetinchem Fb
46 Dohad Eg
44 Doi Luang, mts. Bb
81 Dolbeau Bb
20 Dôle Db
7 Dolgellau Ce
72 Delisle Ad
93 Dolores Df
31 Dombas Bc
72 Dombe Grande Af
20 Dombes, dist. Cc
32 Domesnes Dd
33 Dominica, I. Fd
91 Dominican Rep, Dc
21 Domodossola Gc
33 Don R. Ge
33 Don R. Hf
6 Doncaster Fd
72 Dondo Ae
44 Dondra Head Dg
8 Donegal, & co. Cb
5 Donegal B. Cb
33 Donetsk Ed
65 Dongara Ad
38 Dongola Ce
72 Dongou Bc
46 Donnelly's
  Crossing Da
20 Donzère Ce
40 Dor (Tantura) Bb
21 Dora Baltea, R. Fc
20 Dora Riparia,
  R. Ej
7 Dorchester Eg
15 Dordogne, R. De
18 Dordrecht Dc
20 Dore, R. Bd
4 Dores Dc
46 Doring R. Hj
12 Dornbirn Hb
8 Dornoch Dc
70 Dorohoi Fb
73 Dorotea Cg
7 Dorset, co. Eg
18 Dorsten Fc
18 Dortmund Fc
71 Dosso Ff
37 Dothan Ce
72 Douai Denain Bd
70 Douala Gh
24 Doubs. R. &
  dept. Bb
5 Doubtful I. B. Be
81 Doucet Bb
8 Douglas, Eng. Cc
6 Douglas, U.S.A. Ee
72 Doumé Ac
7 Dover, Eng. Hj
89 Dover, U.S.A. Rc
4 Dover, Str. of Jg
11 Doverfjell Bc
73 Dowa Ef
80 Dowagiac Bc
6 Down, co. Fb
5 Downpatrick Fb
20 Dra, R. Dc
20 Drac, R. De
33 Dragobych Df
19 Draguignan Gf
96 Drake Passage Cd
9 Drakensberg,
  mts. Dc
27 Dráma Ba
11 Drammen Cd
19 Draveil Bf
22 Drawsko Cb

16 Dresden Ec
30 Drina, R. Sb
9 Drogheda Ec
9 Droichead Dc
9 Dromahair Cb
20 Drôme, R. &
  dept. Ce
47 Drug Hh
80 Drumheller Cb
88 Drummond I. Db
62 Drummond Ra. Cc
33 Drummondville Jb
96 Drygalski I. Fc
81 Du Bois Fd
80 Dubawit, L. Da
80 Dubawnt, R. Da
61 Dubbo Cb
9 Dublin, Ire. Ec
87 Dublin, U.S.A. Hd
9 Dublin, Co. Ec
33 Dubovka Hf
71 Dubréka Cg
28 Dubrovnik Gd
62 Duchess Ac
34 Dudinka Lc
7 Dudley Fe
26 Duero, R. Aa
24 Dugiotok, I. Eb
62 Duifken Pt. Ba
18 Duisburg Fb
73 Duk Faidat Eb
71 Duku Hf
49 Dulawan Dc
86 Duluth Bb
40 Duma Cc
41 Dumaran, I. Cb
8 Dumbarton De
8 Dumfries & co. Ee
18 Dümmer See Hb
9 Dun Laoghaire Ec
30 Duna, R. Bb
30 Dunafoldvar Bb
30 Dunaujvaros Bb
67 Dunback Cf
8 Dunbar Fd
8 Dunbarton, co. Dd
30 Dunblane Ed
8 Duncan Bb
85 Duncan Bd
5 Dundalk Eb
75 Dundee, Nat. Ec
8 Dundee, Scot. Fd
67 Dunedin Cf
8 Dunfermline Ed
9 Dungannon Eb
46 Dungarpur Dg
9 Dungarvan, B. Dd
5 Dungeness Hg
9 Dungloe Cb
61 Dungog Db
73 Dungu Dc
8 Dunkeld Ed
9 Dunkery Beacon Df
14 Dunkirk, Fr. Eb
8 Dunkirk, U.S.A. Fc
9 Dunmanway Be
9 Duns Fd
7 Dunstable Gf
61 Dunwich Da
20 Durance, R. De
70 Durango, Mex. Dc
85 Durango,
  U.S.A. Ed
87 Durant Ae
75 Durban Ec
18 Düren Fd
6 Durham, Eng. Fc
6 Durham, Co. Fc
8 Durness Db
75 Durres Be
32 Dushanbe Jf
18 Düsseldorf Fc
83 Dutch Harbor Cd
14 Dvina, R. Eb
46 Dwarka Bg
8 Dyceon Fc
15 Dzamyn Ude Fb
33 Dzaudzhikau, see
    Ordzhonikidze
32 Dzerzhinsk Hd
34 Dzhambul Kc
33 Dzhankoi Ff
50 Dzhargalantu Db
50 Dzhargalantu Ra.,
    Mts. Qd
33 Dzialdow, R. Fb
33 Dzialdovo Eb
51 Dzun-Mod Eb
50 Dzungaria, reg. Cb

75 East London Dd
8 E. Lothian, Co. Fe
47 E. Pakistan, st. Mf
18 East Schelde, R. Cc
35 East Siberian S. Tb
7 Eastbourne,
  England Hg
67 Eastbourne,
  N.Z. Ed
57 Easter I. He
44 Eastern Ghats,
  mts. Df
7 Eastleigh Fg
81 Eastmain Ba
89 Easton Hd
86 Eau Claire Bc
7 Ebbw Vale Df
12 Ebeltoft Dc
19 Eberbach Je
16 Eberswalde Eb
21 Ebingen Ha
71 Ebolova Hh
65 Ebro, R. Ca
8 Ecclefechan Ee
12 Ecuador, rep. Bc
36 Ed Damer Cd
36 Ed Debba Cd
36 Ed Dirr Cc
39 Ed Dueim Cc
18 Edam Eb
18 Ede Eb
19 Edea Hh
65 Edel Land Ad
75 Edenburg Dc
9 Edenderry Ec
18 Eder See Hc
27 Edhessa Ba
60 Edievale Bf
8 Edinburgh Ee
21 Edirne Ca
36 Edmonton Db
81 Edmundson Cb
27 Edremit Cb
80 Edson Cb
73 Edward, Dd
32 Eekloo Cc
29 Egadi Is. Df
30 Eger Cb
11 Egersund Bd
13 Egilsau Ca
36 Egridir Db
27 Egridir, L. Db
92 Egua Cb
76 Egypt (U.A.R.) Ec
5 Ehime, pref. Bd
18 Eigg I. Bd
24 Eight Degree
    Chan. Cg
8 Eighty Mile
    Beach
39 Eil De
62 Einasleigh & R. Bb
18 Eindhoven Ec
13 Einsiedeln Ca
17 Eisenach Dc
16 Eisenhütten-
  stadt Fb
36 Eisleben Ec
70 Eketahuna Ed
70 El Aaiún Cd
73 El Agowa Da
38 El Arish Cc
85 El Centro Ce
94 El Cerro Cc
94 El Chorro Cd
90 El Cuyo Gd
90 El Djouf Dd
67 El Dorado Be
38 El Faiyûm Cc
68 El Fasher Ed
90 El Fuerte Cb
91 El Gallo Ad
61 El Geneina Ed
70 El Goléa Eb
70 El Jadida Db
67 El Jauf Dd
73 El Jebelein Ea
38 El Juwara Ed
39 El Kamlin Cd
39 El Khandaq Cd
16 El Kharga Cc
39 El Muglad Bd
39 El Obeid Cd
68 El Odaiya Bd
70 El Oued Gb
71 El Oulg Fe
85 El Paso Ee
11 El Qantara Cc
81 El Suweis
    (Suez) Dg
94 El Zappallar De
22 Elazig Db
28 Elba, I. Cc
33 Elbag Ea
31 Elbasan Ce
16 Elbe, R. Cb
35 Elbrus, mt. Hg
45 Elburz, mts. Gb
74 Eldoret Fc
48 Electra Ge
29 Elena Dc
74 Elephant, R. Bb

85 Elephant Butte
    Reservoir Ee
18 Escalona Ba
91 Eleuthera I. Ca
8 Elgin Fc
31 Elgon, mt. Fc
39 Elhur Dc
81 Elie Ed
72 Elila, R. Dd
60 Elizabeth,
    Australia Ab
89 Elizabeth,
    U.S.A. Hd
89 Elizabethton Df
88 Elkhart Cd
31 Elkhovo Fd
88 Elkins Fe
84 Elko Cc
84 Ellensburg Bb
79 Ellesmere I. Ja
56 Ellice Is. Dd
75 Elliot Dd
8 Ellon Fc
44 Ellore Ee
96 Ellsworth Land Pb
27 Elmali Cb
49 Elmira Gc
18 Elmshorn Ja
28 Elota, R. Cc
16 Elwood Cd
7 Ely, Eng. He
86 Ely, U.S.A. Bb
7 Ely, I. of He
88 Elyria Dd
94 Embarcacion Cd
73 Embu Fd
16 Emden Ga
62 Emerald Cc
80 Emerson Ec
61 Emmaville Da
18 Emmen Fb
13 Emmental dist. Bb
18 Emmerich Fc
75 Empangeni Ec
94 Emperado Be
28 Empoli Cc
85 Emporia, Kan. Ad
85 Emporia, Va. Gd
18 Ems, R. Gb
18 Emsdetten Gb
73 Emu Park Dc
39 En Nahud Bd
60 Encarnacion De
60 Encounter B. Ac
95 Encruzilhada Ef
44 Ende Dd
62 Endeavour Str. Ba
12 Endelave I. Dd
56 Enderbury I. Dd
73 Enderby Land Dc
89 Endicott Gc
69 Enes Fg
13 Engadin Eb
13 Engelberg Cb
34 Engels Je
6-7 England, King.
47 Englehart Ab
47 English Bazar Mf
85 Enid Gd
75 Enkeldoorn Ec
18 Enkhuizen Eb
29 Enna Ef
81 Ennis Bd
9 Enniscorthy Ed
9 Enniskillen Db
18 Enschede Fb
60 Ensenada Aa
73 Entebbe Ed
94 Entre Rios Df
71 Enugu Gg
71 Enugu Ezike,
62 Epa Gh
14 Epernay Ec
14 Epinal Gc
77 Epirus, dist. Bb
7 Epping Hf
51 Er Rahad Ea
21 Erba Hd
27 Ercivas, mts. Eb
27 Eregli, Turkey Da
27 Eregli, Turkey Db
17 Erfurt Dc
70 Erg Chech Ed
70 Erg Edehan Hc
16 Erithem Fb
88 Erie Ec
88 Erie, L. Ec
54 Erimo, C. Dd
17 Erlangen Dd
65 Erldunda Ed
75 Ermelo Ec
44 Ernakulam Dg
9 Erne, L., Bb
44 Erode Df
74 Erundu Bb
22 Erz Gebirge (Ore)
42 Erzincan Db
42 Erzurum Eb
54 Esan, C. Dd
11 Esbjerg Bd
88 Escanaba Bb

19 Esch Ee
18 Eschweiler Fd
26 Escorial Ba
70 Escuinapa de
    Hidalgo Dc
30 Esfahan Gc
40 Esh Sham
    (Damascus) Cc
75 Eshowe Ec
10 Eskifjördur Ca
11 Eskilstuna Dd
27 Eskisehir Db
7 Essex, co. Hf
  Esperance Ce
26 Espichet, C. Ab
26 Espinho Aa
92 Espirito Santo,
    prov. Ed
  Estcourt Dc
30 Estergon Bb
  Estevan Bc
32 Estonia, S.S.R. Ed
26 Estrela, Sa. da Aa
92 Estremadura,
    prov. Bb
26 Estremozo Ab
19 Etaples Ad
71 Etawah Ge
13 Ethiopia, st. Fe
8 Etive, L. Cd
29 Etna, Mt. Ef
26 Eton Cc
74 Etosha Pan Bc
8 Ettrick Ee
73 Eucalyptus Bc
65 Eucla De
18 Euclid Ed
60 Eudunda Ab
34 Eugene Bc
60 Eulo Ba
42 Euphrates (Firat),
    R.
84 Eureka Bc
34 Euroa Cc
2 Europe, cont. Hc
60 Euston Bb
88 Evanston Bc
88 Evansville Bf
65 Everard L. Ee
47 Everest, Mt. Le
87 Everglades Dc
88 Everett Bb
7 Evesham Fe
20 Évian Ec
26 Évora Ab
16 Évreux Dc
32 Evrykhou Db
27 Evvoia, I. Bb
49 Ewab Is. Ed
34 Exaltación Bb
7 Exeter Dg
74 Exmoor Dd
7 Exmouth Dg
46 Exmouth G. Ac
73 Eyasi, L. Ed
8 Eyemouth Fe
10 Eyrabakki Ab
8 Eyre
63 Eyre, L. Ad
8 Eyre Peninsula Fe
27 Ezine Cb

76 Fabriano Dc
71 Fachi He
45 Fada Ed
28 Faenza Cb
50 Fagaras Ec
8 Fair I. Ca
82a Fairbanks Db
47 Fairlie Cf
38 Faizabad,
    Afghanistan Gb
47 Faizabad, India Je
45 Fakfak Ef
90 Falcon Dam Eb
93 Falkland Is. Dc
93 Falkland Is.
    Dependencies Sa
89 Fall River Kd
7 Falmouth Bg
7 Falmouth Cg
71 False B. Bd
12 Falster, I. Ed
31 Falun Da
22 Famagusta Db
39 Famaka Cd
11 Fanø, I. Ab
28 Fano Dc
22 Farafangana Gh
74 Farafra Oasis Eb
74 Farah Ab
39 Farasan, Is. Dd
7 Fareham Fg

78 Farewell, C. Nc
84 Fargo Gb
86 Fairbault Bd
71 Farim Bf
60 Farina Aa
7 Farnborough Gf
27 Farnham Gf
26 Faro, Portugal Ab
11 Faró, Sweden Dd
27 Fársala Bb
11 Farsund Bd
43 Fasa Gd
9 Fastnet I. Be
46 Fatehgarh (Farrukhabad) Ge
46 Fatehpur, Raj. Ee
47 Fatehpur, Ut.P. Hf
51 Fatshan Fd
46 Faucilles, Mts. Da
29 Favara Df
10 Faxaflói Ab
87 Fayetteville Cd
46 Fazilka Dc
87 Featherston Ed
66 Feilding Ed
21 Feldkirch Hb
90 Felipe Carillo Puerto Gd
7 Felixstowe Jf
28 Feltre Ca
51 Fengkieh Ec
41 Fenyang Fc
33 Feodosiya Gf
9 Fermanagh, Co. Db
28 Fermo Cd
9 Fermoy Cd
71 Fernando Póo,l. Gh
46 Ferozepore Ec
28 Ferrara Cc
20 Ferrières Aa
26 Ferrol Aa
70 Fès Db
90 Fesnillo Dc
8 Fetlar Inset
65 Fianarantsoa Gh
75 Ficksburg Dc
28 Fidenza Je
9 Fife, co. Ed
26 Figueras Ca
71 Figuig Eb
66 Fiji Is. Gk
75 Filyas Da
27 Filyos, R. Da
21 Finale Ligure Je
8 Findhorn Ec
26 Findlay Cd
26 Finisterre, C. Aa
5 Finland, Rep. Lc
11 Finland, G. of Dd
90 Finlay Forks Bb
21 Finnmark, dist. Eb
10 Finnsnes Db
62 Finschhafen Gh
21 Finsteraarhorn, mt. Cb
3 Fintona Db
21 Fiorenzuola d'Arda He
42 Firat (Euphrates), R. Db
21 Firenze, see Florence
20 Firminy Cd
46 Firozabad Ge
7 Fishguard Cf
89 Fitchburg Kc
84 FitzroyCrossing Db
21 Fivizzano Je
85 Flagstaff Cd
18 Flandre Orientale, prov. Cc
18 Flandres, Plaines des Cc
10 Flateyr Aa
62 Flattery C. Cb
6 Fleetwood Dd
11 Flekkefjord Bd
12 Flensburg Ca
80 Flin Flon Db
65 Flinders B. Be
11 Flinders I. Cd
62 Flinders Ras. Ab
82 Flinders R. Bb
88 Flint Dc
8 Flint, co. Da
87 Florence, Ala. Ce
87 Florence, S.C. Ee
28 Florence (Firenze) Cc
94 Florencia Cd
49 Flores, I. Dd
21 Flores S. Cd
95 Florianópolis Fe
21 Florida, B. Df
83 Florida, st. Ed
87 Florida Keys Df
91 Florida Str. Bb
27 Florina Bb
21 Floró Bc
95 Fluela P. Eb
18 Flushing (Vlissingen) Cc
62 Fly R. Fh

30 Focsani Fc
62 Fofo Fofo Gh
29 Foggia Ed
71 Foix Df
10 Folda Cc
28 Foligno Dc
7 Folkestone Hj
28 Folonica Cc
88 Fond du Lac, Canada Db
86 Fond du Lac, U.S.A. Cc
91 Fonseca, G. of Ad
19 Fontainebleau Bf
51 Foochow Fd
19 Forbach Fe
61 Forbes Cb
87 Fordyce Be
28 Forécariah Cg
79 Forel, Mt. Ob
20 Forez, Monts du Bd
10 Forfar Fd
28 Forlì Db
20 Formentera, I. Cb
51 Formosa I., see Taiwan
94 Formosa, Arg. De
95 Formosa, Braz. Fc
46 Forres Ec
62 Forsayth Bb
16 Forst Fc
81 Fort Albany Aa
68 Fort Archambault Gd
84 Fort Augustus Dc
94 Fort Ayacucho Dc
75 Fort Beaufort Dd
81 Fort Charlet, see Djanet Gd
84 Fort Collins Ed
94 Fort Corrales Cd
72 Fort Crampel Bb
90 Fort Dauphin Gh
91 Fort de France Fd
86 Fort Dodge Bc
94 Fort D'Orbigny Cd
88 Fort Erie Fc
70 Fort Flatters Gc
86 Fort Frances Bb
90 Fort Fraser Bb
81 Fort George Ba
80 Fort Gouraud (Idjil) Cd
80 Fort Grahame Bb
94 Fort Guachalla Cd
73 Fort Hall Fd
73 Fort Jameson Ef
69 Fort Johnston Fg
68 Fort Lamy Dd
80 Fort Laperrine (Tamanrasset) Gd
87 Fort Lauderdale Df
80 Fort Liard Ba
80 Fort Mackay Cb
80 Fort McMurray Cb
78 Fort McPherson Db
80 Fort Morgan Fd
46 Fort Munro Bf
87 Fort Myers Df
80 Fort Nelson Bb
78 Fort Norman Eb
84 Fort Peck, Res. Eb
80 Fort Providence Cb
80 Fort Reliance Ca
80 Fort Resolution Ca
80 Fort Sandeman Bc
81 Fort Severn Aa
72 Fort Sibut Bb
80 Fort Simpson Ba
94 Fort Siracusa Cd
80 Fort Smith, Can. Cb
87 Fort Smith, U.S.A. Bd
75 Fort Vermilion Cb
75 Fort Victoria Eb
88 Fort Wayne Cd
80 Fort William, Can. Bd
8 Fort William, Scot. Cd
85 Fort Worth Ge
80 Fort Yukon Dd
92 Fortaleza Ec
64 Forte Coimbra Bd
64 Forte Rocades Ba
8 Forth, Firth of Fd
21 Fossano Fe
14 Fougères Cc
19 Fourchambault Bb
19 Fourmies Dd
71 Fouta Djalon, mt. Cf
67 Foveaux Str. Bg
72 Fowey Cg
65 Fowlers B. Ee
83c Fox Is. Eb
79 Foxe Basin Kb
79 Foxe Channel Jb
78 Foxe Pen. Kb
9 Foxford Cb
10 Foxton Ed
9 Foyle De

9 Foynes Bd
95 Foz de Iguaçú Ee
29 Franca Fd
23 Francavilla Fd
4 France, Rep. Ff
72 Franceville Ad
20 Franchecomte, dist. Dc
75 Francistown Db
88 Frankfort, Ind. Bd
86 Frankfort, Ky. Ce
16 Frankfurt a.O. Fb
19 Frankfurt a.M. Hd
88 Franklin Kd
78 Franklin, terr. Haa
60 Frankston Cc
84 Fransfontein Ab
81 Franz Ab
29 Franz Josef Ld., Is. Ga
63 Fraser I. Dd
74 Fraserburg Cd
8 Fraserburgh Fc
20 Frasne Ec
13 Frauenfeld Ca
93 Fray Bentos Df
12 Frederica Cd
89 Frederick Ge
89 Fredericksburg Fe
12 Frederikshaab Nb
12 Frederikshavn Db
12 Frederiksvaerk Ed
11 Fredrikstad Cd
18 Freetown Cg
21 Freiburg Fb
27 Freising Dd
45 Fremantle Be
46 Fremont, Mich. Bc
88 Fremont, Ohio Dd
72 French Guiana Db
39 French Somaliland Dd
90 Fresnillo Dc
85 Fresno Cd
19 Freudenstadt Hf
65 Freycinet Estuary Ad
13 Fribourg, & cant. Bb
79 Friedberg Hd
21 Friedrichshaab Hb
66 Friendly Is., see Tonga Is.
18 Friesland, prov. Ea
8 Fröckelnhm Fd
92 Frutti Venezia Giulia, reg. Db
80 Frobisher, L. Db
78 Frobisher B. Lb
79 Frobisher Bay Lb
10 Frohavet Bc
33 Frolovo Hf
7 Frome Ef
60 Frome L. Ab
29 Frosinone Dd
18 Frostburg Fe
10 Fróya, I. Bc
34 Frunze Ke
5 Fruchow Fd
90 Fuerte, R. Cb
70 Fuerteventura B. Cd
53 Fuji-san, mt. Cc
53 Fujimiya Cc
53 Fujisawa Cc
53 Fujiyama, mt., see Fuji-san Cb
53 Fukien, prov. Fd
53 Fukuchiyama Cc
53 Fukui Cc
53 Fukui & pref. Cd
54 Fukuokab pref. Bd
54 Fukushima, & pref. Dc
53 Fukuyama Bd
91 Fulda & R. Jd
89 Fulton Gd
53 Funabashi Dc
70 Funchal Bb
81 Fundy, B. of Cb
13 Funta F.P. Cb
71 Fürth Jd
75 Fuse Cd
21 Füssen Jb
71 Fushin Gb
64 Futuna, I. Hj
51 Fuyang Fb
14 Fuyu Gb

87 Gainesville, Ga. De
87 Gainesville, Fla. Df
65 Gardner I. Fe
92 Galapagos Is. Ad
8 Galashiels Ee
30 Galati Fc
29 Galatina Gd
11 Galdhöpiggen, mt. Bc
90 Galeana Ca
86 Galesburg Bc
32 Galich Hd
26 Galicia, prov. Aa
40 Galilee, S. of Bc
62 Galilee L. Cc
39 Gallabat Cd
21 Gallarate Gd
44 Galle Dg
12 Gallipoli, Italy Fd
27 Gallipoli, Turkey, see Gelibolu
10 Gällivare Eb
8 Galloway Df
85 Gallup Ed
87 Galveston Bf
9 Galway & co. Bc
9 Galway B. Bc
71 Gambaga Ef
18 Gambia, st. Ad
72 Gambia, R. Cf
72 Gambona Bd
73 Ganale Dorya, R. Gb
73 Gandar Fa
28 Gander Gb
24 Gandia Bb
47 Ganga, Mouths of the Mh
47 Ganga (Ganges), R. Lf
46 Ganga Nagar Dd
71 Gangtok Me
92 Gannat Bc
65 Gantheaume B. Ad
73 Gao Ee
70 Gap Ee
39 Garad De
24 Garah Ca
21 Garda, dept. Be
21 Garda, L. di Jd
73 Gardaia Fb
85 Garden City Fd
9 Garmisch-Partenkirchen Fa
14 Garonne, R. Cd
28 Garoua Ab
71 Garraway Dh
84 Garrison Res. Fb
50 Gartok Cc
68 Garua Bd
48 Garut Bd
88 Gray Bd
21 Gascony Cf
53 Gascony, reg. Df
65 Gaspéyne R. Ad
72 Gashaka Ab
62 Gasmata Hh
21 Gaspé R. Hb
71 Gaspé Pen. Cb
26 Gata, C. de Bd
6 Gateshead Fc
10 Gatinais, dist. Aa
75 Gatooma Da
47 Gauhati Ne
27 Gávdhos, I. Bc
11 Gävle Dd
6 Gawler Ab
65 Gawler Ranges Fe
71 Gaya, Dahomey Ff
47 Gaya, India Kf
28 Giulianova Dc
25 Gaylord Dd
63 Gayndah Dd
40 Gaza Bd
22 Gdansk (Danzig) Ea
22 Gdansk Bay Ea
22 Gdynia Ea
39 Gedaref Cd
27 Gediz, R. Cb
60 Geelong Bc
18 Geeraardsbergen Dd
61 Geeveston Cd
71 Geidam Hf
73 Geita Ed
13 Gek Ab
29 Gela Ef
13 Geldrop Ec
18 Geleen Ed
27 Gelibolu (Gallipoli) Ca
18 Gelsenkirchen Gc
72 Gendringen Fc
95 General Carneiro Ec
72 General Machado Bf
13 Geneva, O.F.S. Gc
13 Geneva, L. of, see Léman, L. Be
13 Genève (Geneva), Switz. Db
20 Genissi Amaat Dc

18 Genk Ed
20 Genlis Db
21 Genoa, see Genova
21 Genoa (Genoa) Ge
21 Genova, G. di Gf
28 Gent Cc
33 Geogievsk Kd
65 Geographe B. Be
65 Geographe Chan. Ac
74 George Cd
96 George V. Coast Jb
13 George, L. Ed
79 George, R. Lc
62 Georgetown, Australia Bb
88 Georgetown, Canada Fc
71 Georgetown, Gambia Cf
92 Georgetown, Guyana Db
48 Georgetown, Malaya Bc
33 Georgia Hg
83 Georgia, st. Ed
88 Georgian B. Eb
62 Georgina R. Ac
17 Gera Ec
65 Geraldton Ad
23 Gerlachovka, mt. Fd
4 Germany, st. He
16 Germiston Dc
26 Gerona Ca
27 Gerze Ea
20 Gevaudan, dist. Be
49 Geelvink B. Ff
39 Gezira Cd
48 Ghaghra (Gogra) R. Je
68 Ghana, st. Be
74 Ghanzi Cb
70 Ghardaïa Fb
70 Ghazaouet Ea
46 Ghaziabad Fd
47 Ghazni Bb
30 Gheorghenl Eb
72 Ghudamis Cb
22 Giant (Krkonose) Mts. Cc
9 Giant's Causeway Ea
74 Gibeon Bc
26 Gibraltar Ab
70 Gibraltar, Str. of Da
64 Gibson Desert Cc
20 Gien Ab
19 Giessen Hd
53 Gifu & pref. Cc
8 Gigha, I. Be
26 Gijon Aa
62 Gilau Gh
56 Gilbert Is. Dc
61 Gilbert R. Bb
61 Gilgandra Cb
13 Gilgit, & Dist. Ca
7 Gillingham Hj
11 Gineifa Cf
25 Gingin Be
84 Girala Ac
6 Girdle Ness Fc
47 Giridih Lf
13 Gironde, R. Ce
8 Girvan De
66 Gisborne Gc
28 Giulianova Dc
35 Gizhiga Tc
73 Gizycho Fa
11 Gjövik Cc
81 Glace Bay Cb
62 Gladstone, Queensland Dc
60 Gladstone, South Australia Ab
88 Gladstone, U.S.A.
7 Glamorgan, co. Df
13 Glarus Da
8 Glasgow De
7 Glastonbury Ef
27 Glauchau Ec
32 Glazov Kd
9 Glen Innes Da
8 Glenbarr Be
75 Glencoe Ec
85 Glendale Ce
9 Glenealy Ed
61 Gleneig Ab
9 Glengarriff De
63 Glenmorgan Cd
20 Glenrothy Cd
61 Glenreagh Db
89 Glens Falls Jc
22 Gliwice Ec
85 Globe De
22 Glogow Dc
32 Glotovo Jc
61 Gloucester, Australia Db

7 Gloucester, & co., England. Ef
89 Gloucester, U.S.A. Kc
16 Glückstadt Cb
33 Glushitsa Ke
17 Gmunden Ee
22 Gniezno Db
44 Goa Ce
74 Gobabis Bb
94 Gobernador Gordillo Bf
50–51 Gobi or Shamo, des. Eb
74 Gochas Bb
48 Göcöng Bb
7 Godalming Gf
47 Godavari, R. Hh
86 Goderich Ec
78 Godhaab Mb
78 Godhavn Mb
44 Godhra Dg
44 Godwin Austen, Mt., see K2
18 Goeree, I. Cc
18 Goes Cc
95 Goiania Fc
95 Goias Ec
92 Goias, st. Ed
46 Gojra Dc
27 Gök, R. Db
84 Golden Gate Bd
87 Goldsboro Ed
22 Goleniow Cb
50 Golma Dc
8 Golspie Dc
33 Gomel Fe
70 Gomera, I. Bc
90 Gomez Palacio Db
43 Gonabad Hc
47 Gonda He
71 Gonaives Dc
39 Gonder Cd
47 Gondia Hh
75 Gonye Rapids Ca
78 Good Hope Eb
74 Good Hope, C. of Bf
61 Goondiwindi Da
61 Goodna Da
75 Goomalling Be
60 Goombalie Ca
78 Goose Lc
46 Gop Bg
47 Gorakhpur Je
47 Gore, N.Z. Bg
72 Goré, Cent. Afr. Bb
9 Gorey Ed
81 Gorgan Gb
18 Gorinchen Dc
33 Goris Jh
28 Gorizia Db
32 Gorki Hd
23 Gorlice Fd
22 Görlitz Fc
23 Gorlouka Gf
9 Gormanston Ec
11 Gorna Oryakhovitsa Ed
62 Goroka Gh
62 Gorongoza Mts. Ed
49 Gorontalo Dc
9 Gort C
22 Gorzów Cb
47 Gosainthan, mt. Kd
13 Goschenen Cc
61 Gosford Db
88 Goshen Cd
28 Gospic Eb
22 Gostyn Dc
14 Göteborg Cd
17 Gotha Dc
11 Gotland I. Dd
55 Goto, Is. Id
11 Gotska Dd
16 Göttingen Cc
22 Gottwaldov (Zlin) Dd
18 Gouda Db
61 Gouin Res. Bb
61 Goulburn Cb
65 Gould Mt. Bb
15 Gourdon De
47 Gourits, R. Cd
71 Gourma-Rarous Ee
44 Goya De
83 Goyders Lagoon Ad
72 Goz Beida Ca
39 Goz Regeb Cd
57 Graaff Reinet Cd
28 Gracac Eb
51 Gracias à Dios, C. Bd
28 Gradisca Db
11 Grafton, Australia Da
84 Grafton, U.S.A. Gb
62 Grafton C. Db
82a Graham I. Zi
82a Graham I.
56 Graham Land Qc
75 Grahamstown Cd
23 Grajewo Gb
8 Grampians, mts. Dd

70 Gran Canaria, I. Bc
94 Gran Chaco, reg. Cd
21 Gran Paradiso, mt. Fd
91 Granada, Nic. Ad
26 Granada, Spain Bb
9 Granard Dc
81 Granby Bb
87 Grand Bahama I. Ef
71 Grand Bassam Eg
85 Grand Canyon Dd
91 Grand Cayman, I. Bc
81 Grand Falls Db
84 Grand Forks Gb
88 Grand Haven Cc
84 Grand Island Gc
84 Grand Junction Ed
71 Grand Lahou Dh
80 Grand Rapids, Canada Eb
88 Grand Rapids, U.S.A. Cc
73 Grande Comore, I. Gf
90 Grande de Santiago, R. Dc
80 Grande Prairie Cb
80 Grandforks Cc
84 Grangeville Cb
66 Granite City Cd
67 Granity Cd
8 Grantown Ec
15 Grasse Gf
13 Graubünden (Grisons) Cb
8 's Gravenhage (The Hague) Db
17 Graz Fe
91 Great Abaco, I. Ca
49 Great Australian Bight De
66 Great Barrier I. Eb
66 Great Barrier Reef Cb
84 Great Basin Cd
78 Great Bear L. Eb
12 Great Belt Dd
74 Great Berg, R. Bd
62 Great Divide, mts. Cc
7 Great Dunmow Hf
78 Great Fish, R. Canada Cb
74 Great Fish, R. South Africa Dd
47 Great Himalaya Ra. Hd
91 Great Inagua I. Db
64 Great Indian Des. (Thar Des.) Ce
72 Great Karasberge, mts. Bc
74 Great Karoo, reg. Cd
51 Great Khingan Mts. Gb
74 Great Namaqualand Bb
64 Great Nicobar I. Gg
62 Great Ruaha, R. Fe
13 Great St. Bernard, Col du, P. Bc
84 Great Salt Lake Dc
80 Great Slave L. Ca
65 Great Victoria Des. Eb
79 Great Whale, R. Kc
75 Great Winterberg, mt. Dd
74 Great Winterhoek, mt. Bd
7 Great Yarmouth Je
42 Great Zab R. Eb
91 Greater Antilles Cc
49 Greater Sunda Is. Cd
27 Greco, C. Dc
26 Gredos, Sa. de, mts. Aa
5 Greece, st. Kh
84 Greeley Fc
88 Green B. Bb
88 Green Bay Bb
26 Green Is. Hg
87 Green Island Cf
65 Greenbushes Be
18 Greencastle Be
89 Greenfield Jc
2 Greenland Eb
8 Greenock De
88 Greensboro Ff
18 Greensburg Ce
71 Greenville, Lib. Dg
88 Greenville, Mich. Cc
89 Greenville, Miss. Be
89 Greenville, N.C. Gg
84 Greenville, S.C. De
87 Greenville, Tex. Ae

7 Greenwich Hf
63 Gregory I. Ad
92 Gregory Ra. Bb
16 Greifswald Ea
12 Grenaa Dc
46 Grenada, I. Bc
91 Grenada, I. Fd
87 Grenade Ce
91 Grenadines, Is. Fd
61 Grenfell Cb
15 Grenoble Cd
62 Grenville C. Ba
61 Greta Db
60 Grey Ra. Ba
67 Greymouth Cc
75 Greytown, Nat. Ec
61 Greytown, N.Z. Ed
60 Griffith Cb
90 Grijalva R. Fd
6 Grimsby Gd
11 Grimstad Bd
13 Grindelwald Cb
74 Griqualand West, dist. Cc
14 Gris Nez, pt. Db
13 Grisons, cant., see Graubünden
23 Grodek Gb
33 Grodno Dc
23 Gródzisk Fb
23 Grójec Fc
18 Gronau Gb
10 Grong Cc
18 Groningen, Netherlands Fa
92 Groningen, Surinam Db
10 Grönöy Cb
74 Grootfontein Ba
62 Groote Eylandt Aa
2 Grosne, R. Cc
26 Grossenhani Ec
28 Grosseto Cc
80 Grouard Cb
33 Groznyy Jg
15 Gstaad Bd
22 Grudziadz Eb
15 Gruyères Bb
33 Gryazi He
33 Gryazovets Hd
23 Grybow Fd
95 Guacu Ed
90 Guadalajara, Mexico Dc
26 Guadalajara, Spain Ba
26 Guadalaviar, R. Bb
26 Guadalcanal Dd
26 Guadalquivir, R. Ab
26 Guadarrama, Sa. de Ba
91 Guadeloupe, I. Fc
26 Guadiana, R. Ab
62 Guaira Ed
94 Guajará-Mirim Bb
50 Guam, I. Cc
90 Guamuchil Cb
90 Guanajuato Cb
91 Guantanamo Cb
95 Guaporé Ae
76 Guarda Aa
39 Guardafui, C. Ed
72 Guastalla Je
72 Guatemala Je
90 Guatemala, rep. Gd
91 Guayabal Cb
91 Guayama Ec
92 Guayaquil Bc
90 Guaymas Bb
43 Gubakha Ld
28 Gubbio Dc
75 Gulu Ec
55 Gumma, pref. Cc
18 Gummersbach Gc
69 Gunedah Db
79 Gunnbjorn Fd. Pb
41 Guntakal De
48 Gunungapi Dd
47 Gurdaspur Eb
47 Gurkha Kd
34 Guryev Ne
71 Gusau Gf
16 Güstrow Eb

18 Gütersloh Hc
90 Gutierrez Gd
92 Guyana, st. Db
15 Guyenne De
61 Guyra Db
44 Gwadar Ac
46 Gwalior Ge
75 Gwanda Db
75 Gwelo Da
63 Gympie Dd
55 Gyoda Cc
30 Gyongyös Cb
30 Györ Ab
80 Gypsumville Db
30 Gyula Cb

11 Haapamaki Ec
32 Haapsala Dd
18 Haarlem Db
40 Habesor, wadi Bd
54 Hachijo Shima, I. Cd
54 Hachinohe Db
8 Haddington Fe
12 Haderslev & co. Cc
50 Hadhal Da
39 Hadhramaut, dist. Dd
52 Haeju Bb
45 Hafar al Batin Fd
40 Haffah Cb
46 Hafizabad Db
10 Hafnarfjördur Ab
16 Hagen Bc
89 Hagerstown Ge
55 Hagi Bd
19 Haguenau Gf
40 Haifa Bc
42 Hail Ed
51 Hailar Fb
84 Halley Dc
81 Haileybury Bb
7 Hailsham Hg
51 Hailun Fb
48 Hailuoto Eb
48 Haiphong Ba
11 Haiti, rep. Dc
39 Haiya Cd
42 Haiyaniya Ed
30 Hajdudoszormeny Cb
23 Hajnowka Gb
54 Hakodate Db
46 Hala Bf
14 Halab (Aleppo) Db
38 Halab Cc
40 Halba Cc
16 Halberstadt Dc
66 Halcombe Ed
11 Halden Cd
46 Haldwanim Gd
45 Hale Mt. Bd
41 Halifax, Can. Cb
6 Halifax, Eng. Fd
62 Halifax B. Cb
17 Hall De
18 Halle, Belg. Dc
16 Halle, Ger. Dc
96 Halley Bay Ab
10 Hällnäs Dc
11 Hall's Creek Db
49 Halmahera, I. Dc
11 Halmstad Cd
12 Hals Dc
11 Hälsingborg Cd
10 Haltiatunturi, mt. Eb
12 Halundborg Ed
46 Halvad Cg
55 Hamada Bd
43 Hamadan Fc
39 Hamah (Hama) Cb
54 Hamamatsu Cd
89 Hamilton, U.S.A. Bc
81 Hamilton, Can. Ab
11 Hamilton, N.Z. Eb
73 Hamilton, Scot. De
88 Hamiltown Ce
7 Hamlin Jb
18 Hamm Gc
73 Hammam Fe
64 Hammersley Range Bc
67 Hampden Cf
67 Hampden Cf
19 Hampton Gf
44 Hamun-I-Mashkel, L. Ac
52 Hanak Dc
19 Hanau Hd
52 Hanchung Ec
55 Handa Cd
85 Hanford Cc
52 Hangchow Fc
11 Hanko Ef

51 Hanku Fc
67 Hanmer De
11 Hann, mt. Db
80 Hanna Cb
16 Hannover Cb
48 Hanoi Ba
89 Hanover Ge
80 Hansard Bb
46 Hansi Ed
11 Hantan Fc
10 Haparanda Eb
46 Hapur Fd
42 Haql Dd
43 Haradh Fe
73 Harer Gb
51 Harbin Gb
88 Harbor Beach Dc
81 Harbour Grace Db
16 Harburg Cb
21 Harbarger Fd. Bc
18 Harderwijk Eb
46 Hardwar Gd
39 Hargeisa De
48 Hari R. Bd
7 Harlech Cc
18 Harlingen, Netherlands Ea
85 Hartingen, U.S.A. Gf
11 Härnösänd Dc
8 Harris, dist. Bc
89 Harrisburg Gd
75 Harrismith Dc
87 Harrison Bd
6 Harrogate Fd
10 Harstad Db
12 Harsyssel dist. Bc
88 Hart Bc
75 Hartebeest Ab
89 Hartford Jd
7 Hartland Pt. Cf
75 Hartley Ea
7 Harwich Jf
46 Haryana, st. Fd
43 Hasa, reg. Fd
27 Hasan, mt. Db
18 Hasselt Ed
70 Hassi Messaoud Gb
7 Hastings, Eng. Hg
84 Hastings, Nebr. Gc
88 Hastings, Mich. Cc
67 Hastings, N.Z. Fc
57 Hatfield Gf
87 Hattieras, C. Ed
80 Hatvan Bb
11 Haugesund Bd
66 Hauraki G. Eb
21 Haut Rhin, dept. Fb
20 Haute Loire, dept.
20 Haute Marne, dept. Da
20 Haute Saône, dept. Db
20 Haute Savoie, dept. Dd
20 Hautes-Alpes, dept. De
70 Hauts Plateaux Fa
80 Havana Bb
87 Havelock Dd
89 Haverhill Kc
47 Havre Eb
72 Havza Ea
52 Hawaii, I. Fc
57 Hawaiian Is. Fb
39 Hawash, R. Dd
66 Hawera Ec
8 Hawick Fe
66 Hawke Bay Fc
66 Hawke's Bay, dist. Fc
60 Hay Bb
80 Hay River Ca
19 Hayange Fe
7 Haywards Heath Gf
88 Hazard Gf
47 Hazaribagh Kg
18 Hazebrouck Bd
80 Hazelton Bd
80 Hazleton Hd
46 Healesville Cc
3 Heard I. Lh
81 Hearst Ab
78 Hebron, Can. Lc
40 Hebron (Al Khalil), Jordan Bb
46 Hedgehope Bg
16 Heemstede Db
18 Heerde Fb
18 Heerenveen Eb
18 Heerlen Ed
30 Hegyeshalom Ab
17 Heidelberg Cd
19 Heidelberg, Ger. He
75 Heidelberg, Transvaal Dc
51 Heilbronn Je
51 Heilungkiang, prov. Gb
11 Heinola Fc

42 Hejez, reg. Dd
10 Hekla, mt. Bb
22 Hel Ea
84 Helena Db
8 Helensburgh Dd
66 Helensville Eb
44 Helmand, R. Ab
18 Helmond Ed
12 Helsingör Fc
11 Helsinki Fc
7 Helston Bg
26 Henares, R. Ba
15 Hendaye Cf
39 Henderson Ff
18 Hengelo Fd
51 Hengyang Fd
19 Hénin Bd
61 Henty Cc
45 Henzada He
44 Herat Ab
7 Herault, R. & dept. Bf
62 Herberton Dd
28 Herceg Novi Cc
7 Hereford & Co. Ee
18 Herentals Dc
18 Herford Hb
43 Heri Rud Jb
51 Herisau Da
64 Hermannsburg Ec
74 Hermanus Bd
7 Hermitage Cf
90 Hermosillo Bb
18 Herne Gc
7 Herne Bay Jf
12 Herning Bc
81 Heron Bay Ab
87 Herrin Cd
18 Hersfeld Jd
18 Herstal Ed
7 Hertford & co. Gf
33 Hervey B. Dc
46 Herzliya Bc
12 Hesselö, I. Ec
86 Heywood Bc
86 Hibbing Bb
88 Hickory Eg
90 Hidalgo del Parral Cb
70 Hierro, I. Bc
70 High Atlas, mts. Eb
88 High Point Fg
83 High River Cb
23 High Tatra, mt. Ed
7 High Wycombe Gf
83 Highland Parks Bc
32 Hiiumaa, I. Dd
54 Hikone Cc
66 Hikurangi Ea
16 Hildesheim Cb
7 Hilla Ec
12 Hilleröd Fd
12 Hillston Cb
83bHilo Dc
18 Hilversum Eb
43 Himachal Pradesh, St. Fc
46 Hiimatnagar Dg
55 Himeji Bd
12 Himmelbjerget Cc
12 Himmerland Cc
40 Hims (Homs) Cb
43 Hinchinbrook I. Cb
7 Hinde Rapids De
44 Hindu Kush, mts. Ba
80 Hines Creek Cb
44 Hingol R. Bc
12 Hinnoy, I. Db
55 Hino, C. Bc
13 Hinterrhein, R. Db
55 Hiroshima & pref. Bd
19 Hirson De
91 Hispaniola, I. Dc
46 Hissar Dd
55 Hitachi Dc
7 Hitchin Gf
40 Hitra, I. Bc
11 Hjaelm, I. Dc
11 Hjälmaren Dd
12 Hjorring & dist. Cb
48 Hoa Binh Ba
61 Hobart Cd
62 Hobro Cc
13 Hochdorf Ca
51 Hochih Kd
87 Hochch Hd
51 Hochwan Fc
19 Hockenheim He
39 Hodeida Dd
88 Hodgson Eb
30 Hódmezö Vasarhely Cb
70 Hodna, Chott de Fa
22 Hodonin Dd
18 Hoek van Holland Db
7 Hof, Ger. Dc
51 Hof, Iceland He
78 Hofei Fc
10 Hofsos Ba
7 Hofuf Fd
70 Hoggar, mts. Gd

51 Hoihow Fd
51 Hokang Hb
57 Hokitika Ce
54 Hokkaido, I., pref. & dist. Db
12 Holbaek & co. Ed
61 Holbrook Cc
84 Holdrege Gc
91 Holguin Cb
88 Holland Cc
85 Hollywood Ce
40 Holon Bc
12 Holstebro Bc
10 Holt Bb
6 Holy I. Cd
6 Holyhead Cd
89 Holyoke Jc
9 Holywood Fb
18 Holzminden Jc
71 Hombori Ée
19 Homburg Ge
82aHomer Cc
68 Homs, Libya Db
40 Homs, Syria, see Hims Cb
51 Honan, prov. Fc
74 Hondeklipp Bd
77 Honduras Kg
91 Honduras, Gulf of Ac
91 Honduras, rep. Ad
11 Hönefoss Cc
14 Honfleur Dc
48 Hong-Ha, R. Ba
51 Hongkong, Br. Crown Colony Fd
57 Honolulu Fb
51 Honshu, I. Cc
18 Hoogeveen Fb
18 Hoorn Eb
18 Hope Be
79 Hopedale Cc
76 Hopei, prov. Fc
65 Hopetoun Ce
15 Hopetown Cc
43 Horal Hammar, L. Fc
18 Hordenberg Fb
39 Hordio Ed
93 Horn, C. Ch
10 Hornavan Db
89 Hornell Gc
61 Hornsby Db
14 Hornslandet Dc
54 Horoizumi Db
54 Horoshiri-dake Db
12 Horsens Cd
61 Horsham, Australia Bc
7 Horsham, Eng. Gf
21 Horten Cd
46 Hoshiarpur Ec
87 Hot Springs Be
35 Hou R. Ba
66 Houhoura Da
87 Houma Bf
87 Houston Af
61 Howe C. Bc
65 Howe C., West, Df
47 Howrah Mg
9 Howth Ec
8 Hoy, I. Eb
11 Hoyanger Bc
27 Hoyran, L. Db
22 Hradec Králové Cc
51 Hsinchu Cd
45 Hsipaw Hd
51 Hualien Gd
51 Huachang Fc
92 Huancayo Bd
94 Haunchaca Cb
90 Huatabampo Cb
44 Hubli Ed
6 Huddersfield Fd
8 Hudson Ba
80 Hudson Bay Junc. Db
80 Hudson Hope Bb
79 Hudson Str. Kb
48 Hué Bb
26 Huelva Ab
26 Huesca Ba
62 Hughenden Bc
87 Hugo Ae
55 Huhehot Fb
90 Huixtla Fd
51 Hulan Fb
51 Huldo Eb
61 Hull, Can. Bb
7 Hull, England Gd
94 Humahuaca Bd
92 Humaita Cc
75 Humandorp Dd
6 Humber, R. Gd
80 Humboldt Db
84 Humboldt B. Bc
84 Humboldt R. Cc
23 Humenné Fd
10 Hunafiöi Aa
51 Hunan, prov. Fd
18 Hundested Ed
4 Hungary, rep. Jj
60 Hungerford Ba
51 Hungnam Bb

51 Hungshui Ho, R. Ed
7 Hunstanton He
18 Hunte, R. Hb
11 Hunter Db
66 Hunterville Ec
7 Huntingdon & Peterborough, Co. Ge
7 Huntington, England Ge
88 Huntington, Indiana Cd
88 Huntington, West Virginia De
6 Huntly, Scot. Ec
66 Huntly, N.Z. Eb
87 Huntsville, Ala. Ce
87 Huntsville, Can. Fb
87 Huntsville, Tex. Ae
51 Hupei, prov. Fc
56 Hurghada Cc
44 Huron Gc
88 Huron, L. Db
10 Husi Gb
85 Hutchison Gd
13 Huttwil Ba
51 Hwaian Fc
51 Hwang Ho, R. Fc
51 Hwangshih Fc
50 Hweiteh Ed
45 Hyden Be
44 Hyderabad, India De
46 Hyderabad, West Pakistan Bf
15 Hyères & Iles.d' Gf
55 Hyogo, pref. Bc
7 Hythe Hj

51 Iasi Ef
71 Ibadan Fg
92 Ibaqué Bb
55 Ibaraki, pref. Cc
18 Ibbenburen Gb
26 Ibiza & I. Cb
73 Ibo Gf
10 Iceland, I., st. Bc
51 Ichang Fc
55 Ichikawa Cc
54 Ichinomiya Cc
54 Ichinoseki Dc
51 Ichun Gb
82 Idaho, st. Bb
84 Idaho Falls Dc
19 Idar Oberstein Ge
72 Idd el Ghanam Ca
38 Idfu Cc
27 Idhi, mt. Cb
70 Idjil (Fort Gouraud) Cd
27 Ierapetra Db
28 Iesi Dc
71 Ife Fg
70 Ifni Cd
23 Iganie Gb
94 Igarka Lc
28 Iglesias Bc
91 Iguacu Ee
93 Iguaçu Falls Ee
90 Iguala Ed
92 Iguaru Fc
10 Iisalmi Fc
51 Ijmuiden Db
18 IJsselmeer Eb
27 Ikaria, I. Cb
55 Iki, I. Ad
23 Ilanz Db
14 Ile de France, prov. Ec
14 Ile et Vilaine, dept. Ce
35 Ilek, & R. Ke
62 Ilfracombe, Australia Bc
7 Ilfracombe, Eng. Cf
27 Ilgin Db
21 Illi, R. Fa
51 Iller, R. Ea
39 Illig Ec
83 Illinois, st. Eb
32 Ilmen, L. Fd
49 Iloilo Db
55 Imabari Bd
32 Imandra L. Fb
28 Imola Cb
21 Imperia Gf
62 Impfondo Bc
58 Imphal Gd
27 Imroz Ca
67 Inangahua Dd
10 Inari & L. Fb
92 Inca Cb
87 Incesu Eb
26 Inchon Bb
45 Indaw Hd
3 Indian Ocean Lf
92 Indian Union, rep. Lg
88 Indiana Fd
83 Indiana, st. Cc
88 Indianapolis Be
94 Indiga Jb
48 Indo China, reg. Bb

37 Indonesia, rep. Fk
61 Indooroopilly Da
46 Indore Eg
46 Indur, R. Bc
46 Indus, Mouths of the Af
48 Indramaju Bd
27 Inebolu Da
72 Ingende Bd
42 Ingham Cb
60 Inglewood, N.Z. Ec
61 Inglewood, Queensland Da
60 Inglewood, Victoria Bc
17 Ingolstadt Dd
75 Inhambane Fb
75 Inhaminga Ea
75 Inharrime Fb
9 Inishmore I. Bc
55 Inland Sea Bd
21 Inn, R. Jb
55 Inner Hebrides Bc
51 Inner Mongolia, Aut. Reg. Fb
62 Innisfail Cb
21 Innsbruck Kb
22 Inowroclaw Eb
44 Inquisivi Bc
13 Interlaken Bb
78 Inuvik Db
67 Invercargill Bg
62 Inverell Da
79 Inverkeithing Ed
8 Inverness & co. Dc
8 Inverurie Fc
75 Inyanga Mts. Ea
75 Inyati Da
33 Inza Je
27 Ioannina Bb
45 Iolanda Cb
8 Iona, I. Bd
27 Ionian Is. Gc
25 Ionian S. Fc
27 Ios, I. Cb
83 Iowa, st. Db
48 Ipoh Bc
61 Ipswich, Australia Da
7 Ipswich, Eng. Je
92 Ipu Ec
94 Iquique Ad
92 Iquitos Bc
27 Iráklion Cb
31 Iran, King. Jf
90 Irapuato Dc
36 Iraq, rep. Hf
91 Irazú, vol. Bd
40 Irbid Bc
21 Irebu Bd
4 Ireland Ce
33 Irgiz Je
6 Irish S. Cd
35 Irkutsk Nd
27 Irmak Db
48 Iron Mt. Ab
86 Iron River Cb
80 Ironton De
63 Ironwood Cb
45 Irrawaddy, R. Hd
34 Irtysh R. Kd
73 Irumu Ec
46 Irún Ba
8 Irvine De
8 Irwin Ec
60 Irymple Bb
55 Isahaya Bd
72 Isangi Cc
29 Ischia Dd
17 Ischl Ee
54 Ise, B. Cd
12 Iseföord Ed
20 Isère, R. & dept. Dd
18 Iserlohn Gc
29 Iserna Ed
21 Iseo, & L. di Jd
54 Ishikari B. Db
55 Ishikawa, pref. Cc
54 Ishinomaki Dc
73 Isiro Dc
27 Iskenderun (Alexandretta) Eb
27 Iskilip Da
80 Island L. Eb
8 Islay, I. Be
6 Isle of Man Cc
7 Isle of Wight Fg
45 Ismâil'iya Cd
27 Isparta Db
40 Israel, st. Bc
27 Istanbul Ca
27 Istiaia Bb
28 Istra, reg. Db
27 Istranca Mts. Ca
93 Itabira Gc
92 Itaeté Ed
95 Itaia Hg
4 Italy, rep. Hg
95 Itambe, mt. Gc
95 Itapura Ed
89 Ithaca Gc
27 Itháki Bb

55 Ito Cd
60 Ivanhoe Bb
33 Ivano-Frankovsk Ef
32 Ivanovo Hd
68 Ivory Coast, rep. Ee
21 Ivrea Fd
55 Iwakuni Bd
54 Iwamizawa Db
54 Iwanuma Dc
54 Iwata Cd
54 Iwate, pref. Dc
71 Iwo Fg
94 Ixiamas Bb
13 Izegem Cd
32 Izhevsk Kd
51 Izhevsk Kd
33 Izmail Ef
27 Izmir (Smyrna) Cb
27 Izmit Da
27 Iznik Ca
41 Izra Cc
55 Izumo Bc

40 Jabal an Nusayriyah mts. Cb
40 Jabal Ash Sharqi (Anti-Lebanon) mts. Cb
43 Jabal at Tuwaiq, mts. Fe
42 Jabal Ibrahim, mt. Ee
42 Jabal Shammar, dists. Dd
47 Jabalpur Gg
40 Jabeah Bb
43 Jabrin Fe
95 Jacareźinho Fd
88 Jackson, Mich. Cc
87 Jackson, Miss. Be
87 Jackson, Ohio De
51 Jackson, Tenn. Cd
35 Jackson Mt. Be
87 Jacksonville, Fla. De
86 Jacksonville, Ill. Bd
10 Jacksons Ce
10 Jackvik Db
91 Jacmel Dc
46 Jacobabad Bd
18 Jade & B. Ha
26 Jaén Bb
43 Jaffna Dg
47 Jagdalpur Hf
25 Jagersfontein Dc
46 Jagraon Ec
46 Jagtial Gj
44 Jaipur Ed
46 Jaipur Ee
79 Jakobshavn Mb
54 Jalalabad Cb
90 Jalapa Enriquez Ed
46 Jalgaon Eh
46 Jalna Ej
23 Jalo Df
46 Jalpaiguri Me
91 Jamaica, I. Cc
47 Jamalpur, East Pakistan Mf
47 Jamalpur, India Lf
49 Jamdena Ed
81 James B. Aa
60 Jamestown, Australia Ab
88 Jamestown, N.D. Gb
88 Jamestown, N.Y. Fc
12 Jammer, B. Cb
24 Jammu Eb
46 Jammu & Kashmir, St. Db
46 Jamnagar Cg
46 Jampur Cd
47 Jamshedpur Lg
54 Jan Mayen I. Bb
46 Jand Db
86 Janesville Cd
46 Janin Bc
75 Jansenville Cd
46 Januária Gc
8 Japan, king. Rf
3 Japan, S. of Od
49 Japen I. & str. Ef
40 Jarash Bc
23 Jaroslaw Gc
46 Jask Hd
54 Jaszbereny Cb
75 Jau Fd
47 Jaunpur Jf
47 Jauru Jd
54 Java S. Bd
40 Jaynagar Le
46 Jazzin Bc
46 Jedburgh Fe
25 Jedrzejów Fc
86 Jefferson City Bd
73 Jegega Gb
12 Jelenia Góra Gb
32 Jelgava Dd

17 Jena Dc
91 Jerémie Dc
26 Jerez Ab
62 Jericho, Austral. Cc
40 Jericho, Jordan Bd
14 Jersey, I. Bc
89 Jersey City Hd
48 Jerusalem Bd
28 Jerzu Bc
49 Jesselton Cc
47 Jessore Mg
47 Jeypore Jj
46 Jhang Maghiana Dc
43 Jhansi Gf
47 Jharsuguda Kh
46 Jhelum Cb
46 Jhunjhunu Ed
42 Jidda Bb
22 Jhlava Cd
73 Jima Fb
30 Jimbolia Cc
90 Jimenez Db
73 Jinja Ec
91 Jinotega Ad
40 Jisr ash Shughur Cb
64 Joanna Spring Cc
92 João Pessoa Fc
22 Joblonec Cc
46 Jodhpur De
19 Joeuf Fe
48 Jogjakarta Cd
75 Johannesburg Dc
8 John-o-Groats Eb
88 Johnson City, Tenn. Df
89 Johnson City, N.Y. Hc
73 Johnston Falls Df
8 Johnstone Dc
89 Johnstown, Pa. Fd
89 Johnstown, N.Y. Hc
48 Johore Bahru Bc
20 Joigny Bb
95 Joinville Fe
10 Jokkmokk Db
88 Jolie Bd
81 Joliette Bb
79 Jones Sd. Ja
87 Jonesboro Bd
11 Jonkoping Cd
48 Jonquiere Bb
54 Joplin Bd
48 Jordan, king. Hf
40 Jorn, R. Bb
10 Jorn Eb
11 Jos Eb
80 Juan de Fuca, Str. Bc
57 Juan Fernandez Is. c
73 Juba Ec
73 Juba, R. Gc
70 Juby, C. Cc
26 Júcar, R. Bb
91 Jucaro Cb
18 Juist Fa
72 Juiz de Fora Gd
46 Jujuy Bd
33 Julfa Jh
94 Juli Bc
94 Juliaca Ac
78 Julianehaab Nb
46 Jullundur Ec
11 Jumet Dd
47 Jumla Id
46 Junagadh Cb
84 Junction City Gd
95 Jundiai Fd
82a Juneau Ec
61 Junee Cb
13 Jungfrau, mt. Cb
48 Juniyah Bc
73 Jur, R. Db
8 Jura, I. Ce
20 Jura, mts. & dept. Db
94 Juruena Db
11 Jylland Cc

44 K2 (Mt. Godwin Austen Da
74 Kaap Plat Cc
71 Kabala Cg
73 Kabale Ed
73 Kabalo Ec
72 Kabongo Dc
44 Kabompo, R. Cf
44 Kabul Bb
45 Kachin, st. Hc
41 Kaddi Gf
60 Kadina Ab
73 Kadugli Da
44 Kaduna Cd
71 Kaedi Ce
71 Kafanchan Gg
73 Kafia Kingi Cb
72 Kafue, R. Df
55 Kagawa, pref. Bd
55 Kagoshima & pref. Bd
55 Kagoshima, B. Bd

83b Kahoolawe, I. Cb
67 Kaiapoi De
51 Kaifeng Fc
66 Kaikohe Da
67 Kaikoura De
66 Kaimanawa Mts. Fc
70 Kairouan Ga
19 Kaiserslautern Ge
66 Kaitaia Da
67 Kaitangata Bg
10 Kajaani Fc
49 Kajan R. Cc
73 Kakamega Ec
74 Kakamas Cc
74 Kakau Veld Cb
46 Kalabagh Cb
27 Kalabáka Bb
33 Kalach He
74 Kalahari, des. Cb
27 Kalamata Bb
88 Kalamazoo Cc
44 Kalat Bc
44 Kalat-i-Ghilzai Bb
51 Kalgan Fb
65 Kalgoorlie Ce
72 Kalima Dc
48 Kalimantan Cd
27 Kalimnos, I. Cb
32 Kalinin Gd
32 Kaliningrad (Königsberg) De
22 Kalisz Ec
73 Kaliua Ee
11 Kalmar Dc
30 Kalocsa Bb
75 Kalomo Da
33 Kaluga Ge
32 Kama Hc
54 Kamaishi Dc
39 Kamaran Is. Dd
73 Kambi Dc
16 Kamchatka Pen. Td
25 Kamenets Podolskiy Ef
33 Kamensk-Shakhtinski Hf
72 Kamina De
80 Kamloops Bb
73 Kampala Ec
48 Kampar R. Bc
18 Kampen Eb
48 Kampot Bb
80 Kamsack Db
54 Kamutaki, Mt. Db
33 Kamyshin Je
55 Kanagawa, pref. Cc
32 Kanash Jd
55 Kanazawa Cc
44 Kancheepuram Df
47 Kanchenjunga, mt. Le
51 Kanchow Fd
72 Kanda Kanda Ce
44 Kandaghat Fc
44 Kandahar Bb
48 Kandangan Cd
46 Kandavu, I. Gk
13 Kandersteg Bb
71 Kandi Ff
44 Kandla Cg
44 Kandy Dg
61 Kangaroo I. Ac
48 Kangean Is. Cd
88 Kankakee Bd
71 Kankan Df
79 Kanlapiskau, L. Kc
32 Kanin, C. Hb
71 Kano Gf
65 Kanowna Ce
55 Kanoya Bd
47 Kanpur He
82 Kansas, st. Dc
86 Kansas City Bd
35 Kansk Md
50-51 Kansu, prov. Ec
55 Kantō, dist. Dc
50 Kantse Ec
55 Kanuma Cc
51 Kaohsiung Gd
74 Kaoko-Otavi Aa
74 Kaoko Veld Aa
72 Kapanga Ce
28 Kapela, mts. Eb
13 Kapoeta Ec
30 Kaposvar Ab
48 Kapuas R. Bd
60 Kapunda Ab
34 Kara Kum Des. He
3 Kara Sea Lb
33 Karachev Ge
44 Karachi Bg
54 Karaganda Ke
49 Karaikal Df
49 Karakelong Dc
44 Karakoram Ra. & mt.
50 Karaman Cb
27 Karaman Db
74 Karamea B. Cd
74 Karasburg Bc

10 Karasjok Fb
72 Karasu Da
55 Karatsu Bd
28 Karawanken, mts. Ea
42 Karbala Ec
50 Karcag Cb
27 Kardhitsa Bb
74 Kareeberge, mts. Cd
75 Kariba Gorge & Lake Da
74 Karibib Bb
48 Karimata Is. Bd
44 Karimata str. Bd
46 Karimnagar Gj
62 Karkar I. Gg
43 Karkheh, R. Fc
17 Karl-Marx Stadt Ec
28 Karlovac (Karlstadt) Eb
27 Karlovy Vary Bc
11 Karlskrona Cd
43 Karlsruhe He
11 Karlstad Cd
46 Karnal Fd
31 Karnobot Fd
73 Karonga Ed
79 Karora Cd
62 Karpathós, I. Cb
34 Karsakpai Je
12 Kartuzy Ea
73 Karungu Ed
22 Karvina Ed
44 Karwar Cf
27 Kaş Cb
72 Kasai, R. Bd
73 Kasama Ef
73 Kasanga Ed
73 Kasangulu Bd
73 Kasange Df
27 Kashan Gc
27 Kashgar Bc
55 Kashiwazaki Cc
44 Kashmir, see Jammu & Kashmir
44 Kashmir Bd
33 Kasimov He
11 Kaskinen Ec
72 Kasongo Lunda Be
27 Kasos, I. Cb
39 Kassala Cd
16 Kassel Cc
27 Kastamonu Da
55 Kastornoye Ge
12 Kastellorizon, I. Cb
44 Kasur Cc
62 Kataio Kombe Cd
28 Katanga Bb
23 Katerini Ba
64 Katherine Ea
72 Katima Rapids Ca
71 Katiola Dg
47 Katmandu Ke
55 Katompe Dc
61 Katoomba (Blue Mts.) Db
22 Katowice Ec
71 Katsina Gf
32 Kattegat Bc
57 Kauai I. Db
21 Kaufbeuren Jb
88 Kaukauna Ab
10 Kauliranta Eb
32 Kaunas Dd
55 Kautokeino Eb
27 Kavalla Bd
55 Kawagoe Cc
55 Kawaguchi Cc
55 Kawakawa De
55 Kawasaki Cc
66 Kawerau Fc
66 Kawhia Harb. Ec
45 Kawthoolei, st. He
71 Kayes Cf
27 Kayseri Eb
34 Kazakhstan He
32 Kazan Jd
31 Kazanluk Ed
43 Kazerun Gd
72 Kazumba Ce
55 Kazunguia Da
27 Kéa Bb
55 Kecskemet Bb
48 Kediri Cd
71 Kédougou Cf
3 Keeling Is., see Cocos Is. Mf
49 Keelung Gd
85 Keene Jc
62 Keerweer C. Ba
74 Keetmanshoop Bc
78 Kefallinia Bb
60 Kefar Ata Bc
55 Keflavik Ab
8 Keith, Austral. Bc
8 Keith, Scotland Fc

32 Keksgolm Fc
48 Kelantan R. Bc
72 Kellé Ad
65 Kellerberrin Be
84 Kellogg Cb
10 Kelloselka Fb
9 Kells, see Caenannus Mor
80 Kelowna Cc
67 Kelso Bf
32 Kem Fb
34 Kemerovo Ld
10 Kemijärvi Fb
96 Kemp Coast Bc
21 Kempten Jb
47 Kendrapara Lh
74 Kenhardt Cc
70 Kenitra Db
9 Kenmare & R. Be
87 Kennedy, C. Df
74 Kenora Ec
68 Kenosha Bc
7 Kent, co. Hf
88 Kentland Bd
83 Kentucky, st. Bc
81 Kentville Cb
68 Kenya, st. Ff
73 Kenya, Mt. Fd
76 Keokuk Bc
62 Keppel B. Dc
44 Kerala, st. Df
46 Kerang Bc
33 Kerch Gf
71 Kerchoual Ef
62 Kerema Gh
32 Kerets, C. Gb
3 Kerguelen, I. Lh
48 Kerintji, mt. Bd
24 Kerkenn Is. Ed
73 Kerkenna Is. Hb
27 Kérkira Ab
27 Kérkira (Corfu) I. Ab
18 Kerkrade Fd
56 Kermadec Is. Ee
43 Kerman Hc
43 Kermanshah Hc
80 Kerrobert Db
9 Kerry, co. Bd
12 Kerteminde Dd
27 Kesan Ca
54 Kesennuma Dc
8 Kessock Dc
32 Kestenga Fb
78 Keszthely Fg
32 Ketapang Bd
28a Ketchikan Ec
71 Kete Krachi Eg
27 Kettering Ge
39 Khamis Mushait Dd
34 Khan Tengri, Mt. Le
43 Khanaqin Fc
46 Khandwa Fh
46 Khanewal Cc
46 Khangai, mts. Eb
44 Khania Bb
46 Khanpur Cd
44 Khanuj Hd
47 Kharagpur Lg
39 Kharg I. Gd
38 Kharga Oasis Cc
33 Kharkov Ge
32 Kharovsk Hc
39 Khartoum Cd
46 Khashm el Girba Cd
31 Khaskovo Ee
33 Khatanga Nb
46 Khavda Bg
46 Khed Brahma Df
70 Khemis Miliana (Affreville) Fa
74 Khenchela Ga
33 Kherson Ff
50 Khersnring Dc
35 Khilok Od
27 Khios Bb
33 Khiva Je
33 Khmelnetskiy Ef
33 Kholm Fd
35 Kholm, see Chelm
71 Khongsomba Dc
33 Khoper, R. He
27 Khotan Bc
70 Khouribga Db

74 Khuis Cc
47 Khulna Mg
45 Khurasan, reg. Hc
46 Khushab Db
44 Khyber P. Cb
51 Kiama Db
51 Kiamusze Hb
51 Kian Fd
51 Kiangsi, prov. Fd
51 Kiangsu Fc
72 Kibangou Ad
72 Kibombo Dd
80 Kicking Horse P. Cb
32 Kichmengski-Gorodok Jd
71 Kidal Fe
7 Kidderminster Ee
16 Kiel, & B. Da
23 Kielce Fc
51 Kienow Fd
50 Kienshui Ed
62 Kieta Jh
33 Kiev Fe
71 Kiffa Cc
73 Kigali Ed
73 Kigoma Dd
55 Kii Chan. Bd
30 Kikinda Cc
27 Kikládhes (Lyclades), Is. Bb
62 Kikori Fh
51 Kichu Ba
73 Kilembe Ec
73 Kilembe Ec
73 Kilesa Fe
73 Kilimanjaro, mt. Fd
73 Kilindi Fd
73 Kilkee Bd
8 Kilkeel Eb
9 Kilkenny & co. Dd
73 Kilialoe Bc
9 Kilkarney Bd
18 Kilkiney Ec
8 Killybegs Cb
73 Kilmallock Cd
8 Kilmarnock De
8 Kilmuir Bc
74 Kilrush Bd
73 Kilwa Kisiwani Fe
73 Kilwa Kivinje Fe
73 Kimba Fe
80 Kimberley Dc
74 Kimberley, dist. Db
72 Kimry Gd
73 Kinabalu, mt. Cc
8 Kincardine, co. Fd
51 Kindia Cg
72 Kindu-Port Empain Dd
32 Kineshma Hd
80 King Bay, see Dampier
51 King I. Bd
54 King Sd. Cb
78 King Christian IX Land Qa
78 King Frederik VI Land Na
65 King George Sd. Bf
78 King William I. Hb
78 King William's Town Dd
53 Kingaroy Dd
7 King's Lynn He
7 Kingsbridge Dg
11 Kingston, Australia Ac
81 Kingston, Can. Bb
91 Kingston, Jam. Cc
66 Kingston, N.Z. Bf
89 Kingston, U.S.A. Hd
91 Kingston Kd
85 Kingsville Gf
51 Kingtehchen Fd
79 Kingwa Kb
13 Kinia Cc
55 Kinki, dist. Cd
60 Kinleith Ec
8 Kinloch Rannoch Dd
8 Kinnaird's Hd. Fc
8 Kinross & co. Ed
9 Kinsale Ce
72 Kinshasa Bd
48 Kintore Ec
8 Kintyre, dist. Ce
27 Kiparissia Bb
72 Kipushi Df
35 Kirensk Nd
34 Kirgizia Jh
51 Kirin Gb
62 Kiriwini Is. Hh
13 Kirkcaldy Ed
8 Kirkcudbright, co. Dc
46 Kirklee Gg
10 Kirkenes Fb
27 Kirklareli Ca
8 Kirkmichael Ed

42 Kirkuk Eb
8 Kirkwall Fb
32 Kirov Jd
33 Kirovabad Jg
33 Kirovograd Ff
32 Kirovsk Eb
8 Kirriemuir Ed
33 Kirsanov He
27 Kirşehir Db
10 Kiruna Eb
72 Kirundu Jd
33 Kiryu Cc
72 Kisangani Dc
55 Kisarazu Cc
46 Kishangarh Ce
33 Kishinev Ef
54 Kishiwada Cd
46 Kishtwar Eb
51 Kisi Hb
73 Kisiju Fe
33 Kisköros Bb
30 Kiskunfelegy-
 haza Bb
30 Kiskunhalas Bb
73 Kismayu Gd
55 Kiso, R. Cc
30 Kisujszállas Cb
54 Kitakami, R. Dc
55 Kitakyūshū Bd
33 Kitale Fc
54 Kitami Db
81 Kitchener Ab
27 Kithira, I. Bb
27 Kithnos, I. Bb
80 Kitimat Bb
73 Kitwe Df
17 Kitzingen Dd
51 Kiukiang Fd
3 Kivu, L. Dd
32 Kizel Ld
27 Kizil, R. Da
33 Kizlyar Jg
22 Kladno Cc
17 Klagenfurt Fe
54 Klaipeda Dd
74 Klamath Falls Bc
51 Klaohsien Fd
13 Klausen P. Cb
74 Klawer Bd
75 Klerksdorp Dc
33 Kletskaya Hf
18 Kleve Fc
32 Klin Gd
2 Klobuck Ec
32 Klodzko Dc
78 Klondike Db
17 Klosterneuburg Gd
13 Klosters Db
35 Klyuchevsk Vol. Td
7 Knighton Ee
17 Knittelfeld Fe
18 Knokke Cc
88 Knoxville Df
74 Knysna Cd
28 Kobaric Da
55 Kobayashi Bd
55 Kobe Cd
52 KøbenhavnsCo. Fd
19 Koblenz Gd
28 Koceyje Eb
55 Kochi & pref. Bd
82aKodiak & I. Cc
71 Koforidua Eg
55 Kofu Cc
12 Köge Fd
74 Kogota Dc
44 Kohat Cb
45 Kohima Gc
55 Kojima Bd
55 Kojonup Be
34 Kokand Ke
34 Kokchetav Jd
50 Kokiu Ed
10 Kokkola Ec
88 Kokomo Bd
55 Kokura Bd
32 Kola Fb
32 Kola Pen. Gb
44 Kolar Df
30 Kolarovgrad Fd
46 Kolayat
 (Srikolayabji) De
71 Kolda Cf
17 Kolding Cd
49 Kolepom I. Fg
32 Kolguyev Jb
34 Kolguyev I. Cc
44 Kolhapur Ce
22 Kolin Cd
16 Köln, see
 Cologne
32 Kolo Eb
22 Kolobrzeg Ca
71 Kolokani Df
32 Kolomna Gd
32 Kolwezi Df
35 Kolyma R. &
 Ra.
42 Köm Ombo Ce
35 Komandorskiye
 Is.
22 Komárno Ec
75 Komatiport Ec
55 Komatsushima Bd

27 Komotiní Ca
48 Kompong Cham Bb
35 Komsomolets I. Ma
96 Komsomolska-
 ya Fb
35 Komsomolsk Qd
32 Kondopoga Fc
32 Konevo Gc
51 Kongmoon Fd
72 Kongolo De
11 Kongsberg Bd
22 Konin Ec
28 Konjic Fc
32 Konosha Hc
33 Konotop Fe
23 Konskie Fc
32 Konstantin-
 ovski Hf
13 Konstanz Da
47 Kontar Hk
27 Konya Db
23 Konza Fd
28 Koper Db
11 Kopervik Bd
28 Koprivnica Fa
48 Korat, see Nakhon
 Ratchasima
18 Korback Hc
27 Korce Ba
28 Korcula, I. Fc
37 Korea, N. & S.
 Reps. Qf
52 Korea Str. Bb
27 Kórinthos Bb
55 Koriyama Dc
27 Korkuteli Db
28 Kornat, I. Fc
66 Koro S. Hk
63 Koroit Bc
33 Korosten Ee
35 Korsakov Re
12 Korsör Ed
33 Korsun Ff
18 Kortrijk Cd
60 Korumburra Cc
27 Kos, I. Cb
22 Koscian Db
11 Kosciusko, mt. Cc
23 Košice Fd
32 Kostroma Hd
22 Kostrzyn Cb
32 Kosvenski
 Kamen Ld
22 Koszalin Da
30 Koszeg Ab
64 Kota Ef
48 Kota Bharu Bc
49 Kotabaru
 Sebuku Cd
72 Kote Cd
32 Kotelnich Jd
31 Kotelnikovski Hf
11 Kotka Fc
32 Kotlas Jc
46 Kotli Db
31 Kotor Bd
46 Kotput Bf
35 Kotuy R. Nb
46 Kouango Cb
70 Kououdou Ef
71 Kouroussa Df
33 Kovel Ee
79 Kovik Kb
32 Kovzhd Gc
50 Kowloon Fd
27 Kozani Bd
44 Kozhikode Df
32 Kozhva Lb
33 Kozienice Fc
22 Kozmin Dc
71 Kpandu Fg
48 Kra, Isthmus of Bb
11 Kragero Bd
30 Kragujevac Cc
48 Krakatau I. Bd
23 Kraków
 (Cracow) Ec
33 Kralicky Sneznik,
 mt. Dc
30 Kraljevo Cd
33 Kramatorsk Gf
75 Kranskop Ec
23 Krasnik Fc
33 Krasnoarmeisk Je
33 Krasnodar Gf
32 Krasnokamsk Ld
32 Krasnoufimsk Ld
34 Krasnovodsk He
35 Krasnoyarsk Md
33 Krasny He
33 Krasny Kut Je
23 Krasnytaw Gc
48 Kratie Bb
18 Krefeld Fb
33 Kremenchug Ff
17 Krems Fd
69 Kribi De
44 Krishna R. Ce
47 Krishnanagar Mg
11 Kristiansand Bd
11 Kristiansund Cd
11 Kristinehamn Cd
27 Kriti, see Crete Bb

33 Krivoy Rog Ff
28 Krk, I. Eb
22 Krkonose (Giant)
 Mts. Cc
22 Kromeriz Dd
10 Kromfors Dc
32 Kronshtadt Fd
75 Kroonstad Dc
33 Kropotkin Hf
23 Krosno Fd
33 Krosno Fd
22 Krotoszyn Dc
28 Krško Eb
75 Krugersdorp Dc
22 Krumlov Cd
30 Krusevac Cd
48 Krui Bc
23 Krzepice Ec
70 Ksar el Kebir Db
48 Kuala Lipis Bc
48 Kuala Lumpur Bc
48 Kuala Selangor Bc
48 Kuala
 Trengganu Bc
33 Kuba Jg
33 Kuban Gf
50 Kucha Cb
48 Kuching Cc
46 Kuda Cg
48 Kudus Cd
32 Kudymkar Kd
43 Kuh-e-Hazaran,
 mt. Hd
10 Kuhmo Fc
10 Kuivaniemi Fb
54 Kuji Db
50 Kuldja Cb
60 Kulwin Bc
71 Kuma Hf
33 Kuma R. Jg
55 Kumamoto &
 pref. Bd
67 Kumara Ce
71 Kumasi Eg
44 Kumbakonam Df
46 Kunch Gf
50 Kungho Ec
32 Kungur Ld
50 Kunlun Shan,
 mts. Cc
55 Kunming Ed
52 Kunsan Bb
10 Kuopio Fc
49 Kupang De
33 Kupyansk Gf
33 Kura R. Jg
55 Kutashiki Bd
48 Kuantan, reg. Db
55 Kure Bd
34 Kurgan Jd
39 Kuria Muria, Is. Ed
35 Kuril Is. Re
32 Kurnatel Dd
34 Kurnool De
67 Kurow Cf
41 Kurrikurri Db
33 Kursk Ge
52 Kursumlija Cd
74 Kuruman & R. Cc
55 Kurume Bd
52 Kurya Lc
54 Kushiro Db
38 Kushka Ef
47 Kushtia Mg
13 Kussnacht Ca
27 Kütahya Cb
33 Kutaisi Hg
41 Kutch, Gulf of Bg
23 Kutno Eb
55 Kutu Bd
68 Kutum Ed
33 Kuvandyk Le
44 Kuwait, st. Fd
54 Kuwana Cc
33 Kuybyshev Ke
33 Kuznetsk Je
52 Kuzomen Gb
51 Kwangchow Fd
52 Kwangju Bb
51 Kwangsi-Chuang
 A.R. prov. Ed
50 Kwantung Ed
51 Kwangtung,
 prov. Fd
51 Kweichow,
 prov. Ed
51 Kweilin Fd
51 Kweiyang Ed
22 Kwidzyn Db
72 Kyabe Bb
35 Kyakhta Nd
45 Kyaukse Hd
8 Kyle of
 Lochalsh Cc
54 Kyo, C. Cc
52 Kyoga, L. Ec
55 Kyogle Da
52 Kyongju Bb
54 Kyoto & pref. Cc
52 Kytiym Ld
55 Kyushu, I. &
 dist. Bd
31 Kyustendil Dd
34 Kzyl-Kum Des. Je
41 Kzyl Orda Je

21 La Bochetta P. Ge
91 La Ceiba Ac
13 La Chaux de
 Fonds Aa
92 La Chorrera Bc
26 La Coruña Aa
11 La Crosse Bc
94 La Esperanza Cb
26 La Estrada Aa
18 La Fayette Bd
8 La Folette Cf
70 La Goulette Ha
13 La Grange Cb
10 la Grand Combe Ce
92 La Guaira Ca
26 La Linea Ab
19 La Louvière Dd
18 La Mancha,
 dist. Bb
93 La Pampa, prov. Cf
92 La Paragua Cb
94 La Paz, Bolivia Bc
93 La Plata, R. de
 la Df
88 La Porte Bd
27 La Rioja Be
16 La Roche sur
 Yon Cd
12 La Rochelle Cd
91 La Romana Ec
94 La Serena Ad
28 La Spezia Bb
32 La Tagua Bb
81 La Tuque Bb
26 La Union Bb
91 La Vega Dc
72 Labe Cf
2 Labe (Elbe) R. Cb
79 Labrador Lc
48 Labuan, I. Cc
49 Labuha Dd
49 Labuk B. Cc
80 Lac la Biche Cb
81 Lac Jeannine Cb
20 Lacaune,Mts.de Af
44 Laccadive Is. Cf
13 Lachen Ca
81 Lachine Bb
60 Lachlan R. Bb
80 Lacombe Cb
89 Laconia Kc
43 Ladis Jd
74 Ladismith Cd
52 Ladoga, L. Fc
56 Ladrone Is, see
 Mariana Is.
75 Ladybrand Dc
80 Ladysmith,
 Canada Bc
75 Ladysmith,
 Natal Dc
62 Lae Gh
12 Laesö, I. Eb
87 Lafayette Be
95 Lages Bc
93 Lagôa dos Patos,
 L. Ef
71 Lagos, Nig. Fg
26 Lagos, Port. Ab
87 Lagrange De
55 Laguna Fe
52 Laguna Madre Gf
46 Lahore Ec
13 Lahti Fc
68 Lai De
61 Laidley Da
43 Laila Fe
74 Laingsburg Cd
87 Lake Charles Be
87 Lake City Df
87 Lake Grace Be
79 Lake Harbour Lb
87 Lakeland Df
71 Lakes Entrance Cc
88 Lakewood Ed
6 Lanark & co. Ee
6 Lancashire, co. Ed
6 Lancaster Ec
52 Lancaster Sd.
33 Lanchow Ec
17 Landeck De
6 Landes, dept. Ce
6 Land's End Bg
12 Landshut Ed
74 Langeberge, mr. Cc
12 Langeland Ee
33 Langenthal Ba

18 Langeoog, I. Ga
8 Langholm Ee
32 Langholt Bb
75 Langkloof Mts. Cd
15 Langon Ce
10 Langöy, I. Cb
20 Langres Db
20 Langres, Plat. Cb
10 Langsele Dc
20 Languedoc, dist. Bf
88 Lansing Cc
28 Lanusei Bc
72 Lanzarote, I. Cf
49 Laoag Db
9 Laoighis, co. Dd
14 Laon Ec
48 Laos, st. Bb
88 Lapeer Dc
10 Lapland, region Fb
3 Laptev Sea Ob
10 Lapua Ec
23 Lapy Gb
43 Lar Gd
70 Larache Da
84 Laramie Ec
85 Laredo Gf
28 Larino Ed
27 Larisa Bb
46 Larkana Be
27 Larnaka Dc
9 Larne Fb
11 Larvik Bd
20 Larzac, Causse du,
 mts. Bf
85 Las Cruces Ee
39 Las Khoreh Dd
85 Las Palmas Ac
55 Las Plumas Cg
90 Las Tres Marias,
 Is. C
85 Las Vegas, Nev. Cd
85 Las Vegas, New
 Mexico Fd
45 Lashio Hd
22 Lask Ec
40 Latakia (Al
 Ladhiqiyah) Bb
29 Latina Dd
8 Latheron Eb
61 Latrobe Cd
32 Latvia Dd
66 Lau or Eastern
 Group, Is. Hk
8 Lauder Fe
13 Lauden Ba
7 Launceston,
 England Cg
61 Launceston, Tas.Cd
62 Laura Bb
87 Laurel Ce
86 Laurium Cb
95 Lauro Müller Fe
13 Lausanne Ab
49 Laut I. Cd
21 Laval Cd
65 Laveron Cd
11 Lavik Bc
93 Lavras Gd
65 Lawlers Cd
71 Lawra Ef
86 Lawrence, Kan. Ad
89 Lawrence,Mass.Kc
67 Lawrence, N.Z. Bf
85 Lawton Ge
7 Laxey Ee
56 Laysan I. Eb
29 Lazio, prov. Dd
20 le Chambon-
 Feugerolles Cd
14 Le Creusot Ec
14 Le Havre Dc
70 Le Kef Ga
13 Le Locle Ab
13 Le Mans Dd
72 Le Marinel Df
20 Le Puy Bd
14 Le Touquet Db
14 Le Tréport Db
84 Leadville Ed
69 Lealui Eg
13 Leamington,
 Canada Dc
7 Leamington,
 England Fe
64 Learmonth Ad
86 Leavenworth Ad
85 Lebanon, Ind. Bd
88 Lebanon, Mo. Bd
88 Lebanon, Pa. Cd
29 Lecce Fg
21 Lecco, & L. di Hd
21 Lechtaler Alpen,
 mts. Fe
22 Leczyca Eb
7 Ledbury Fe
80 Leduc Cb
65 Leeds Fd
66 Leeton Cb
55 Leeuwarden Ea
65 Leeuwin C. Bc
91 Leeward Is. Fc
49 Legaspi Db

28 Leghorn
(Livorno) Cc
28 Legnago Cb
21 Legnano Gd
22 Legnica Dc
44 Leh Db
16 Lehe Cb
74 Lehututu Cb
7 Leicester & co. Fe
62 Leichhardt Ra. Cc
62 Leichhardt R. Ab
18 Leiden Db
60 Leigh Creek Ab
9 Leinster, prov. Ec
16 Leipzig Ec
26 Leiria Ab
11 Leirvik Bd
80 Leismer Cb
8 Leith Ke
9 Leitrim, co. Cb
9 Leixlip Ec
13 Léman, L. (L. of Geneva) Ab
12 Lemvig Bc
35 Lena, R. Pc
34 Leninabad Je
33 Leninakan Hg
32 Leningrad Fd
34 Leninogorsk Ld
34 Leninsk Kuznetski Ld
21 Leno Jd
14 Lens Eb
29 Lentini Ef
13 Lenzburg Ca
17 Leoben Fe
91 Leogane Dc
7 Leominster, England Ea
89 Leominster, U.S.A. Jc
91 Leon,Nicaragua Ad
90 Leon, Mexico Dc
26 León & prov. Aa
60 Leongatha Cc
65 Leonora Cd
72 Leopold II, L. Bd
91 Lerdo Db
26 Lérida Ca
27 Léros, I. Cb
8 Lerwick Inset
19 Les Cayes Dc
31 Leskovac Cd
8 Leslie Ed
32 Lesnoi Fb
75 Lesotho, st. Dc
91 Lesser Antilles Fd
49 Lesser Sunda Is. Ce
18 Lessines Cd
27 Lésvos, I. Cb
22 Leszno Dc
80 Lethbridge Cc
45 Letpadan He
9 Letterkenny Db
13 Leukerbad Bb
18 Leuven Dd
27 Levádhia Bb
18 Levanto Bb
8 Leven Fd
8 Leven, L. Ed
64 Levêque C. Cb
18 Leverkusen Fc
13 Levier Ab
60 Levin Ed
61 Levis Bb
23 Levoca Fd
27 Levkas, I. Bb
66 Levuka, I. Gk
7 Lewes Hg
8 Lewis, dist. Bb
81 Lewisporte Db
84 Lewiston Cb
84 Lewistown Eb
88 Lexington Ce
49 Leyte, I. Db
23 Lezajsk Gc
50 Lhasa Hd
51 Liaoning, prov. Gb
51 Liaoyang Gb
51 Liaoyuan Gb
74 Libebe, see Andara Ca
85 Liberal Fd
22 Liberec Cc
68 Liberia, rep. Aft.Be
19 Libreville De
68 Libya, king. Dc
38 Libyan Des. Bc
29 Licata Df
7 Lichfield Fe
75 Lichtenburg Dc
23 Lidzbark Fa
21 Liechtenstein, st. Hb
19 Liège Ed
17 Lienz Ee
32 Liepaja Dd
18 Lier Dc
13 Liestal Ba
19 Liétard Bd
9 Liévin Bd
71 Liguria, prov. Ge
28 Ligurian S. Bc
72 Likasi Df

72 Likati Cc
32 Likhoslavl Gd
14 Lille Eb
11 Lillehammer Cc
11 Lillesand Bd
80 Lillooet Bb
92 Lima, Peru Bd
88 Lima, U.S.A. Cd
23 Limanowa Fd
27 Limassol Dc
23 Limavady Ea
17 Limburg Cc
95 Limeira Fd
9 Limerick, & co. Cd
12 Limfjord Bc
27 Limnos, I. Cb
15 Limoges De
91 Limón Be
15 Limousin De
75 Limpopo, R. Db
7 Limuru Fd
42 Lina Ed
93 Linares, Chile Bf
90 Linares, Mexico Ec
7 Linaskes Db
6 Lincoln & co., England Gd
67 Lincoln, N.Z. De
84 Lincoln, U.S.A. Gc
21 Lindau Hb
11 Lindesnes Bd
73 Lindi Fe
27 Líndos Cb
49 Lingayen & G. Db
18 Lingen Gb
48 Lingga Arch. Bc
26 Lingres Bb
29 Linguaglossa Ef
70 Linguéré Be
11 Linköping Dd
7 Linney End Dd
51 Linsia Ec
17 Linz Fd
15 Lions, G. of Ff
29 Lipari, Is. Ee
13 Lipetsk Ge
23 Lipno Eb
18 Lippstadt Hc
73 Lira Ec
73 Lisala Cc
26 Lisbon Ab
9 Lisburn Eb
56 Lisianski I. Eb
33 Liski Ge
61 Lismore, Australia Da
9 Lismore, Ire. Cd
9 Lisnaskea Db
88 Listowel, Can. Ec
9 Listwel, Ire. Bd
61 Lithgow Db
27 Lithium, C. Bc
32 Lithuania Dd
22 Litomerice Cb
87 Little Abaco, I. Ef
15 Little Barrier I. Eb
21 Little Belt Cd
88 Little Current Eb
86 Little Falls, Minn. Bb
89 Little Falls, N.Y. Hc
46 Little Rann Cg
87 Little River De
87 Little Rock Be
7 Littlehampton Gg
51 Liuchow Ed
61 Liverpool, Australia Db
61 Liverpool, Can. Cb
6 Liverpool, Eng. Ed
24 Livingston Db
75 Livingstone Da
13 Livny Ge
55 Livramento Df
20 Livron Ce
7 Lizard Pt. Bg
28 Ljubljana Ea
11 Ljusdal Dc
6 Llandudno Dd
7 Llanelli Cf
7 Llanfyllin De
85 Llano Estacado Fe
69 Loango Df
69 Loangwa Fg
75 Lobatsi Dc
72 Lobito Af
13 Locarno Bb
8 Lochaber Cd
8 Lochmaddy Ac
69 Loch Haven Gd
61 Lockhart Cc
67 Lockport Fc
40 Lod (Lydda) Bd
46 Lodhran Cd
21 Lodi Hd
72 Lodja Cd
6 Lódz Ec
11 Lofoten Is. Cb
88 Logan Df
21 Logan, Mt. Db
88 Logansport Ad
26 Logroño Ba
19 Lohr Jd

20 Loire,R.&dept. Cd
15 Loire-Atlantiqué, dept. Dc
20 Loiret, dept. Ab
18 Lokeren Cc
72 Lokolama Bd
12 Lolland, I. Ee
30 Lom, Bulgaria Dd
11 Lom, Norway Bc
72 Lomami, R. Cd
21 Lombardia, prov. Hd
49 Lomblen I. Dd
49 Lombok, I. Cd
71 Lome Fg
72 Lombela & R. Cd
72 Lomé Ac
8 Lomond, L. Dd
23 Lomza Gb
81 London, Can. Ab
7 London, Eng. Hf
9 Londonerry & co. Eb
30 Lugoj Cc
85 Long Beach Ce
9 Long Eaton Fe
91 Long I., Bahamas Cb
26 Long I., U.S.A. Jd
48 Long Xuyen Bb
61 Longford, Australia Cd
9 Longford & co., Ireland Dc
81 Longlac Ab
62 Longreach Bc
87 Longview Be
19 Longwy Ee
18 Loningen Gb
20 Lons le Saunier Dc
10 Lonsdal Db
7 Looe Cg
65 Loongana De
9 Loop Hd. Bd
10 Lopphavet Ea
88 Lorain Ad
44 Loralai Bb
86 Lorca Bb
56 Lord Howe I. Ce
85 Lordsburg Ee
95 Lorena Ed
28 Loreto Dc
16 Lörient Bd
21 Lörrach Fb
14 Lorraine, reg. Gc
85 Los Alamos Ed
56 Los Angeles Ce
50 Los Mochis Cb
32 Loshkar Ola Jd
28 Lošinj, I. Eb
8 Lossiemouth Ec
20 Lot, R. Ae
73 LotagipiSwampEh
72 Loto Cd
13 Lötschberg Tunnel Bb
71 Louga Be
7 Loughborough Fe
7 Loughrea Cc
75 Louis Trichardt Eb
56 Louisiade Arch. Cd
83 Louisiana, st. Dc
88 Louisville Ce
75 Lourdes Cf
72 Lourenço Marques Ec
9 Louth, co. Ec
52 Lovat Fd
11 Lovisa Fc
23 Low Tatra, mt. Ed
72 Lowa Dd
89 Lowell Kc
90 Lower California Bb
67 Lower Hutt Ed
35 Lower Tunguska, R. Mc
7 Lowestoft Je
23 Lowitz Eb
56 Loyalty Is. De
51 Loyang Fc
20 Lozere, dept. Be
72 Luanda Ae
48 Luang Prabang Bb
73 Luangwa, R. Ef
73 Luanshya Df
73 Luapula, R. Df
72 Lubaczów Gc
22 Luban Cc
23 Lubartów Gc
33 Lubawa Eb
85 Lubbock Fe
16 Lubeck Db
22 Lubicz Bb
23 Lublin Gc
33 Lubny Fe
72 Lubumbashi Df
72 Lubutu Dd
28 Lucca Cc
24 Lucena Bb
23 Lucenec Ed
9 Lucera Fd
51 Lucknow Jd

16 Luckenwalde Eb
47 Lucknow He
18 Lüdenscheid Gc
74 Lüderitz (Angra Pequena) Bc
46 Ludhiana Ec
88 Ludington Bb
7 Ludlow Ee
11 Ludvika Dc
19 Ludwigsburg Jf
19 Ludwigshafen He
72 Luebo Ce
72 Lufira, R. De
87 Lufkin Be
32 Luga Ed
13 Lugano Cb
33 Lugansk (Voro-shilovgrad) Gf
73 Lugenda, R. Ff
73 Lugh Ferrandi Gc
26 Lugo, Spain Aa
26 Lugo, Italy Cb
30 Lugoj Cc
39 Luhaiya Dd
21 Luino Gd
72 Luisa Ce
72 Lukenie, R. Bd
72 Lukolela Bd
23 Luków Gc
10 Lulea Eb
27 Lüleburgaz Ca
72 Lulonga, R. Bc
72 Lulua, R. Ce
72 Luluabourg Ce
45 Lumding Gc
67 Lumsden Bf
11 Lund Cd
7 Lundy I. Cf
16 Lüneburg Db
16 Lüneburg HeathCb
18 Lünen Gc
19 Lunéville Ff
46 Luni Df
33 Luninets Ee
73 Luofo Dc
9 Lurgan Eb
69 Lusaka Eg
72 Lusambo Cd
73 Lushoto Fd
51 Lü-ta (Port Arthur-Dairen)Gc
7 Luton Gf
33 Lutsk Ee
4 Luxembourg, st. Gf
38 Luxor Cc
13 Luzern Ca
95 Luziania Fc
22 Luzicke Hory Cb
49 Luzon, I. Db
35 Lvov Df
35 Lyakhov Is. Rb
46 Lyallpur Dc
10 Lycksele Dc
7 Lydd Hg
40 Lydda (Lod) Bd
75 Lydenburg Ec
67 Lyell Dd
7 Lyme Regis Eg
7 Lymington Fg
88 Lynchburg Ff
60 Lyndhurst Ab
89 Lynn Kc
20 Lynn Lake Db
20 Lyon (Lyons) Cd
20 Lyonnais, dist. Cd
11 Lysekil Cd
67 Lyttelton De
33 Lyudinovo Fe

62 Mackenzie R., Australia Cc
78 Mackenzie, R., Canada Eb
78 Mackenzie, terr. Fb
88 Mackinaw City Cb
82a McKinley, mt. Cb
61 Macksville Db
61 Maclean Da
75 Maclear Dd
80 McLennan Cb
80 Macleod Cc
96 McMurdo Sd. Kb
8 Macnee Bd
29 Macomer Bd
20 Mâcon, France Cc
87 Macon, U.S.A. De
72 Macondo Cf
3 Macquarie I. Ph
62 Madagascar, I. Gg
62 Madang Gh
43 Madaripur Ng
68 Madeira, I. Ab
90 Madera Cb
4 Madhya Pradesh, st. Hg
72 Madimba Ad
72 Madingou Ad
88 Madison, Ind. Ce
86 Madison, Wis. Cc
88 Madisonville Bf
49 Madjene Cd
44 Madras, & st. Df
90 Madre, de la Sc
93 Madre de Dios I.Bh
26 Madrid Ba
48 Madura, I. Cd
44 Madurai Dg
55 Maebashi Cc
80 Mafeking, Can. Db
75 Mafeking, Cape Province Dc
61 Mafra Cc
73 Mafia, I. Fe
95 Mafra Fe
35 Magadan Sd
73 Magadi Fd
75 Magato Hills Eb
71 Magburaka Cg
39 Magdala Cd
81 Magdalen Is. Cb
94 Magdalena Cb
16 Magdeburg Db
48 Magelang Cd
9 Magellan's str. Bh
21 Magenta Gd
20 Mageride, Monts de la, mts. Be
21 Maggiore, Lago Gd
96 Magnetic South Pole Jc
34 Magnitogorsk Hd
43 Magos Jd
66 Mahabaleshwar Dk
48 Mahakam R. Cc
46 Maharashtra,st. Ce
44 Mahé Df
67 Maheno Cf
26 Mahón Cb
43 Maidan-i-Naftan Fc
7 Maidstone Hf
68 Maiduguri Dd
33 Maikop Hg
38 Maimana Fb
83 Maine, st. Gb
14 Maine-et-Loire, dept. Cc
43 Mainpuri Fd
19 Mainz Hd
31 Maira, R. Fe
70 Maison Carrée Fa
43 Maitland Db
32 Maizuru Cc
26 Majorca, see Mallorca, I. Cb
69 Majunga Gg
71 Maka-Koulibentane Cf
75 Makarikari Salt-pan Cb
79 Makasar Cd
49 Makasar Str. Cd
71 Makeni Cg
33 Makeyevka Gf
33 Makhachkala Jg
73 Makindu Fd
46 Makó Fc
33 Makov Ee
43 Makran, prov. Hd
75 Makurazaki Bd
71 Makurdi Cg
44 Makwar Coast Df
48 Malacca Bc
48 Malacca, str. of Bc
84 Malad City Dc
26 Maladetta, Mt. Ca
36 Málaga Bb
69 Malagasy Rep. Gg
75 Malakal Ed
73 Malakand Ec
32 Malang Cd
82 Malanje Be
11 Malaren, L. Dd
75 Malatiele Dd

42 Malatya Db
69 Malawi Fg
48 Malay Pen. Ac
37 Malaya, st. Oj
43 Malaysia, st. Bc
65 Malcolm Cd
18 Maldegem Cc
44 Maldive Is. Cg
7 Maldon Hd
42 Maléa, C. Bb
46 Malegaon Eh
69 Mali, st. Df
73 Malindi, Kenya Gd
75 Malindi, Rhod. Da
8 Mallaig Cd
26 Mallorca (Majorca),
I. Cb
9 Mallow Cd
10 Malmberget Fd
19 Malmedy Fd
7 Malmesbury, Cape
Province Bd
7 Malmesbury,
England Ff
11 Malmö Cd
43 Maloshulka Gc
42 Malta, I. Ec
74 Maltahohe Bb
44 Maivan Ce
1 Malvern Ee
7 Mamou Cg
6 Man, I. of Ce
49 Manado Dc
43 Managua Ad
61 Manapouri Af
43 Manass Cb
43 Manaus Cc
6 Manchester,
England Ed
89 Manchester,
U.S.A. Jc
37 Manchuria, reg. Qe
11 Mandal Bd
45 Mandalay Hd
3 Mandeb, Bab el,
Str. of Dd
47 Mandla Hg
45 Mandsaur Ef
46 Mandvi Bg
29 Manfredonia Ed
60 Mangalore,
Austral. Cc
9 Mangalore,
India Cf
66 Mangaweka Ef
66 Mangonui Da
50 Mangyai Dc
44 Manicoré Cc
92 Manifa Fd
7 Manikput Hf
49 Manila Db
61 Manilla Db
45 Manipur Gd
27 Manisa Cb
88 Manistee Bb
88 Manistique Bb
88 Manitoba, L. Bb
78 Manitoba, prov.Ec
88 Manitoulin I. Db
88 Manitowoc Bb
92 Manizales Bb
66 Manjhand Bf
88 Mankato Bc
11 Manly Db
46 Manmad Eh
44 Mannar, & G. Dg
11 Mannheim He
49 Manokwari Ef
77 Mansel I. Jb
70 Mansfield,
Australia Cc
88 Mansfield,
U.S.A. Dd
38 Mansura Cb
88 Manton Cb
31 Mantova Jd
92 Manturovo Hd
62 Manus I. Gg
63 Many Peaks Dc
73 Manyara, L. Fd
38 Manych Hf
15 Manyoni Ee
46 Manzai Cb
41 Manzala, L. Bb
91 Manzanillo,
Cuba Cb
90 Manzanillo,
Mexico Dd
62 Maprik Fg
42 Maqdala Cd
43 Magna Dd
74 Maquaile Cd
93 Mar del Plata Df
62 Maracaibo & L. Ba
92 Maracay Ca
43 Maragheh Fb
92 Marajo I. Ec
65 Maralinga Ed
92 Maranhao, st. Ec
63 Maranoa R. Cd
27 Marathón Bb
7 Marazion Bg
92 Marbat Ed
64 Marble Bar Bc

18 Marburg Hd
7 March He
28 Marche, reg. Dc
8 Maree, L. Cc
62 Mareeba Cb
85 María Fe
92 Margarita Ca
7 Margate Hj
73 Margherita Gc
12 Mariager &
Fjord Dc
65 Mariana or
Ladrone Is. Cc
91 Marianao Bb
14 Maribo, co. Ee
28 Maribor Ea
27 Maric, R. Ca
11 MarieGalante, I. Fc
62 Marienburg Fg
74 Mariental Bb
11 Mariestad Cd
87 Marietta, Ga. De
88 Marietta,W.Va. Ee
35 Mariinsk Ld
88 Marinette Bb
95 Maringa Ed
88 Marion, Ind. Cd
88 Marion, Mich. Cb
88 Marion, Ohio Dd
31 Marisa, R. Ed
40 Marj Uyun Bc
7 Market Drayton Ee
7 Market
Harborough Ge
6 Market
Weighton Gd
96 Markham, Mt. Ja
23 Marlbork Ea
7 Marlborough Ff
7 Marlborough,
dist. Dd
27 Marmara, S. of Ca
27 Marmaris Cb
19 Marne, R. Ce
60 Maroona Bc
57 Marquesas Is. Gd
86 Marquette Cb
70 Marrakesh Db
60 Marree Aa
75 Marromeu Fa
70 Marsa Fatma Dd
29 Marsala Df
15 Marseilles Ff
71 Marshall, Lib. Cg
87 Marshall,U.S.A.Be
56 Marshall Is. Dc
86 Marshalltown Bc
12 Marstal De
11 Marstrand Cd
45 Martaban, & G.
of He
91 Marti Cb
67 Martinborough Ed
91 Martinique, L. Fd
88 Martins Fy Ed
89 Martinsburg Fe
88 Martinsville,
Ind. Be
88 Martinsville, Va. Ff
66 Marton Ed
55 Marugame Bd
66 Marupa Fc
66 Marupara Fc
34 Mary Jf
82 Maryborough,
Queens. Dd
60 Maryborough,
Vic. Bc
83 Maryland, st. Fc
84 Marysville Bd
68 Marzuq Dc
73 Masaka Ed
52 Masan Bb
91 Masaya Ad
49 Masbate & I. Db
70 Mascara Fa
75 Maseru Dc
43 Mashhad Hb
74 Mashonaland,
dist. Ea
73 Masindi Ec
38 Mashra .G. of Ed
41 Masjed Soley-
man Fc
43 Maskel, R. Jd
86 Mason City Bc
11 Mass Cd
28 Massa Cb
28 Massa
Maritima Cc
83 Massachusetts,
st. Fb
75 Massangena Eb
89 Massena Hb
20 Massif Central,
plat. Bd
67 Masterton Ed
44 Mastuj Ca
75 Masuda Bd
44 Masulipatam Ee
75 Masurian Lakes Fb
75 Matabeleland,
dist. Da

51 Matadi Fb
72 Matadi Ae
43 Matagalpa Ad
71 Mataham Ce
90 Matamoros Eb
27 Matane Cb
82aMatanuska Db
49 Matanzas Bb
27 Matapan, see
Tainaron Bb
49 Mataram Cd
26 Mataró Ad
67 Mataura isg
90 Matehuala Dc
29 Matera Fd
30 Mateszalka Db
46 Mathura Fe
15 Matiesfontein Cd
92 Mato Grosso st. Dd
75 Matobe Ed
73 Matopo Hills Db
55 Matsue Bc
55 Matsumae Db
55 Matsumoto Cc
55 Matsuyama Bd
55 Matsuzaka Cd
13 Matterhorn, mt. Bc
31 Mau Ranipur Gf
19 Maubeuge Cd
55 Maubin He
23 Mauer L. Fa
57 Maui I. Fb
57 Maun Ca
83bMaurua Loa, vol. Dc
20 Maurienne, dist. Ed
68 Mauritania, rep. Bc
3 Mauritius, I. Kg
37 Maushij Dd
96 Mawson Ec
51 Mayaguana, I. Db
19 Mayaguez Ec
8 Maybole De
87 Mayfield Cd
9 Maynooth Ec
50 Mayo, co. Bc
38 Mazari-i-Sharif Fb
90 Mazatlan Cc
32 Mazelkia Dd
75 Mazoe Ea
29 Mazzard Df
75 Mbabane Ea
73 Mbale Ec
71 Mbaimayo Hh
72 Mbandaka Bc
74 M'Bomu, R. Cc
72 Mbuji-Mayi Ce
78 M'Clintock
Chan. Ga
78 M'Clure Str. Ea
85 Mead, L. Dd
88 Meadville Ed
9 Meath, co. Ec
14 Meaux Ec
42 Mecca De
18 Mechelen Dc
71 Mechéria Eb
48 Medan Ac
70 Médéa Fa
92 Medellín Bb
71 Mederdra He
36 Medias Eb
88 Medicine Hat Cb
42 Medina,
Saudi Arabia De
26 Medina, Spain Ba
26 Medinaceli Ba
4 Mediterranean
Sea Jh
15 Medoc, dist. Ce
65 Meekatharra Bd
46 Meerut Fd
27 Megara Bb
46 Mehsana Dg
51 Meihsien Fd
45 Meiktila Hd
13 Meitingen Cb
26 Meissen Ec
92 Meiyanga Ab
20 Mejean, Causse,
mts. Be
46 Mekele Cd
46 Mekhtar Bc
46 Meknès Db
48 Mekong R. Ea
49 Melalap Cc
60 Melbourne Bc
21 Melegnano Hd
29 Melfi Ed
44 Melfort Db
70 Melilla Ea
33 Melitopol Gf
95 Melo Ef
7 Melsetter Ea
7 Melton
Mowbray Ge
26 Melville Bb
62 Melville B. Aa
71 Melville C. Ba
64 Melville I.,
Australia Ea
78 Melville I., Can. Fa
79 Melville Pen. Jb
69 Memba Gg

21 Memmingen Jb
87 Memphis Cd
42 Menaal Ahmadi Fd
88 Menasha Ab
27 Menderes, R. Cb
93 Mendoza, &
prov. Cf
27 Menemen Cb
29 Menfi Df
48 Menggala Bd
48 Menin Cd
60 Menindee Bb
45 Menkong Hc
88 Menominee Bb
26 Menorca, I. Cb
48 Mentawai Is. Ad
21 Menton Ff
70 Menzel Temime Ha
55 Menzies Cd
18 Meppen Gb
21 Merano Kc
45 Merauke Gg
39 Merca De
44 Mercara Df
44 Mercedes De
66 Mercer Eb
45 Mergui & Arch. Hf
90 Merida, Mexico Gc
26 Merida, Spain Ab
92 Merida, Cord. de Bb
87 Meridan Ce
89 Meriden Jd
7 Merioneth, co. De
16 Merksem Dc
65 Merredin Be
86 Merrill Cb
7 Mersea, I. Jf
16 Merseburg Dc
6 Mersey, R. Ed
27 Mersin Db
7 Merthyr Tydfil Df
19 Merzig Fe
85 Mesa De
7 Mesewa Cd
73 Meshra er Req Db
27 Mesolóngion Bb
42 Mesopotamia,
reg. Ec
29 Messina, Italy Ee
75 Messina, Trans. Db
27 Messini, G. of Bb
28 Mestre Db
73 Metehil Fa
8 Methil Ed
67 Methven Ce
28 Metlika Eb
44 Metró Gf
42 Mexicali Aa
90 Mexico Ed
72 Mexico, Rep. Hf
72 Mexico, G. of Kf
32 Mezen & R. Hb
36 Mézières De
30 Mezotur Cb
46 Mhow Eg
87 Miami Df
43 Mianeh Fb
46 Mianwali Cb
71 Miaoli Gd
88 Michigan, L. Bb
83 Michigan, st. Eb
88 Michigan City Bd
81 Michipicoten
Harb. Ab
31 Michurin Fd
73 Middelburg Hc
70 Middle Atlas,
mts. Db
75 Middelburg, Cape
Province Dd
18 Middelburg,
Netherlands Cc
75 Middelburg,
Transvaal Dc
12 Middlefart Cd
6 Middlesbrough Fc
55 Middlesex Gd
89 Middletown,
Conn. Jd
89 Middletown,
New York Hd
88 Middletown,
Ohio Ce
7 Midhurst Gg
88 Midland, Can. Fb
55 Midland, Mich. Cc
88 Midland, Tex. Fe
65 Midland
Junction Be
9 Midleton Ce
8 Midlothian, co. Ee
47 Midnapore Lg
56 Midway I. Eb
7 Midye Cb
55 Mie, pref. Cd
38 Miechcód Db
22 Miedzychod Db
23 Miedzyrzec Dc
23 Miedzyrzecz Cb
30 Miercurea Cluc Eb
26 Miéres Aa
55 Mihara Bd
11 Mikkeli Fc
27 Mikonos Cb

21 Milano (Milan) Hd
27 Milás Cb
7 Mildenhall He
60 Mildura Bb
63 Miles Dd
84 Miles City Eb
89 Milford He
7 Milford Haven Bf
70 Miliana Fc
65 Miling Be
20 Millau Be
18 Milieliand
Kanal Gb
81 Millerton Db
60 Millicent Bc
27 Milos Bb
7 Milton Cg
9 Milton Malbay Cd
88 Milwaukee Bc
43 Minab Hd
26 Minamata Be
92 Minas Gerais, st. Ed
45 Minbu Ge
21 Mincio, R. Jd
49 Mindanao,I.& S.Dc
21 Mindel, R. Ja
16 Minden Hb
49 Mindoro, I. Db
72 Mindouli Ad
7 Minehead Df
81 Mingan Ca
39 Mingary Bb
54 Mingenew Bd
26 Minho Aa
31 Minna Gg
86 Minneapolis Bc
80 Minnedosa Eb
83 Minnesota, st. Db
26 Miño, R. Aa
84 Minot Fb
18 Minsen Ga
33 Minsk Ee
23 Minsk
Mazowiecki Fb
35 Minusinsk Md
38 Minya Cb
54 Minya Konka,
mt. Ed
81 Miquelon I. Cb
44 Miraj Ce
46 Miram Shah Cb
94 Miranda, Braz. Dd
26 Miranda, Spain Ba
21 Mirandola Ke
20 Mirecourt Ea
43 Mirfa Ge
48 Miri Cc
96 Mirny Fc
46 Mirpur Khas Df
47 Mirzapur Jf
43 Misbaah Fd
51 Mishan Hb
88 Mishawaka Bd
30 Miskolc Ca
43 Misool, I. Ed
86 Mississippi, R. Bd
83 Mississippi, st. Fc
84 Missouri, R. Eb
83 Missouri, st. Dc
81 Mistassini, L. Ba
29 Mistretta Ef
3 Mitchell,
Australia Cd
84 Mitchell, U.S.A. Gc
62 Mitchell R. Bb
9 Mitchelstown Cd
27 Mitilini Cb
55 Mito Dc
30 Mitrovica Bc
54 Mitsugo, I. (Tori
Shima) Cd
61 Mittagong Db
13 Mittenwald Fa
21 Mirzick Ac
54 Miyagi, pref. Dc
54 Miyake Jima I. Cd
54 Miyako Dc
55 Miyakonojo Bd
54 Miyasu Cc
55 Miyazaki, &
pref. Bd
22 Mladá Boleslav Cb
10 Mo Cb
23 Mlawa Fb
54 Mobaye Cc
86 Moberly Bd
87 Mobile Ce
84 Mobridge Fb
39 Mocha Dd
73 Mocimboa da
Praia Gf
72 Modane Ed
21 Modena Je
85 Modesto Bd
29 Modica Ef
8 Moffat Ed
39 Mogadishu De
45 Mogaung Hc
95 Mogi das Cruzes Fd
95 Mogi Mirim Fd
33 Mogilev Fe

33 Mogilev
  Podolski Ef
22 Mogiño Db
30 Monacs Bc
9 Mohill Ec
81 Moisie Ca
85 Mojave Des. Ce
55 Moji Bd
66 Mokai Ec
52 Mokpo Bb
18 Mol Ec
29 Mola Fd
33 Moldavia Ef
10 Molde Bc
29 Molfetta Fd
28 Molise, reg. Ed
92 Mollendo Bd
10 Molndal Cd
33 Molodechno Ee
32 Mologa Fd
83b Molokai, I. Cb
61 Molong Cb
75 Molopo, R. Cc
45 Molucca S. & Is. Dc
73 Mombasa Fd
54 Mometsu Db
31 Momchilgrad Ee
12 Mön Ef
91 Mona Pass. Ec
21 Monaco, st. Ff
9 Monaghan, & co. Eb
21 Moncalieri Cb
18 Mönchenglad-bach Fc
90 Monclova Db
81 Moncton Cb
26 Mondego Aa
21 Mondovi Fe
88 Monessen Fd
9 Moneymore Eb
28 Monfalcone Db
47 Monghyr Lf
37 Mongolia, Rep. Oe
8 Monifieth Fd
72 Monkoto Cd
7 Monmouth, co. Ef
21 Monnow De
29 Monopoli Fd
28 Monreale Dc
87 Monroe, Canada Be
88 Monroe, U.S.A. Dd
71 Monrovia Cg
9 Mons Cd
15 Mont Blanc Ge
20 Mont Cenis Frejus Tunnel Cf
20 Mont d'Or Tunnel Ec
20 Mont Dore, mt. Ad
14 Mont St. Michel Cc
74 Montagu Cd
82a Montague I. Dc
26 Montalbán Ba
21 Montalcino Cc
52 Montana, st. Bb
20 Montargis Aa
15 Montauban De
20 Montbéliard Eb
20 Montceau les Mines Cc
21 Monte Carlo Ff
91 Monte Cristi Dc
13 Monte Rosa, mt. Bc
51 Monte S. Angelo Ed
91 Montego Bay Cc
20 Montélimar Ce
90 Montemorelos Eb
31 Montenegro, / dist. Bd
28 Montepylciano Cc
20 Montereau Aa
85 Monterey Bd
90 Monterrey Db
95 Montes Claros Gc
86 Montevideo, U.S.A. Ac
93 Montevideo, Uruguay Df
87 Montgomery, U.S.A. Ce
7 Montgomery, & co., Wales Ee
19 Montigny les Metz Fe
14 Montmorillon Dd
89 Montpelier Jb
20 Montpellier Bf
81 Montreal Hb
14 Montreuil Db
13 Montreux Ab
8 Montrose Fd
91 Montserrat, I. Fc
45 Monywa Hd
41 Monza Hd
75 Monze Da
65 Moora Be
8 Moore L. Bd
74 Mooreesburg Bd
8 Moorfoot Hills Ee
86 Moorhead Ab
80 Moose Jaw Db
83 Moosomin Dc
81 Moosonee Aa

71 Mopti Ef
11 Mora Cc
46 Moradabad Gd
22 Morava, R. Dd
30 Morava, R. Cc
22 Moravian Heights Cd
8 Moray, co. Ec
8 Moray Firth Ec
80 Morden Ec
6 Morecambe Ec
61 Moree Ca
90 Morelia Dd
26 Morena, Sa. de Bb
63 Moreton B. & I. Dd
21 Morgan Ab
87 Morgan City Bf
88 Morgantown Ed
60 Moriarty's Ra. Ca
54 Morioka Dc
44 Mormugao Ce
62 Mornington I. Ab
26 Morobe Gb
73 Morocco, king. Bb
73 Morogoro Fd
70 Moron Cb
69 Morondavo Gh
49 Morotai, I. Dc
33 Morozovsk Hf
95 Morrinhos Fc
66 Morrinsville Eb
88 Morristown Df
12 Mors, I. Bc
3 Morshansk He
21 Mortara Gd
7 Morte Pt. Cf
20 Morteau Eb
94 Morteros Cf
61 Moruy Dc
20 Morvan, Mts. du Cc
8 Morven, dist. Cd
84 Moscow, U.S.A. Cb
32 Moscow, U.S.S.R. Gd
20 Moselle, R. Eb
67 Mosgiel Cf
73 Moshi Fd
11 Mosquito Coast Bd
61 Moss Vale Db
72 Mossaka Bd
69 Mossâmedes Gg
67 Mossburn Bf
74 Mossel Bay Cd
22 Most Bc
70 Mostaganem Fa
28 Mostar Ec
95 Mostardas Ef
42 Mosul Eb
73 Mota Fd
94 Motacucito Cc
81 Motala Dd
8 Motherwell Ee
47 Motihari Ke
87 Motril Bb
67 Motueka Dd
20 Moulins Bc
45 Moulmein He
88 Moundsville Fe
60 Mount Barker, S. Austral. Ac
65 Mount Barker, W. Austral. Be
88 Mount Clemens Dc
62 Mount Carbet Ad
66 Mount Eden Eb
90 Mount Gambier Bc
47 Mount Golds-worthy Bc
62 Mount Isa Ac
65 Mount Magnet Bd
66 Mount Maunganui Fb
90 Mount Morgan Dc
65 Mount Morgans Cd
82 Mount Mulligan Bb
63 Mount Perry Dd
60 Mount Pleasant, Australia Ab
88 Mount Pleasant, U.S.A. Cc
38 Mount Sinai, & Pen. Cc
65 Mount Sir Samuel Cd
44 Mount Tom Price Bc
88 Mount Vernon Dd
9 Mountmellick Dc
92 Moura, Braz. Cc
26 Moura, Port. Ab
9 Mourne, Mts. Eb
12 Mouscron Cd
13 Mouthe Ee
66 Moutohora Fc
9 Moville Da
71 Moyamba Cg
69 Mozambique Gg
69 Mozambique, Port. terr. Fg
69 Mozambique Chan. Gg
31 Mozdok Jg
33 Mozy Ee
74 Mpanda Ee

70 Msaken Ha
73 M'Salu, R. Ff
31 Mtsensk Ge
73 Mtwara Gf
92 Muana Bd
48 Muaraenim Bd
73 Mubende Ec
8 Mucki Bd
27 Mudanya Ca
61 Mudgee Cb
27 Mudurnu Da
73 Mufulira Df
37 Muğla Cb
72 Mugtad Da
47 Mugu Jd
16 Mühlhausen Dc
9 Muine Bheag Ed
8 Muirkirk De
39 Mukalla Dd
51 Mukden, (Shenyang) Gb
44 Muktsar Ec
90 Mulege Bb
81 Mulgrave Cb
26 Mulhacen Bb
16 Mülheim Bc
21 Mulhouse Fb
8 Mull, I. Cd
48 Müller, mts. Cc
62 Muller Ra. Fb
9 Mullet Pen. Ab
65 Mullewa Bd
9 Mullingar Dc
61 Mullumbimby Da
46 Multan Cc
48 Mun R. Bb
49 Muna, I. Dd
46 Munabao Cf
21 München (Munich) Ka
88 Muncie Cd
73 Mungbere Dc
61 Mungindi Ca
72 Munhango Bf
21 Munich, see München
35 Munku-Sadyk, Mt. Nd
18 Münster, see.
9 Münster, prov., Ireland Ed
10 Muonio Eb
10 Muonio, R. Eb
32 Murashi Jd
67 Murchison Dd
65 Murchison R. Bd
26 Murcia & prov. Bb
30 Mures, R. Db
53 Murgon Dd
32 Murmansk Fb
32 Murom Hd
54 Muroran Db
60 Murray Bridge Ac
60 Murray R. Bb
60 Murrayville Bc
60 Murrumbidgee R. Cb
61 Murrumburrah Cb
61 Murrurundi Db
13 Murten Bb
65 Musgrave Ra. Ed
72 Mushie Bd
86 Muskegon Bc
87 Muskogee Ad
39 Mussali, mt. Dd
14 Mustagh P. Ca
61 Muswellbrook Db
27 Mut Db
74 Mutanna Ba
51 Mutankiang Gb
72 Mutshatsha Cf
12 Mutsu, B. Db
46 Muttaburra Bc
42 Muwaih Ee
46 Muzaffarnagar Fd
47 Muzaffarpur Ke
44 Mugtadh, mt. Cc
73 Mwanza Ed
72 Mwea Cd
73 Mwenga Dd
73 Mweru, & Swamp De
45 Myaungmya Ge
49 Myitkyina Hc
47 Mymensingh Nf
22 Myslibörz Db
44 Mysore, & st. Df

91 Nacaome Ad
73 Nachingwea Ff
90 Nacozari Ca
46 Nadiad Dg
30 Nadiac Cb
11 Naerbö Bd
12 Naestyed Ed
71 Nafada Hf
13 Näfels Da
38 Nag Hammadi Cc
49 Naga Db
45 Naga Hills Hc
45 Nagaland Gc
55 Nagano & pref. Cc
55 Nagaoka Cc
46 Nagar Parkar Cf
55 Nagasaki & prefecture Ad
55 Nagaur De
44 Nagercoil Dg
55 Nagoya Cc
46 Nagpur Gh
30 Nagykanizsa Ab
55 Nagykorös Bb
47 Nainpur Hg
8 Nairn & co. Ec
73 Nairobi Fd
73 Naivasha Fd
43 Najafabad Gc
55 Nakano Shima Ad
55 Nakatsu Bd
48 Nakhon Ratchasima (Korat) Bb
33 Nakhichevan Jh
81 Nakina Aa
80 Nakomis Db
74 Nakop Cc
12 Nakskov Ee
73 Nakuru Fd
69 Nalolo Eg
48 Nam Dinh Ba
50 Nam Tso, L. Dc
34 Namangan Ke
73 Namapa Ff
74 Namaqualand, dist. Bc
63 Nambour Dd
50 Namcha Barwa Dd
54 Namib Des. Bb
52 Namlea Dd
52 Nampo Bb
10 Namsen, R. Cc
10 Namsos Cc
19 Namur Dd
74 Namutoni Ba
12 Namyslow Dc
48 Nan Bb
84 Nan R. Bb
50 Nanaim, mts. Dc
80 Nanaimo Bc
63 Nanango Dd
55 Nanao Cc
51 Nanchang Fd
51 Nanchung Ec
14 Nancy Gc
46 Nander Fj
46 Nandi Gk
46 Nandurbar Eh
51 Nanking Fc
65 Nannine Bd
51 Nanning Ed
51 Nanping Fd
15 Nantes Cd
89 Nantucket I. Kd
51 Nanyang, Fc
26 Nao, C. de la Cb
46 Napier Ej
29 Naples (Napoli) Ed
55 Nara & pref. Cd
60 Naracoorte Bc
50 Naradhan Cb
47 Narayanganj Ng
7 Narberth Cf
15 Narbonne Ef
29 Nardo Gd
65 Naretha Ce
23 Naserw, R. Fb
61 Narrabri Cb
65 Narrandera Cb
65 Narrogin Be
46 Narromine Cb
55 Naruto Bd
52 Narva Ed
32 Narvik Db
88 Narwalk Dd
32 Naryan-Mar Kb
67 Naseby Cf
89 Nashua Kc
88 Nashville Bf
28 Nasice Gb
90 Nasirabad Fd
91 Nassau, I. Cb
49 Nassau mts. Fd
92 Natal, Braz. Fc
75 Natal, prov. South Africa Ec
81 Natashquan Ca
86 Nathdwara Df
95 Natividade Fb
73 Natron, L. Fd
55 Natuna Is. Ac
66 Naturaliste C. Ae

16 Naumburg Dc
40 Naur Bd
56 Nauru, I. Dd
92 Nauta Bc
32 Nautsi Eb
87 Navarre, prov. Ba
87 Navasota Ae
90 Navojoa Cb
27 Navpaktos Bb
27 Navplion Bb
46 Navsari Dh
46 Nawabshah De
47 Nawakot Ke
46 Nawalgarh Ee
27 Naxos Cb
14 Nay Bend Gd
28 Nazareth Bc
92 Nazas, R. Db
7 Naze, The Jf
73 Ndola Df
9 Neagh, L. Eb
83c Near Is. Ab
7 Neath Df
62 Nebraska, st. Cb
76 Necker I. Eb
56 Necochea Df
93 Necochea Df
7 Needham Market Je
7 Needles, The Fg
80 Neepawa Eb
70 Nefta Gb
44 Negapattinam Df
45 Negrais, C. Ge
49 Negros, I. Db
43 Neh Hc
45 Nehbandan Hc
68 Neheim Gc
73 Nekemte Fb
46 Nellore Df
88 Nelson, Canada Cc
67 Nelson, N.Z. Dd
67 Nelson, disc. King. Ge
21 Neu Ulm Ja
16 Neubrandenburg burg Eb
13 Neuchâtel Aa
13 Neuchâtel, L. de Ab
20 Neufchâteau Da
14 Neufchâtel Dc
13 Neumünster Ca
16 Neumünster Ca
19 Neunkirchen Ge
93 Neuquen, prov. Cf
16 Neuruppin Eb
16 Neuss Fc
20 Neussargues Bd
16 Neustrelitz Eb
19 Neuwied Gd
87 Nevada Bd
92 Nevada, Sa. Bb
82 Nevada, st. Bc
32 Nevel Fd
20 Nevers Bc
33 Nevinnomyssk Hg
91 Nevis, I. Fc
27 Nevsehir Db
New Albany Ce
92 New Cumnock Be
81 New Glasgow Cb
62 New Guinea, Terr. of Gg
83 New Hampshire, st. Fb
84 New Hanover, I. Hg
89 New Haven Jd
56 New Hebrides Dd
86 New Iberia Be
62 New Ireland, I. Hg
83 New Jersey, st. Fc
83 New Kensington Fd
89 New London Jd
90 New Mexico, st. Cc
61 New Norfolk Cd

87 New Orleans Bf
88 New
  Philadelphia Hd
66 New Plymouth Ec
91 New Providence
  I. Ca
7 New Quay Ce
7 New Radnor De
9 New Ross Ed
35 New Siberian Is. Qb
59 New South Wales,
  st. He
86 New Ulm Bc
80 New
  Westminster Bc
89 New York Jd
83 New York, st. Fb
66 New Zealand,
  st. Dc
73 Newala Ff
89 Newark, N.J. Hd
89 Newark, N.Y. Gc
89 Newark, Ohio Dd
88 Sewaygo Cc
89 Newburgh Hd
7 Newbury Ff
89 Newburyport Kc
61 Newcastle,
  Australia Db
81 Newcastle, Can. Cb
6 Newcastle, Eng. Fb
9 Newcastle, Ire. Bd
75 Newcastle, Nat. Dc
9 Newcastle, N.
  Ire. Fb
64 Newcastle
  Waters Eb
8 Newcastleton Fe
65 Newdegate Be
79 Newfoundland,
  prov. Lc
7 Newhaven Hg
7 Newmarket Fe
87 Newport, Ark. Bd
7 Newport, Eng. Fg
9 Newport, Ire. Bc
89 Newport, R.I. Kd
8 Newport, Scot. Fd
7 Newport, Wales Ef
89 Newport News Gf
7 Newquay Eg
9 Newry Eb
86 Newton, Iowa Bc
89 Newton, Mass. Kc
7 Newton Abbot Dg
7 Newtown
  Forbes Dc
8 Newtown
  Stewart
6 Newtownards Fb
35 Nezhin Fe
43 Neyriz Gd
41 Neyshabur Hb
33 Nezhin Fe
74 Ngami, Former
  L. Cb
68 Ngaoundere De
67 Ngapara Cf
71 Nguru Hf
60 Nhill Bc
83 Niagara Falls Fc
71 Niamey Ff
48 Nias, I. Ac
77 Nicaragua, rep. Kg
91 Nicaragua, L. Ad
29 Nicastre Fe
21 Nice Ff
45 Nicobar Is. Gg
29 Nicosia, Italy Ef
27 Nicosia, Cyprus Db
91 Nicoya Pen. Ad
81 Niedersachsen,
  prov. Hb
16 Nienburg Cb
91 Nieuw Nickerie Db
18 Nieuwpoort Bc
20 Nievre, dept. Bb
27 Niğde Db
71 Niger Delta Gh
68 Niger, rep. Dd
71 Niger, R. Df
68 Nigeria, Fed. of Ce
8 Nigg Ec
67 Nigtchaps Bf
54 Nii Shima, I. Cd
54 Niigata & pref. Cc
55 Niihama Bd
82b Niihau, I. Aa
54 Niitsu Cc
18 Nijmegen Ec
35 Nikolayevsk Rd
35 Nikolayevski Je
33 Nikolayew Ff
32 Nikolsk Jd
33 Nikopol Ff
31 Nikšic Bd
38 Nile, R. Cc
88 Niles Ed
44 Nilgiri Hills Df
21 Nîmes Cf
31 Nimmitabel Cc
44 Nine Degree
  Chan. Cg
51 Ningpo Gd

51 Ningsia Hui, Aut.
  Reg. Ec
51 Ningteh Fd
18 Ninove Dd
15 Niort Cd
80 Nipawin Db
81 Nipigon Ab
88 Nipissing, L. Fa
31 Nis Cd
23 Nisko Gc
12 Nasum Fd.
95 Niteroi Gd
22 Nitra Ed
66 Niuafu, I. Hk
56 Niue I. Ed
19 Nivelles Dd
20 Nivernais, dist. Bc
46 Nizamabad Gj
35 Nizhne Kolymsk Sc
32 Nizhne Toyma Hc
35 Nizhneudinsk Md
34 Nizhniy Tagil Hd
84 Njole De
29 Nocera Ed
55 Noda Cc
70 Nogales Ba
55 Nogata Bd
33 Noginsk Mc
33 Noginsk Gd
22 Nolima Ea
82a Nome Bb
48 Nong Khoi Bb
18 Noord Beveland,
  I. Cc
18 Noord Brabant,
  prov. Db
18 Noord Holland,
  prov. Db
18 Noordoost
  Polder Eb
72 Noqui Ae
32 Norcia Dc
22 Norddy Bd
80 Nordegg Cb
10 Norden Ga
16 Nordenham Ha
12 Norderney, I. Ga
11 Nordfjordeid Bc
16 Nordhausen Dc
10 Nordhorn Gb
10 Nordkinn, C. Fa
10 Nordreisa Eb
10 Nordvik Ob
84 Norfolk, Neb. Cc
89 Norfolk, Va. Gf
7 Norfolk, co. He
56 Norfolk I. De
35 Norilsk Lc
62 Norman R. Bb
62 Norman Wells Eb
14 Normandy, reg. Cc
62 Normansby I. Hh
62 Normanton Bb
12 Nörresundby Cb
89 Norristown Hd
11 Norrköping Dd
11 Norrsundet Dc
11 Norrtalje Dd
65 Norseman Ce
2 North America Bc
92 North Atlantic
  Ocean Eb
80 North
  Battleford Do
81 North Bay Bb
84 North Bend Ea
8 North Berwick Fd
10 North C. Fa
83 North Carolina,
  st. Ec
88 North Chan., L.
  Huron Da
82 North Dakota,
  st. Cb
7 North Downs Hf
62 North-East New
  Guinea Fg
7 North Foreland Hj
16 North Frisian Is. Ca
81 North Island Ec
78 North Magnetic
  Pole Ha
8 North Minch Cb
48 North Pagai, I. Bd
84 North Platte Fc
96 North Pole Ca
8 North Ronaldsay
  I. Fa
4 North Sea Fd
89 North
  Tonawanda Fc
8 North Uist, I. Ac
64 North West C. Ac
8 Northam Be
65 Northampton,
  Australia Ad
7 Northampton &
  co., England Ge
89 Northampton,
  U.S.A. Jc
9 Northern
  Ireland Eq
58 Northern
  Territory Ec

6 Northumberland,
  co. Eb
81 Northumberland,
  Str. Cb
78 Northwest
  Territories Hb
89 Norwalk Jd
4 Norway, King. Gc
2 Norwegian S. Gb
7 Norwich Je
54 Noshiro & I. Db
74 Nossob, R. Cc
29 Nota Ef
22 Notec, R. Cb
81 Notre Dame B. Db
6 Nottingham &
  co. Fe
75 Notwani Db
71 Nouakchott Ce
72 Nova-Chaves Cf
44 Nova Goa Ce
95 Nova Granada Fd
92 Nova Lima Gd
72 Nova Lisboa Bf
75 Nova Mambone Eb
79 Nova Scotia,
  prov. Ld
31 Nova Zagora Ec
21 Novara Gd
34 Novaya Zemlya,
  Is. Hb
22 Nové Zámky Ed
32 Novgorod Fd
28 Novi Eb
31 Novi Ligure Ge
31 Novi Pazar Cd
30 Novi Sad Bc
28 Novigrad Bb
72 Novo Redondo Af
33 Novocherkassk Hf
34 Novokuznetsk Ld
33 Novomoskovsk Ge
33 Novorossiysk Gg
34 Novosibirsk Ld
33 Novozbkov Fe
34 Novy Port Kc
23 Nowa Huta Fc
23 Nowemiastro Fc
61 Nowra Db
44 Nowshera Cb
23 Nowy Dwór Gb
23 Nowy Sacz Fd
3 Nowy Targ Fd
22 Nowy Tomysl Cb
8 Noss Head Eb
13 Nsawam Eg
71 Nsukka Gg
2 Nua Bc
38 Nubian Des. Cc
80 Nueva Rosita Db
91 Nuevitas Cb
20 Nuits Cb
20 Nuits St. George Cb
3 Nukha Jg
7 Nullagine Cc
65 Nullarbor Plain De
71 Numan Hg
55 Numazu Cc
7 Nuneaton Fe
51 Nunkiang Gb
82a Nunivak, I. Bb
29 Nuoro Bd
10 Nurmes Fc
17 Nürnberg
  (Nuremberg) Dd
28 Nuri Bc
44 Nushki Bc
74 Nuweveldberge,
  mts. Cd
65 Nuyts Arch. Ee
65 Nuyts Pt. Bf
68 Nyala Ed
72 Nyamlell Db
12 Nyborg Dd
30 Nyiregyhaza Cd
12 Nykobing Ee
75 Nylstroom Db
11 Nynashamn Dd
12 Nyngan Cb
22 Nysa Dc

49 Obi Is. Dd
92 Obidos Dc
54 Obihiro Db
39 Obok Dd
33 Oboyan Ge
32 Obozerskaya Hc
77 Obuasi Eg
89 Ocean City He
39 Ochil Hills Ed
88 Oconto Bb
35 October
  Revolution I Mb
54 Odate Db
55 Odawara Cc
27 Odemis Cb
75 Odendaalsrus Dc
12 Odense & co. Dd
22 Oder, R. Cb
28 Oderzo Db
65 Odessa, U.S.A. Fe
33 Odessa, U.S.S.R. Ff
71 Odienne Dg
42 Odokanow Dc
30 Odorhei Eb
42 Odra, R. Cc
22 Odra Port Cb
42 Oeiras Ec
39 Odweina De
28 Odzak Gb
92 Oeiras Ec
71 Offa Fg
9 Offaly, co. Dc
19 Offenbach Hd
21 Offenburg Fa
28 Ogaki Cc
54 Ogaki Cc
71 Ogbomosho Fg
64 Ogden Dc
89 Ogdensburg Hd
21 Oglio, R. Jd
54 Ogoouhe, st. De
28 Ogulin Eb
66 Ohakune Ec
87 Ohio, R. Cd
83 Ohio, st. Eb
22 Ohre, R. Bc
66 Oil City Fd
19 Oise, R. Be
55 Oita & pref. Bd
94 Ojos del Salado,
  mt. Ca
32 Oka, R. Hd
74 Okahandja Bb
74 Okaputa Bb
28 Okarito Ce
74 Okavango R. Ba
74 Okavango
  Swamp Ca
55 Okayama &
  pref. Bd
55 Okazaki Cd
11 Okeechobee, L. Df
7 Okehampton Dg
71 Okene Gg
35 Okha Rd
35 Okhotsk, & S. of Rd
55 Oki Shima Bc
54 Okiep Bc
83 Oklahoma, st. Dc
85 Oklahoma City Gd
33 Okrika Gh
32 Oktiabrski Hb
67 Okuru Be
54 Okushiri, I. Cb
10 Olafsvik Ab
11 Öland Dd
29 Olbia Bd
26 Old Castile,
  prov. Ba
18 Oldenburg Ha
18 Oldenzaal Fb
6 Oldham Ed
89 Olean Fc
55 Olekminsk Pc
32 Olenya Fb
15 Oléron, Ile d' Ce
22 Olesnica Dc
28 Olib Eb
54 Oliague Bd
32 Olomouc Dc
32 Olonets Fc
35 Olovyannaya Od
23 Olsztyn Fb
30 Olt, R. Ec
13 Olten Ba
30 Oltenito Fc
27 Olympus, mt. Ba
9 Omagh Db
64 Omaha Gc
48 Oman, G. of Hf
74 Omaruru Bb
49 Omtrai str. Dd
59 Omdurman Cd
21 Omegma Gd
55 Ometepec Ed
18 Omiya Cc
55 Omiya Cc
13 Ommen Fb
34 Omsk Kd
74 Omua Matako,
  R. Bb
55 Omuta Bd
71 Onda Fg

74 Ondangua Ba
32 Onega Gc
32 Onega, G. of Gc
32 Onega, L. Gc
32 Onega R. Gc
66 Onehunga Eb
89 Oneida Hc
89 Oneonta Gc
66 Ongarue Ec
65 Ongerup Be
71 Onitsha Gg
55 Onoda Bd
35 Onomichi Bd
64 Onslow Bc
87 Onslow B. Ee
31 Onstwedde Fa
55 Ontake, mt. Cc
89 Ontario, L. Fc
79 Ontario, prov. Jc
65 Oodnadatta Fd
65 Ooldea Ee
18 Oostende
  (Ostend) Bc
18 Oosterhout Dc
44 Ootacamund Df
72 Opala Cd
62 Opalton Bc
22 Opava Dd
23 Opoczno Fc
22 Opole Dc
26 Oporto (Pôrto) Aa
66 Opotiki Fc
11 Oppdal Bc
66 Opua Ea
44 Opunake Dc
43 Oqair Gd
30 Oradea Dc
46 Orai Gf
52 Oran, Algeria Ea
94 Orán, Arg. Cd
72 Orange, France Ce
61 Orange, N.S.W. Cb
87 Orange, U.S.A. Bf
74 Orange, R. Bc
75 Orange Free State,
  prov. Dc
16 Oranienburg Eb
33 Orany De
28 Orbetello Cc
61 Orbost Cc
42 Ordu Da
33 Ordzhonikidze Hg
12 Ore (Erz Gebirge)
  Mts. Bc
11 Orebro Cd
4 Oregon, st. Ab
32 Orekhovo
  Zvyevo Gd
33 Orel Ge
33 Orenburg Le
26 Orense Aa
67 Orepuki Ag
28 Orihuela Bb
10 Orillia Fa
21 Orinoco, R. Cb
47 Orissa, st. Kh
28 Oristano Be
90 Orizaba Ed
8 Orkney, co Ea
8 Orkney Is. Fb
87 Orlando Df
20 Orléamais, dist. Ab
55 Orleans Dd
44 Ormara Ac
49 Ormoc Db
56 Ormond Fc
10 Ornans Aa
10 Ornskoldsvik Dc
29 Oron Gh
14 Orontes (Asi) R. Cb
29 Orosei Bd
21 Orsa Cc
33 Orsha Fc
33 Orsk Le
28 Orte Dc
28 Ortona Ec
94 Oruro Bd
28 Orvieto Dc
21 Orzinuovi Hd
55 Osaka & pref. Cd
88 Oscoda Db

81 Oshawa,
  Canada Bb
89 Oshawa, U.S.A. Fc
71 Oshogbo Fg
90 Osijek Bc
86 Oskaloosa Bc
11 Oslo & Fd. Cd
27 Osmancik Da
27 Osmaneli Da
18 Osnabüch Hb
95 Osorio He
93 Osorno Bg
18 Oss Ec
18 Ostend, see
  Oostende Bc
18 Osterholz-
  Scharmbeck Ha
10 Ostersund Cc
22 Ostia Dd
22 Ostrava Ec
23 Ostroda Eb
23 Ostroleka Fb
23 Ostrów Dc

23 Ostrow
  Mazowiecka Fb
23 Ostrowiec Swieto-
  krzyski Fc
22 Ostrzeszów Dc
55 Osumi Chan. Bd
89 Oswego Gc
7 Oswestry De
67 Otago, dist. Bf
66 Otaki Ed
54 Otaru Db
74 Otavi Ba
74 Otjiwarongo Bb
28 Otocac Eb
54 Otoineppu Db
66 Otorohanga Ec
29 Otranto Gd
54 Otsu Cc
81 Ottawa Bb
11 Ottenby Dd
86 Ottumwa Bc
23 Otwock Fb
21 Otztaler Alpen,
  mts. Jc
71 Ouagadougou Ef
71 Oualata De
72 Ouanda Djalé Cb
72 Ouango Cc
70 Ouargla Gb
72 Oubangi, R. Bc
18 Oude, R. Db
74 Oudtshoorn Cd
72 Ouesso Bc
70 Ouezzane Db
10 Oulu & R. Fc
10 Oulujärvi, L. Fc
93 Ouro Preto Ee
7 Ouse, R., Beds Ge
6 Ouse, R., Yorks Gd
8 Outer Hebrides Ac
18 Outreau Ad
40 Ouyen Bc
10 Öv Tornea Eb
94 Ovalle Af
74 Ovamboland,
  dist. Ba
18 Over Flakkee, I. Dc
26 Oviedo Aa
33 Ovruch Ee
67 Owaka Bg
55 Owase Cd
86 Owatonna Bc
81 Owen Sound Ab
62 Owen Stanley
  Ra. Gh
88 Owensboro Bf
88 Owosso Cc
11 Oxelösund Dd
7 Oxford & co.,
  England Ff
67 Oxford, N.Z. De
72 Oyem Ac
81 Oyo Fg
20 Oyonnax Dc
49 Ozamiz Dc
67 Ozark Plat. Bd
29 Ozieri Bd
21 Ozorkow Ec

48 Pa Sak R. Bb
50 Paan (Batang) Da
74 Paarl Bd
23 Pabianice Ec
47 Pabna Mf
46 Pachhadra Df
90 Pachuca Ec
56-57 Pacific Ocean
48 Padang Bd
48 Padang
  Sidimpuan Ac
18 Paderborn Hc
7 Padstow Cg
28 Padua (Padova) Db
47 Paducah Cd
66 Paeroa Eb
75 Pafuri Eb
28 Pag, I. Eb
49 Pagadian Dc
66 Pago Pago Dj
48 Pahang R. Bc
66 Pahiatua Ed
74 Paignton Dg
11 Päijanne, L. Fc
88 Painesville Ed
8 Paisley De
51 Paiyin Ec
51 Paiyunopo Eb
10 Pajala Eb
44 Pakala Df
51 Pakhoi Ed
44-45 Pakistan, St. Bc
30 Paks Bb
75 Pala Bb
46 Palanpur Df
75 Palapye Db
45 Palau Is. Ec
45 Palawan, I. Cc
48 Palembang Bd
26 Palencia Ba
29 Palermo De
47 Palestine Ae
44 Paighat Df
46 Pali Df
46 Palitana Ch

21 Pallanza Gd
29 Palma, Italy Df
73 Palma, Mozam. Gf
26 Palma, Spain Cb
70 Palma I. Bc
85 Palmares Ef
29 Palmarola, I. Dd
21 Palmas, C. Dh
95 Palmeria Ee
72 Palmeirinhas, Pta.
  das Ae
62 Palmerston Cf
61 Palmerston C. Cc
56 Palmerston I. Bd
66 Palmerston
  North Ed
29 Palmi Ee
42 Palmyra Dc
26 Palos Ab
26 Palos, C. de Bb
34 Pamirs, Mts. Kf
87 Pamlico Sd. Ed
85 Pampa Fd
93 Pampas, reg. Cf
26 Pamplona Ba
91 Panama Ce
92 Panama, rep. Ab
91 Panama Canal
  Zone Ce
49 Panay, I. Db
32 Pancevo Cc
64 Pandharpur De
73 Pangani Fe
48 Pangkalpinang Bd
46 Pangkiang Fb
44 Panjgur Ac
29 Pantelleria, I. Cf
90 Panuco, & R. Ec
51 Paoki Ec
51 Paoshan Dd
51 Paoting Fc
51 Paotow Eb
30 Papa Ab
8 Papa Stour, I. Inset
66 Papakura Eb
79 Papantia de
  Olarte Dc
25 Paphos Dc
62 Papua, G. of Fh
72 Papua, Terr. of Fh
92 Para, state Dc
48 Paracel Is. Cb
54 Paraguari De
93 Paraguay, rep. De
94 Paraguay, R. Dd
92 Paraiba, state Fc
32 Paramaribo Db
94 Parana, Braz. Fb
94 Parana, Par. Cf
94 Parana, R. Cf
94 Parana, st. Ed
95 Paranaguá Fe
20 Paray le Monial Cc
46 Parbhani Fj
11 Parchim Db
22 Pardubice Cc
49 Parepare Cd
81 Parent Bb
14 Paris, France Ec
37 Paris, U.S.A. Ae
81 Parkersburg Fe
61 Parkes Cb
21 Parma Je
92 Parnaiba Ec
92 Parnaiba Ec
11 Pärnu Dd
27 Paros I. Bb
61 Parramatta Db
78 Parry Is. Ga
81 Parry Sd. Bb
87 Parsons Ad
29 Partanna Df
47 Parvatipuram Jj
65 Pasadena Ce
84 Pasco Cb
9 Passage West Ce
92 Passo Fundo Ee
92 Pasto Bb
93 Pasuruan Cd
93 Patagonia, reg. Cg
46 Patan Dg
66 Patea Ec
29 Paterno Ef
89 Paterson Hd
46 Pathankot Eb
48 Patiala Cd
46 Patiala Fc
27 Pátmos, I. Cb
47 Patna Kf
47 Pátrai, & G. Bb
48 Pattani Bc
11 Pattani Ee
7 Pau Cf
51 Pavia Hd
34 Pavlodar Kd
33 Pavlograd Gf
33 Pavlovo Hd
21 Pavullo nel
  Frignano Je
29 Pawtucket Kd
27 Paxói, I. Bb
84 Payette Cc

94 Paysandu Df
31 Pazardzhik Ed
28 Pazin Db
80 Peace, R. Cb
80 Peace River Cb
65 Peak Hill Bd
62 Peak Ra. Cc
83b Pearl Harbor Cb
2 Peary Ld. Fa
32 Pechenga Fb
62 Philippi L. Ac
32 Pechora, G. Kb
85 Pecos Cb
85 Pecos, R. Fe
30 Pécs Bb
67 Peebing Bb
8 Peebles & co. Ee
63 Peera Peera
  Poolana L. Ad
45 Pegu He
45 Pegu Yoma,
  Mts. He
51 Pehpei Ec
48 Pekalongan Bd
86 Pekin Cc
51 Peking Fc
49 Feleng, I. Dd
74 Pelican Pt. Ab
74 Pella Bc
78 Pelly, L. Gb
27 Peloponnese,
  dist. Bb
95 Pelotas Ef
20 Pelvoux, Massif
  du, mt. Ee
73 Pemba, I. Fe
51 Pemberton Be
81 Pembroke, Can. Bb
7 Pembroke & co.,
  Wales Cf
7 Pembroke Dock Cf
48 Penang, I. Bc
93 Penas, G. de Bg
84 Pendleton Cb
62 Penedo Fd
88 Penetanguish-
  ene Fa
51 Pengpu Fc
48 Penida, I. Cd
51 Penki Gb
44 Penner R. Df
49 Pennine Ra. Ec
83 Pennsylvania,
  st. Fb
62 Penong Ee
61 Penrith Db
87 Pensacola Ce
60 Penticton Cc
62 Pentland Cc
32 Pentland Firth Eb
23 Penza Je
7 Penzance Bg
13 Penzberg Fa
86 Peoria Cc
18 Petak R. Bc
92 Pereira Bb
33 Perekop Ff
33 Pereyaslav-
  Khmelnitski Fe
93 Pergamino Cf
73 Périgueux De
73 Perim, I. Ga
32 Perm Ld
92 Pernambuco, st. Fc
75 Perpignan Ef
36 Persia, sec Iran Jf
11 Persian G. Fd
61 Perth, Australia Be
81 Perth, Canada Cb
8 Perth & co.,
  Scotland Ed
48 Peru Bd
92 Peru, rep. Bc
28 Perugia Dc
22 Pesaro Dc
28 Pescara Ec
44 Peshawar Cb
71 Pesqueira Fc
40 Petah Tiqva Bc
19 Petange Ee
81 Petrborro Bb
70 Peterborough,
  Australia Ab
7 Peterborough,
  England Ge
6 Peterhead Gc
82 Petermann Pk. Pa
82a Petersburg,
  Alaska Ec
89 Petersburg, Va. Gf
46 Peto Gd
67 Petone Ed
88 Petoskey Cb
31 Petrich De
30 Petrinja Fb
31 Petrovpavlovsk Jd
35 Petropavlovsk-
  Kamchatskiy Sd
95 Petrópolis Gd
30 Petrosul, Mt. Eb
30 Petrovaradin · Cc

35 Petrovsk Nd
32 Patrozavodsk Ec
19 Pforzheim Hf
46 Phagwara Ec
46 Phalodi De
48 Phan Rang Bb
48 Phan Thiet Bb
48 Phanom Dong
  Raek, mts. Bb
62 Philippi L. Ac
49 Philippines, Is. &
  Rep. Db
48 Phitsanulok Bb
85 Phoenix De
56 Phoenix Is. Ed
21 Piacenza Hd
28 Pianosa, I. Ec
30 Piatro Fb
92 Piaui, state Ec
94 Pica Bd
14 Picardy, reg. Ec
87 Picayune Ce
61 Picton, Austral. Db
67 Picton, N.Z. Ed
87 Pictou Cb
44 Pidurutalagala,
  Mt. Dg
29 Piedimonte Ed
90 Piedras Negras Db
51 Pieksämäki Fc
10 Pielinen, & L. Fc
21 Piemonte, prov. Fe
84 Pierre Fc
10 Pietarsaari Ec
75 Pietermaritz-
  burg Ec
75 Pietersburg Db
28 Pieve Da
10 Pihtipudas Fc
74 Piketberg Bd
94 Pilar De
64 Pilbara Bc
94 Pilcomayo, R. Cd
23 Pilica, R. Fc
27 Pilos Bb
22 Pilsen, see Pizen Bd
32 Pimba Fe
94 Pimenta Bueno Cb
91 Pinar del Rio Bb
23 Pinczów Fc
87 Pindus Mts. Bb
87 Pine Bluff Be
64 Pine Creek Ea
32 Pinega Hc
32 Pinega R. Hc
21 Pinerolo Fe
48 Ping R. Ab
65 Pingelly Be
51 Pingliang Ec
59 Pingnarup Be
51 Pingtung Gd
65 Pinjarra Be
32 Piombino Cc
23 Pionsk Fb
23 Piotrków Ed
88 Piqua Cd
27 Piraiévs Bb
28 Piran Db
92 Piranhas Fc
95 Pirapora Gc
95 Piray Be
27 Pirgos Bb
19 Pirmasens Ge
31 Pirot Dd
33 Piryatin Fe
33 Pisa Cc
94 Pisagua Ac
22 Pisek Cd
28 Pistoia Cc
22 Pitea Db
57 Pitcairn I. De
10 Pitea Eb
30 Pitesti Ec
87 Pittsburg Bd
88 Pittsburgh Fd
61 Pittsworth Da
48 Phuket Ac
29 Pizzo Fe
81 Placentia Db
93 Plata, Rio de la Df
89 Plattsburg Jb
85 Plenty, B. of Fb
32 Plesetsk Hc
22 Pleszew Dc
26 Plettenberg B. Cd
30 Pleven Ed
31 Plievlja Bd
23 Plock Eb
31 Plovdiv Ed
20 Plomb du Cantal,
  mt. Ad
28 Pluj Ea
7 Plymouth, Eng. Cg
88 Plymouth, Ind. Bd
31 Plymouth, Mont-
  serrat Fc

88 Plymouth,
  Wisc. Bc
22 Pizen (Pilsen) Bd
48 Pnom Penh Bb
21 Po, R. Jd
34 Pobeda Pk. Ke
84 Pocatello Dc
89 Pocomoke City He
95 Pocos de Caldas Fd
22 Podmokly Cc
32 Podolsk Gd
71 Podor Ce
52 Podulloaei Fb
44 Point Pedro Dg
91 Pointe à Pitre Fc
15 Poitiers Dd
15 Poitou Cd
46 Pokaran Ce
61 Pokataroo Ca
4 Poland, st. Je
27 Polatli Db
72 Poli Ab
29 Policastro Ed
10 Polmak Fa
32 Polotsk Ed
33 Poltava Ff
91 Ponce Ec
79 Pond Inlet Ka
44 Pondicherry Df
32 Pongoma Fb
32 Ponoi & R. Hb
19 Pont à Mousson Ff
95 Ponta Grossa Ee
95 Ponta Pora Dd
26 Pontarlier Ec
87 Pontchartrain,
  L. Ce
28 Pontebba Da
29 Pontecorvo Dd
88 Pontiac Dc
45 Pontianak Bd
52 Pontine Is. Dd
26 Pontoise Be
12 Pontremoli Cd
21 Pontypool Df
7 Pontypridd Cf
29 Ponza, I. Dd
7 Poole Fg
46 Poona Cc
94 Poopó, L. Bc
32 Popayan Bb
18 Poperinge Bd
84 Poplar Bluff Bd
90 Popocatepetl,
  mt. Ed
72 Popokabaka Be
46 Porbandar Bh
28 Pordenone Db
28 Porec Db
10 Pori Ec
10 Porjus Db
11 Porkkala Ec
27 Porsuk, R. Db
13 Port Aa
60 Port Adelaide Ab
80 Port Alberni Bc
60 Port Albert Cc
44 Port Albert
  Victor Ch
75 Port Alfred Dd
91 Port Antonio Cc
80 Port Arthur,
  Canada Fc
91 Port Arthur-Dairen
  (Lü-ta) Gc
87 Port Arthur,
  U.S.A. Bf
91 Port au Prince Dc
60 Port Augusta Ab
81 Port aux Basques
  Db
45 Port Blair Df
26 Port Bou Ca
60 Port Broughton Ab
81 Port Cartier Ca
67 Port Chalmers Cf
68 Port Colborne Fe
91 Port de Paix Dc
87 Port Dickson Bd
62 Port Douglas Cb
75 Port Elizabeth Dd
8 Port Ellen Be
28 Port Erie Be
64 Port Fairy Bc
72 Port Francqui Cd
8 Port Glasgow De
91 Port Harcourt Gh
51 Port
  Hawkesbury Cb
64 Port Hedland Bc
81 Port Huron Dc
61 Port Jackson Db
9 Port Laoise Dc
65 Port Lincoln Fe
64 Port Louis Cc
61 Port Macquarie Db
62 Port Moresby Gh
80 Port Nelson Eb
8 Port of Ness Bb
91 Port of Spain Fd
67 Port Pegasus Ag
60 Port Phillip B. Bc
81 Port Pirie Ab

78 Port Radium Fb
64 Port Roper Fa
41 Port Said (Bûr Sa'îd) Ca
75 Port Shepstone Ed
38 Port Sudan Cc
48 Port Swettenham Bc
7 Port Talbot Df
15 Port Vendres Ef
60 Port Wakefield Ab
9 Portadown Eb
20 Portage la Prairie Ec
26 Portalegre Ab
26 Portimao Ab
60 Portland, Me. Kc
61 Portland, N.S.W. Cb
84 Portland, Ore. Bb
60 Portland, Vic. Bc
7 Portland Bill Eg
8 Portlethen Fc
7 Portmadoc Ce
8 Portmahomach Ec
95 Pôrto (Oporto) Aa
95 Porto Alegre Ef
72 Porto Amboim Af
73 Porto Amélia Gf
29 Porto Anzio Dd
95 Porto Artur Eb
29 Porto Empedocle Df
94 Porto Esperanca Dc
94 Porto Murtinho Dd
95 Porto Nacional Fb
71 Porto Novo Fg
95 Porto Pres Vargas Ef
28 Porto Recanati Dc
70 Porto Santo, I. Bb
92 Porto Seguro Fd
94 Porto Socompa Bd
29 Porto Torres Bd
95 Porto União Ee
92 Porto Velho Cc
28 Portoferrazo Cc
8 Portpatrick Cf
8 Portree Bc
8 Portrush Ea
7 Portsmouth, England Fg
89 Portsmouth, N.H. Kc
88 Portsmouth, Ohio De
89 Portsmouth, Va. Gf
4 Portugal, Rep. Db
72 Portugália Ce
6 Portuguese Guinea Ad
9 Portumna Cc
20 Posadas De
13 Poschiavo Eb
70 Poste Maurice Cortier (Bidon 5) Fg
7 Postmasberg Cg
75 Potchefstroom Dc
26 Potenza Ed
75 Potgietersrus Db
33 Poti Fb
94 Potosi Bc
51 Potow Fc
16 Potsdam Eb
89 Pottsville Gd
89 Poughkeepsie Hd
9 Poulaphouca, Res. Ec
94 Pouso Alegre Eg
32 Povenets Gc
64 Powell Creek Eb
88 Powers Bb
20 Pozarevac Cc
22 Poznan Db
94 Pozo Almonte Bd
12 Praded, mt. Dc
15 Prades Ef
12 Praesto & co. Fd
22 Prague (Praha) Cc
62 Prairie Bc
25 Prata Fc
28 Prato Cc
85 Pratt Gd
16 Prenzlau Eb
22 Prerov Db
25 Prescott De
95 Presidente Epitacio Ed
94 Presidente Hermes Cb
95 Presidente Murtinho Ec
95 Presidente Prudente Ed
85 Presidio Ff
23 Presov Fd
6 Preston Ed
8 Prestwick De
75 Pretoria Dc
27 Prevéza Bb
27 Pribram Cd
84 Price Dd

74 Prieska Cc
31 Prilep Ce
33 Priluki Fe
80 Prince Albert, Canada Db
78 Prince Albert Pen. Fa
79 Prince Charles Is. Kb
3 Prince Edward Is. Jh
80 Prince George Bb
81 Prince of Wales, Is. Ha
80 Prince Rupert Ab
62 Princess Charlotte B. Ba
7 Princetown Dg
94 Principe da Beira Cc
74 Prins Albert Cd
33 Pripyat, R. Ee
33 Pripyat Marshes Ee
31 Pristina Cd
34 Prokopevsk Ld
33 Proletarski Hf
45 Prome He
62 Proserpine Cc
22 Prostejov Dd
31 Provadiya Fd
20 Provence, dist. Df
15 Provence, reg. Ff
89 Providence Kd
91 Providencia, I. Bd
19 Provins Ef
84 Provo Dc
32 Prudnik Dc
33 Prut R. Ef
25 Przemysl Gd
23 Przeworsk Gc
34 Przhevalsk Ke
32 Psará, I. Cb
32 Pskov Ed
90 Puebla Ed
85 Pueblo Fd
90 Puerto Barrios Gd
91 Puerto Cabezas Bd
91 Puerto Cortés Ac
70 Puerto de Cabras Cc
95 Puerto Deseado Cg
94 Puerto Heath Bb
95 Puerto Madryn Cg
91 Puerto Montt Bg
90 Puerto Morales Gc
91 Puerto Plata Dc
49 Puerto Princesa Cc
91 Puerto Rico, I. Ec
91 Puerto Suarez Dc
33 Pugachey Je
92 Puget Sd. Bb
29 Puglia, reg. Fd
70 Puisaye, Collines de la, mts. Bb
76 Pukekohe Eb
28 Pula (Pola) Db
33 Pulawy Fc
94 Puna, reg. Bc
94 Puna de Atacama Be
45 Punaka Gc
17 Punakha Me
94 Punata Bc
44 Punch Ce
75 Punguè Ea
46 Punjab, st. Ec
94 Puno Ac
95 Punta Arenas Bh
94 Puntarenas Bd
94 Puquios Bc
47 Puri Kj
90 Purisima Bb
47 Purnea Lf
47 Purulia Lg
31 Purvomai Ed
52 Pusan Bb
33 Pushkino Je
66 Putaruru Ec
34 Putih I. Kb
18 Putten Eb
12 Puttgarden Ec
20 Puy de Dôme, mt. & dept. Ad
84 Puyallup Bb
73 Pweto De
32 Pya I. Eb
45 Pyapon He
33 Pyatigorsk Hg
52 Pyinmana He
52 Pyongyang Bb
5 Pyrenees, mts. Df
45 Pyu He

42 Quadhinna De
31 Qualat at el Mudauwara Dd
40 Qalqilyah Ec
39 Qamr B. Ed
43 Qasr Umm Ramad Fe
40 Qatana Ec
43 Qatar, pen. Gd
43 Qazvin Fb
38 Qena Cc
43 Qeshm, I. Hd
39 Qishn Ed
30 Quatsino Bb
75 Que Que Da
61 Queanbeyan Cc
81 Quebec & prov. Bb
78 Queen Charlotte Is. Dc
80 Queen Charlotte Sd. Bb
96 Queen Elizabeth Is. Qb
96 Queen Mary Coast Fc
96 Queen Maud Land Bb
60 Queenscliff Bc
59 Queensland, st. Cc
75 Queenstown, Cape Province Dd
67 Queenstown, N.Z. Bf
61 Queenstown, Tas. Cd
92 Queimados Fd
92 Quela Be
86 Quelimane Fg
90 Queretaro Dc
81 Quesnel Bb
44 Quetta Bc
29 Quezon City Db
48 Qui Nhon Bb
94 Quillagua Bd
44 Quilon Dg
43 Quilpie Bd
14 Quimper Ac
86 Quincy, Ill. Ad
89 Quincy, Mass. Kc
26 Quintanar Ba
61 Quirindi Db
92 Quito Bc
43 Quom Gc
60 Quorn Ab
38 Quseir Cc

30 Raab, R. Ab
10 Raabe Fc
8 Raasay, Sd. of Bc
49 Raba Cd
70 Rabah Gd
70 Rabat Bb
62 Rabaul Hg
32 Rabigh Be
81 Race, C. Cc
22 Racibórz Ec
88 Racine Bc
30 Radauti Eb
60 Radium Hill Bb
7 Radnor, co. De
23 Radom Fc
23 Radomsko Ec
7 Radstock Ef
33 Radzymin Fb
80 Rae Ca
57 Rae Bareli Ne
66 Raetihi Ec
74 Rafaela Cf
42 Rafha Ed
72 Raga Db
13 Ragaz Da
26 Raglan Eb
29 Ragusa Ef
48 Rahaeng, see Tak
44 Raichur De
47 Raigarh Jh
42 Raiis De
84 Rainier, Mt. Bb
85 Rainy L. Cc
44 Raipur Hh
45 Rajahmundry Ee
46 Rajasthan, st. De
62 Rajkot Cg
54 Rajpipla Dh
17 Rajshahi Mf
67 Rakaia De
75 Rakops Cb
9 Raleigh Fg
60 Ram Allah Bd
78 Ramah Lc
6 Ramgarh Ce
42 Ramla Bd
36 Ramnicu Sarat Fc
30 Râmnicu Vâlcea Ec
16 Rampur Gd
43 Ramsgate Ge
7 Ramsgate Hj
93 Ranaghat Mg
47 Ranchi Kg
72 Randers & co. Cc
67 Rangia Gc
66 Rangiora Ge
43 Rangoon He
47 Rangpur Mf
47 Raniganj Lg
46 Raniwara Df
46 Rann of Kutch Cf
49 Rantekombola, mt. Dd

21 Rapallo He
84 Rapid City Fc
13 Rapperswil Ca
56 Rarotonga I. Gd
43 Ras al Hadd,C. He
38 Ras Banas Cc
39 Ras Dashan, mt. Cd
43 Ras Rakan, C. Ge
43 Ras Tanura Fd
40 Rashayya Ec
43 Rasht Fb
33 Rasskazovo He
83 Rat Is. Bb
46 Ratangarh Ed
9 Rathkeale Cd
9 Rath Luirc Cd
9 Rathdrum Ed
16 Rathenow Eb
9 Rathlin, I. Ea
9 Rathnew Ec
46 Ratlam Eg
86 Raukumara Ra. Fc
11 Rauma Ec
43 Ravar Hc
28 Ravenna Db
21 Ravensburg Db
65 Ravensthorpe Ce
62 Ravenswood Cc
44 Rawalpindi Cb
66 Rawene Da
22 Rawicz Dc
84 Rawlins Ec
30 Rawson Cg
81 Ray, C. Db
80 Raymond Cc
30 Razgrad Fd
15 Ré, Ile de Cd
7 Reading, Eng. Gf
89 Reading, U.S.A. Hd
26 Real de Antonio Ab
54 Rebun, I. Da
92 Recife Fc
18 Recklinghausen Gc
60 Red Cliffs Bb
80 Red Deer Cb
80 Red Oak Ac
87 Red R. Be
3 Red Sea Jd
84 Redding Bc
7 Redditch Fe
7 Redruth Bg
85 Redlands Ce
9 Ree, L. Cc
67 Reefton Ce
17 Regensburg De
17 (Ratisbon) Ed
30 Reghin Eb
29 Reggio di Calabria Ee
21 Regio nell Emilia Je
80 Regina Db
44 Registan, Dist. Ab
95 Registro do Araguaia Ec
74 Rehoboth Bb
40 Rehovot Bd
17 Reichenbach Ec
88 Reicheville Ff
7 Reigate Gf
14 Reims Fc
80 Reindeer L. Db
10 Reinosa Eb
23 Rejowiec Gc
84 Remeshk Hd
20 Remiremont Ea
18 Remscheid Gc
16 Rendsburg Ca
8 Renfrew & co., Scotland De
84 Renfrew, U.S.A. Gb
18 Renkum Ec
60 Renmark Bb
14 Rennes Cc
84 Reno, R. Je
94 Resistencia De
30 Resita Cc
59 Resolution, I. Lb
23 Reszel Fa
27 Rethimnon Bb
3 Réunion, I. Kg
26 Réus Ca
13 Reuss, R. Ca
19 Reutlingen Jf
86 Revelstoke Cb
77 Revilla Gigedo Is. Gg
3 Rewa Gf
46 Rewari Fd
84 Rexburg Dc
10 Reykjanes Ab
10 Reykjavik Ab
42 Rezayeh Eb
32 Rezekne Ed
21 Rhätikon, mts. Hb
18 Rheden Fb
18 Rhein, see Rhine
18 Rheine Fc
13 Rheinfelden Ba

18 Rheydt Fc
18 Rhine (Rhein) R.
86 Rhinelander Cb
21 Rho Hd
83 Rhode I., st. Fb
27 Rhodes, the Rhódos Ed
68 Rhodesia Eg
31 Rhodope Mts. Ce
7 Rhondda Df
20 Rhône, R. & dept. Cd
2 Rhum I. Bc
6 Rhyl Dd
46 Riasi Eb
48 Riau Arch. Bc
12 Ribe, co. & R. Bd
95 Riberão Preto Fd
67 Riccarton De
84 Richfield Dd
62 Richmond, Australia Bc
84 Richmond, Calif. Bd
88 Richmond, Ind. Ce
89 Richmond, Ky. Cf
87 Richmond, Va. Gf
89 Richmond, New Zealand Dd
7 Rietfontein Cc
28 Rieti Dc
50 Ritstangi Ba
32 Riga, & G. of Dd
54 Riishiri, I. Da
28 Rijeka (Fiume) Eb
18 Rijn, R. Db
18 Rijswijk Db
28 Rimini Db
81 Rimouski Bb
49 Rindjani, mt. Cd
12 Ringkøbing & co. Bc
12 Ringkøbing Fjord Bd
12 Ringsted Ed
10 Ringvassoy Dd
94 Rio Branco Ba
95 Rio Cuarto Cf
95 Rio de Janeiro, & st. Cd
95 Rio Gallegos Ch
95 Rio Grande Ef
85 Rio Grande, R. Ee
95 Rio Grande do Norte, st. Fc
95 Rio Grande do Sul, st. Ee
93 Rio Muni, prov. Cg
95 Rio Pardo Gc
95 Rio Verde Ec
92 Riobamba Bc
20 Riom Bd
29 Rionero Ed
13 Rioz Aa
6 Ripon Fc
11 Risör Bd
10 Ristijärvi Fc
21 Riva Jd
20 Rive de Gier Cd
94 Rivera Df
71 River Cess Dg
89 Riverhead Jd
74 Riversdale Cd
80 Riverton, Can. Bb
67 Riverton, N.Z. Bg
21 Riviera Ce
18 Rivière du Loup Cb
21 Rivoli Fd
43 Riyadh Fe
30 Riyan Dd
42 Rize Ea
26 Roanne Cc
89 Roanoke Ff
89 Roanoke Rapids Gf
60 Robe Ac
34 Robertson Cd
71 Robertsport Cg
60 Robertstown Ad
81 Robertsbrown Ab
81 Robervaln Bb
26 Roca, C. da Ab
93 Rocha Df
6 Rochdale Ed
13 Rochefort Ce
19 Rochester, Minn.
89 Rochester, N.Y. Gc
86 Rock Island Bc
84 Rock Springs Ec
85 Rocky Ford Fd
89 Rocky Mount Gg
84 Rocky Mts. Db
86 Rockford Cc
89 Rockhampton Dc
12 Rockingham B. Cb
11 Rodberg Bc
12 Rødbyhavn Ec
15 Rodez Ef
27 Ródhos (Rhodes), I. Cb
30 Rodna Eb

64 Roebourne Bc
64 Roebuck B. Cb
18 Roermond Ec
18 Roeselare Cd
88 Rogers City Db
74 Roggeveldberge, mts. Cd
10 Rognan Db
46 Rohri Be
46 Rohtak Fd
90 Rojo, C. Ec
95 Rokugo, C. Cc
95 Rolandia Ed
43 Roma Cd
28 Romagna, reg. Cb
30 Roman Fb
20 Romanche, R. Bd
20 Romans Dd
28 Rome, Italy Dd
89 Rome, U.S.A. Hc
7 Romford Hf
12 Rōmo, I. Bd
26 Ronda Ab
92 Rondônia, st. Cd
12 Rönne Fa
18 Ronse Cd
18 Roosendaal Dc
96 Roosevelt I. La
42 Roraima, st. Cb
11 Røros Cc
13 Rorschach Da
10 Ros Vatn Cb
93 Rosario, Arg. Cf
90 Rosario, Mexico Cc
9 Roscommon, & co. Dc
9 Roseau Fd
39 Roseires Cd
18 Rosendael Bc
17 Rosenheim Ee
80 Rosetown Db
61 Rosewood Da
12 Roskilde Ed
33 Roslavl Fe
7 Ross, England Ef
67 Ross, N.Z. Ce
8 Ross & Cromarty, co. Dc
96 Ross Dependency Lc
96 Ross I. Lb
96 Ross Sea Lb
96 Ross Shelf Ice La
80 Rossland Cc
9 Rosslare Ed
11 Rosso Bd
33 Rossosh Ge
88 Rosthern Db
16 Rostock Ea
33 Rostov Gf
85 Roswell Fe
8 Rosyth Ed
18 Rotenburg Ja
7 Rother Hg
6 Rotherham Fg
8 Rothesay Fe
27 Roto Cb
66 Rotorua Fc
18 Rotterdam Dc
21 Rottweil Ga
18 Rotummeroog, I.
14 Rouen Fa
18 Rousay, I. Fa
15 Roussillon Ef
11 Rouyn Bb
21 Rovato Jd
21 Rovereto Kd
28 Rovigo Cb
28 Rovinj Db
33 Rovno Ad
67 Roxburgh, N.Z. Bf
8 Roxburgh, & co., Scotland Fe
47 Royagada Jj
86 Royale, I. Cb
7 Royston Ge
23 Roznava Fd
33 Rtishchevo He
66 Ruapehu, mt. Ec
39 Rub al Khali, des. Dd
32 Rudnichny Kd
30 Rudok Bc
73 Rudolf, L. Fc
73 Rudolstadt Dc
88 Rudyard Ca
73 Rufiji, R. Fe
71 Rufisque Bf
7 Rugby Fe
16 Rügen, I. Ea
11 Ruhr, R. Fc
72 Rukl, R. Bd
73 Rukwa, L. Ee
30 Ruma Bc
5 Rumania, st. Kf
73 Rumbek Cd
54 Rumoi Db
47 Runanga Ce
9 Rush Bc
60 Rushworth Bc
30 Ruse Fd

87 Russelville Bd
34-35 Russian Soviet Federal Socialist Republic Lc
75 Rustenburg Dc
7 Rutland, co., England Ge
89 Rutland, U.S.A. Jc
73 Ruvuma, R. Ff
73 Ruwenzori, mt. Dc
33 Ruzaevka Je
23 Ruzomberok Ed
73 Rwanda, st. Dd
33 Ryazan Ge
33 Ryazhsk He
32 Rybinsk Gd
32 Rybinsk Res. Gd
7 Ryde Fg
7 Rye Hg
32 Rynda Gb
23 Rypin Eb
56 Ryukyu Is. Bb
23 Rzeszów Fc
32 Rzhev Fd

19 Saarbrücken Fe
19 Saarburg Fe
32 Saaremaa, I. Dd
19 Saar, land Fe
19 Saarlouis Fe
26 Sabadell Ca
54 Sado, I. Cc
12 Saeby Db
55 Saeki Bd
7 Saffron Walden He
70 Safi Db
32 Safonovo Jb
27 Safranbolu Da
55 Saga & pref. Bd
45 Sagaing Hd
46 Sagar Gd
88 Saginaw & B. Cc
50 Sagli Da
91 Sagua La Grande Bb
26 Sagunto Bb
68 Sahara Des. Cc
70 Saharan Atlas, mts. Fb
46 Saharanpur Fd
46 Sahiwal (Montgomery) Dc
72 Sa'id Bundas Cb
32 Saïda Guba Fb
43 Saidabad Hd
48 Saigon-Cholon Bb
39 Saihut Ed
55 Saijo Bd
11 Saimaa Fc
51 Sain Shanda Fb
32 St. Albans Gf
20 St. Amour Cf
67 St. Andrews, N.Z. Cf
8 St. Andrews, Scotland Fd
91 St. Ann's Bay Cc
50 St. Arnaud Bc
81 St. Augustin Di
87 St. Augustine Df
7 St. Austell Cg
19 St. Avold Fe
13 St. Bernard, Col du Gd. Bc
80 St. Boniface Ec
31 St. Brieuc E
55 St. Catherines Fc
20 St. Chamond Cd
91 St. Christopher, see St. Kitts
88 St. Clair, L. Dc
50 St. Claude Dc.
86 St. Cloud Bb
55 St. Croix, I. Fc
14 St. Denis Ec
20 St. Dié Ea
19 St. Dizier Df
20 St. Eloy Ac
31 St. Etienne Cd
20 St. Florentin Ba
13 St. Gallen Da
85 St. George, Australia Ca
85 St. George, U.S.A. Dd
91 St. George's Fc
91 St. George's (Chan. Ee
19 St. Germain Bf
30 St. Germain des Fosses Bc

13 St. Gotthard P. Cb
12 St. Heddinge Fd
74 St. Helena B. Bd
69 St. Helena, I. Bb
6 St. Helens Ed
31 St. Hyacinthe Bb
88 St. Ignace Cb
19 St. Ingbert Ge
7 St. Ives Bg
89 St. Jean Jb
89 St. Jerome Jb
81 Saint John Cb
91 St. John's, Antigua Fc
81 St. John's, Can. Db
88 St. Joseph, Mich. Bc
88 St. Joseph, Miss. Bd
7 St. Juan Gf
13 St. Julien Ab
67 St. Kilda Cf
91 St. Kitts (St. Christopher), I.
62 St. Lawrence Cc
81 St. Lawrence, G. of Cb
82a St. Lawrence I. Bb
81 St. Lawrence, R. Cb
13 St. Lô Cf
86 St. Louis, Sen. Be
86 St. Louis, U.S.A. Bd
91 St. Lucia, I. Fd
18 St. Malo Dc
91 St. Marc Dc
91 St. Martin, I. Fc
91 St. Marys Fd
85 St. Mary's Pk. Ab
91 St. Maur Bf
13 St. Moritz Db
15 St. Nazaire Bd
7 St. Neots Ge
91 St. Nicolas Ff
14 St. Omer Eb
92 St. Paul, French Guiana Db
87 St. Petersburg Df
81 St. Pierre I. Db
18 St. Pol-sur-Mer Bc
17 St. Pölten Fd
14 St. Quentin Ec
15 St. Raphael Gf
54 St. Sebastian B. Cd
88 St. Thomas Bc
91 St. Thomas, I. Ec
18 St. Trond Ed
15 St. Tropez Gf
76 St. Veit Fe
84 St. Vincent, C. Ab
60 St. Vincent, G. Ad
91 St. Vincent, I. Fd
69 Ste. Marie, C. Gh
21 Saitama, pref. Cc
70 Sakaï Cd
55 Sakaiminato Bc
42 Sakaka Ec
73 Sakania Df
27 Sakarya, R. Da
54 Sakata Cc
35 Sakhalin I. Rd
94 Sakhnin R. Ke
11 Sakskøbing Ed
11 Sala Cc
30 Salala Ed
26 Salamanca, Sp. Aa
89 Salamanca, U.S.A. Fc
74 Saldanha, B. Bd
61 Sale, Austral. Cc
70 Salé, Morocco Db
44 Salem, India Df
89 Salem, Mass. Kc
84 Salem, Ohio Ed
84 Salem, Ore. Bc
29 Salemi Df
83 Salen Cf
29 Salerno Ed
6 Salford Fd
73 Salima Ef
90 Salina Cruz Ed
85 Salinas, Braz. Gc
85 Salinas, U.S.A. Bd
7 Salisbury, Eng. Ff
75 Salisbury, Rhod. Ea
89 Salisbury, U.S.A. He
40 Salhad Cc
32 Salla Eb
12 Salling, dist. Bc
29 Sallom Cd
84 Salmon Db
20 Salon Ee
54 Salonta Cb
5 Salsk Hf
21 Salsomaggiore He
40 Salt Ac
65 Salt L. Ac
84 Salt Lake City Dc
29 Saltash Cg
7 Saltcoats Ec
12 Saltholm Fd

90 Saltillo Db
94 Salto Df
53 Salton Sea Ce
38 Salum Bb
47 Salur Jj
21 Saluzzo Fe
92 Salvador Fd
77 Salvador, Rep. Ac
45 Salween, R. He
33 Salyany Jh
17 Salzburg Dd
16 Salzgitter Db
49 Samar, I. Db
52 Samarai Hj
48 Samarinda Jf
46 Samarkand Jf
46 Samarra Fc
47 Sambalpur Jh
20 Sambre, R. Dd
54 Samchok Bb
73 Same Fd
43 Samnan Gb
66 Samoa Is. Ch
27 Sámos, I. Cb
48 Sampit, & B. Cd
51 Samshui Fd
12 Samsö, I. Dd
27 Samsun Ea
51 San, R. Gc
43 San Andreas, I. Bd
26 San Andres Tuxtla Ed
85 San Angelo Ed
26 San Antioco, I. Bc
85 San Antonio Cf
91 San Antonio, C. Bb
72 San Antonio do Zaire Cc
21 San Benedetto al Po Cd
85 San Bernardino Ce
90 San Carlos Db
93 San Carlos de Bariloche Bg
85 San Clemente, I. Ce
94 San Cristobal, Argentina Cf
90 San Cristobal, Mexico Fd
92 San Cristobal, Venezuela Bb
85 San Diego Ce
90 San Felipe Bf
90 San Fernando, Mexico Ec
26 San Fernando, Spain Ab
84 San Francisco Bd
91 San Francisco de Macoris Dc
21 San Giovanni in Persecento Ke
21 San Ignacio Cc
90 San Jorge, B. Ba
94 San Jorge, G. de Cg
94 San José, Bol. Cc
94 San José, Rica Be
49 San José, Phil. Db
85 San José, U.S.A. Bd

28 San Sepolcro Dc
28 San Severo Ed
90 Sa'na Db
71 Sanaga, R. Hh
43 Sanandaj
21 (Sinneh) Fb
20 Sancerre Ab
20 Sancerrois, Collines du, mts. Ab
91 Sancti Spiritus Cb
49 Sandakan Cc
8 Sanday, I. Fa
74 Sandfish B. Ab
27 Sandikli Db
11 Sandnes Bd
11 Sandnessjöen Cb
72 Sandoa Cc
11 Sandön Dd
7 Sandown Fg
84 Sandpoint Cb
7 Sandringham He
65 Sandstone Bd
88 Sandusky Da
11 Sandvig Allinge Fa
63 Sandy C. Dc
72 Sanga, R. Bc
30 Sangihe Is. Dc
72 Sangmelina Ac
50 Sangsang Cd
72 Sangwa De
55 Sanjo Cc
72 Sankuru, R. Cd
26 Sanlúcar Ab
55 Sano Cc
23 Sanok Gd
8 Sanquhar Ee
94 Santa Ana, Bol. Bb
85 Santa Ana, U.S.A. Ce
94 Santa Bárbara, Brazil Dc
85 Santa Barbara, U.S.A. Ce
85 Santa Barbara Is. Ce
85 Sta. Catalina, I. Ce
95 Santa Catarina, st. Ee
91 Santa Clara, Cuba Cb
85 Santa Clara, U.S.A. Bd
93 Santa Cruz, Arg. Cj
94 Santa Cruz, Bol. Cc
68 Santa Cruz, Canary Is. Ac
85 Santa Cruz, U.S.A. Bd

28 San Sepalcro Dc
28 San Severo Ed
95 Santa Cruz, I. Ce
93 Santa Cruz, prov. Bg
90 Santa Eugenia, Pt. Ab
94 Santa Fé, Arg. Cf
85 Santa Fé, U.S.A. Ed
94 Santa Isabel, Bolivia Cb
95 Santa Isabel, Brazil Eb
71 Santa Isabel, Sp. Guin. Gh
81 Sta. Margherita Ligure He
95 Santa Maria, R. Ca
90 Santa Maria, R. Ca
26 Santa Maria d'Ortigueira Aa
95 Santa Maria da Vitória Gb
92 Santa Marta Ba
93 Santa Rosa, Arg. Cf
95 Santa Rosa, Brazil Ee
93 Santa Rosa, Honduras Ad
84 Santa Rosa, U.S.A. Bc
26 Santander Ba
26 Santarém Ab
93 Santiago, Chile Bf
91 Santiago, Dom. Rep. Dc
26 Santiago, Spain Aa
91 Santiago de Cuba Cb
90 Santiago del Estero Ca
90 Santiago Ixcuintla Cc
95 Santo Angelo Ee
94 Santo Corazón Dc
94 Santo Domingo Ec
94 Santo Rafael Cc
95 Santos Fa
74 Santos Bd
53 São Carlos Fd
95 São Domingos Db
93 São Francisco, R. Da
95 São Francisco, R. Gb

95 Sao Gabriel Ef
95 São João Fd
95 São José de
Norte Ef
95 São Lourenço Ec
92 São Luis Ec
95 São Paulo & st. Fd
95 São Sebastião Fd
69 São Tomé, I. Ce
20 Saône, R.
20 Saone et Loire,
dept. Cc
76 Saoura, prov. Ec
71 Sapele Gg
54 Sapporo Db
73 Sagota Fa
46 Saradiya Bh
28 Sarajevo Gc
35 Saraktash Le
31 Saransk Je
32 Sarapul Kd
89 Saratoga
Springs Jc
33 Saratov Je
37 Sarawak, st. Pj
46 Sardarsharh Ed
29 Sardinia, I. Bd
13 Sargans Da
46 Sargodha Db
14 Sark, I. Bc
27 Sarkişla Eb
27 Sarnia Ab
33 Sarny Ee
21 Saronno Hd
87 Sarosota Df
11 Sarpsborg Gf
19 Sarrebourg Gf
19 Sarreguemines Ge
71 Sarro Df
46 Sarupsa Dd
43 Sarur He
33 Sarych, C. Fg
47 Sasaram Kf
55 Sasebo Ad
78 Saskatchewan,
prov. Gc
80 Saskatchewan,
R. Db
80 Saskatoon Db
73 Sasobani Gb
33 Sasovo He
71 Sassandra & R. Dh
29 Sassari Bd
71 Satadougou Cf
46 Satara Dk
47 Satna Hf
30 Satoraljoujhely Ca
30 Satu Mare Db
36 Saudi Arabia,
King. Hg
81 Sault Ste. Marie,
Canada Ab
88 Sault Ste Marie,
U.S.A. Cc
15 Saumur Cd
39 Sauqira B. Ed
71 Saurboer Ab
30 Sava, R. Bc
46 Savali, I. Ch
91 Savanna la Mar Cc
87 Savannah De
44 Savantvadi Ce
75 Save, R. Eb
21 Savigliano Fe
20 Savoie, dist. &
dept. Ed
21 Savona De
55 Sawara Dc
49 Sawu Is. De
40 Sayda (Sidon) Bc
8 Scalasaig Bd
8 Scalloway Inset
10-11 Scandinavia
6 Scarborough Gc
33 Schaffhausen Ca
79 Schefferville Lc
89 Schenectady Hc
18 Schiedam Dc
18 Schiermonnikoog,
I. Fa
19 Schiltigheim Gf
28 Schio Cb
16 Schleswig Ca
13 Schopfneim Ba
49 Schouten Is. Ff
18 Schouwen, I. Cc
75 Schuckmann-
burg Ca
21 Schwabischer Jura,
mts. Ha
13 Schwanden Da
48 Schwaner mts. Cd
51 Schwangyashan
Hb
13 Schwarzenburg Bb
21 Schwarzwald,
mts. Gb
13 Schwaz Db
17 Schweinfurt Dc
21 Schwenningen Ga
13 Schwerin Db
19 Schwetzingen Ge
13 Schwyz, & cant. Ca
29 Sciacca Df

61 Scone Db
8 Scotland Ec
96 Scott I. Lc
84 Scotts Bluff Fc
61 Scottsdale Cd
89 Scranton Hd
7 Seaton Dg
84 Seattle Bb
90 Sebastien Vizcaino
B. Ab
44 Secunderabad De
60 Sedan Ab
67 Seddon Ed
67 Seddonville Dd
71 Sedhiou Bf
74 Seeheim Bc
71 Ségou Df
26 Segovia Ba
46 Sehore Fg
20 Seille, R. Dc
14 Seine, R. Ec
44 Seistan, Dist. Ab
12 Sejero, I. Ed
21 Sekondi-
Takoradi Eg
21 Selestat Fa
71 Selibaby Ce
38 Selima Oasis Dc
33 Selitrenoye Jf
80 Selkirk, Canada Eb
8 Selkirk, & co.,
Scotland. Ee
80 Selkirk Mts. Cb
47 Selma Ce
7 Selsey Bill Gg
75 Selukwe Ea
42 Selvas, reg. Cc
62 Selwyn Bc
48 Samarange Cd
32 Semenovskoe Hd
48 Semeru, mt. Fc
34 Semipalatinsk Ld
33 Sempach Ca
23 Sempacher See Ca
75 Sena Ea
54 Sendai, Honshu Dc
55 Sendai,
Kyushu Bd
68 Senegal, rep. Ad
71 Senegal, R. Cf
75 Senekal Dc
33 Sengilev Je
28 Senigallia Dc
8 Senj Eb
10 Senja Db
39 Sennar Cd
81 Senneterre Bb
20 Sens Bc
33 Sera Cc
52 Seoul Bb
62 Sepik R. Fg
43 Sept Iles Ca
10 Seraing Ed
47 Serampore Mg
30 Serbia, dist. Cd
33 Serdobsk He
21 Seregno Hd
48 Seremban Bc
92 Sergipe, st. Fd
27 Sérifos, I. Ab
33 Serov Jd
33 Serpukhov Ge
69 Serra da
Bandeira Dg
92 Serra de Tumuc
Humac Db
95 Serra do
Espinhaco Gc
95 Serra do Mar Fe
94 Serra do Norte Db
95 Serra do
Roncador Eb
94 Serra do
Tombador Db
94 Serra dos
Parecis Cb
27 Sérrai Ba
92 Sertania Fc
74 Sesfontein Aa
75 Sesheke Ca
32 Sessa Dd
21 Sesto Hd
21 Sestri Levante He
15 Sète Ef
30 Sétif Ga
55 Seto Uchi, see
Inland Sea Bd
70 Settat Db
26 Setúbal Ab
21 Setumo Fd
33 Sevastopol Fg
20 Séverac De
55 Severn, R. De
35 Severnaya Zemlya,
Is. Mb
26 Sevilla Ab
82a Seward Db
82a Seward Pen. Bb
50 Seydisfjördur Ca
27 Seyham, R. Eb
33 Seym Fe

30 Sfantu
Gheorghe Ec
70 Sfax Hb
39 Shabale, Webi,
R. De
75 Shabani Db
46 Shahdadk Ae
47 Shahdol Hg
46 Shahgarh Be
88 Shahhat Eb
47 Shahjahanpur Ge
43 Shahreza Gc
43 Shahrud Gb
43 Shahsavat Gb
33 Shakhty Hf
32 Shakhunya Jd
73 Shala, L. Fb
43 Shamil Hd
73 Shamo, L. Fb
75 Shamva Ea
45 Shan States Hd
51 Shanghai Gc
51 Shangjao Fd
51 Shangkiu Fc
66 Shannon Ed
9 Shannon, R. Bd
51 Shansi, prov. Fc
35 Shantar Is. Qd
51 Shantung, prov. Fc
51 Shaohing Gc
54 Shari, B. Db
33 Sharja, B. Ad
43 Sharka He
88 Sharon Ed
32 Sharya Jd
51 Shasi Fc
33 Shatsk He
80 Shaunavon Dc
81 Shawinigan Dc
85 Shawnee Gd
88 Sheboygan Bc
7 Sheerness Hf
6 Sheffield, Eng. Fd
61 Sheffield, Tas. Cd
46 Shekhupura Dc
51 Shelburne Cb
88 Shelbyville Bg
35 Shelekhov G. Ad
33 Shemakha Jg
86 Shenandoah Ac
27 Shendi Cd
32 Shenkursk Hc
51 Shensi, prov. Ec
33 Shentala Ke
50 Shentsa Cc
51 Shenyang, see
Mukden Gb
35 Shepetovka Ee
50 Shepparton Cc
7 Sheppey, I. of Hf
7 Sherborne Eg
71 Sherbro, I. Cg
81 Sherbrooke Cb
84 Sheridan Ec
85 Sherman Ge
18 's Hertogen-
bosch Ec
8 Shetland Is. Inset
33 Shevchenko Kd
9 Shibam Dd
54 Shibata Cc
54 Shibetsu Db
55 Shich-to, Is. Ad
32 Shiga, pref. Cc
50 Shigatze Cd
51 Shihkiachwang Fc
46 Shikarpur Be
55 Shikoku, I. &
dist. Bd
45 Shillong Gc
55 Shimabara Bd
54 Shimada Cd
55 Shimane, pref. Bd
54 Shimizu Cc
44 Shimoga Df
75 Shimonoseki Bd
8 Shin, L. Db
43 Shin Dand Hb
55 Shinano, R. Cc
55 Shingu Cd
54 Shinjo Cc
72 Shinkolobwe Df
73 Shinyanga Dd
55 Shio, C. Cd
54 Shiogama Dc
55 Shirakawa Dc
54 Shiraoi Db
43 Shiraz Gd
44 Shiriya, C. Db
47 Shitapur He
54 Shizuoka & pref. Cd
31 Shkoder & L. Bd
62 Shoalwater B. Dc
51 Shoayang Fd
44 Sholapur De
47 Shoshone Cc
75 Shoshong Db
87 Shreveport Be
7 Shrewsbury Ee
7 Shropshire, co. Ee

39 Shuqra Dd
43 Shushtar Fc
32 Shuya Hd
45 Shwebo Hd
45 Shweli R. Hd
44 Shyok R. Da
50 Siakwan Ed
46 Sialkot Eb
48 Siam, G. of Bc
51 Sian Fc
51 Siangfan Fc
51 Siangtan Fd
32 Siauliai Dd
28 Sibenik Ec
48 Siberut, I. Ad
44 Sibi Bc
50 Sibui Ec
48 Sibolga Ac
50 Sichang Ed
29 Sicily, I. Df
27 Sidheros, C. Cb
70 Sidi bel Abbes Ea
7 Sidmouth Dg
84 Sidney Fc
40 Sidon, see Sayda
23 Siedice Gb
18 Siegburg Gd
18 Siegen Hd
23 Siemiatycze Gb
28 Siena Cc
22 Sieradz Ec
94 Sierra de
Cordoba Cf
63 Sierra Leone, st. Ae
90 Sierra Madre,
mts. Cb
84 Sierra Nevada Bc
27 Sifnos Bb
30 Sighet Db
30 Sighisoara Eb
48 Sihanoukville Bb
46 Sikar Ee
35 Sikhote Alin Ra. Qe
47 Sikkim, st. Me
45 Silchar Gd
27 Silifke Db
47 Siliguri Me
30 Silistra Fc
12 Silkeborg Cc
72 Silva Porto Bf
23 Silvaplana Db
85 Silver City Ee
60 Silverton Bb
13 Silz Ea
48 Simeulue, I. Ac
33 Simferopol Fg
46 Simla Fc
30 Simleul
Silvaniei Db
74 Simonstown Bd
13 Simplon P. &
Tunnel Cb
90 Sinaloa Cb
48 Singapore Bc
48 Singaradja Cd
21 Singen Gb
27 Singitkos G. Bd
48 Singkawang Bc
61 Singleton Db
51 Singtai Fc
51 Sinhailien Fc
50 Sining Ec
49 Sinkat Cd
50 Sinkiang-Uigur,
Aut. Reg. Cb
43 Sinneh
(Sanandaj) Fb
30 Sinoe, L. Gc
75 Sinoia Ea
27 Sinop Ea
51 Sinsiang Fc
54 Sintai Ec
48 Sintang Cd
26 Sintra Ab
52 Sinuiju Bb
51 Sinyang Fc
13 Sion Bb
54 Sioux City Gc
33 Sioux Falls Gc
60 Sioux Lookout Ec
62 Sir Edward Pellew
Group Ab
29 Siracusa Ef
47 Sirajganj Mf
39 Siret, & R. Eb
26 Sirohi Df
27 Siros, I. Bb
46 Sirsa Ed
68 Sirte Db
28 Sisak Fb
47 Sitapur He
18 Sittard Ed
47 Sivas Dd
37 Sivrihisar Db
38 Siwa Bc
47 Siwan Ke
12 Sjaelland, I. Cd
12 Sjaellands Odde Ed
12 Skaelskör Cd
50 Skagafjördur Ba
12 Skagen Db

11 Skagerrak Bd
82a Skagway Ec
12 Skanderborg,
co. Cd
44 Skardu Db
6 Skegness He
10 Skelleftea Ec
9 Skerries Ec
22 Skien Bd
23 Skierniewice Fc
70 Skikda Ga
27 Skiros Bb
12 Skive Bc
12 Skjern & R. Bd
31 Skoplje Cd
35 Skovorodino Pd
8 Skye, dist. I. Bc
12 Slagelse Ed
22 Slakov Dd
27 Slatina Df
30 Slatina Ec
75 Slavgorod Fe
33 Slavyansk Gf
6 Sleaford Gd
23 Sliavnico Ed
18 Sliedrecht Dc
9 Slieve Mish, mt. Bd
9 Sligo & co. Cb
11 Sliven Fd
32 Slobodskoi Kd
7 Slough Gf
23 Slovakian Ore
Mts.
28 Slovenia, prov. Ea
22 Slupca Db
22 Slupsk Da
33 Slutsk Ee
9 Slyne Head Ac
70 Smara Cc
7 Smethwick Fe
79 Smith Sd. Ka
75 Smithfield Dd
61 Smithton Cd
10 Smöla, I. Bc
33 Smolensk Fe
27 Smolikas, mt. Ba
35 Smolyan Se
27 Smyrna, see
Izmir
18 Sneek Ea
22 Snezka, mt. Cc
58 Snoksdalar Ab
49 Snow Mt. Ff
6 Snowdon, mt. Dd
60 Snowdrift Ca
60 Snowtown Ab
60 Soalalo Gg
73 Sobat, R. Eb
92 Sobral Ec
33 Sochi Ga
57 Society Is. Fd
85 Socorro Ee
39 Socotra, I. Ed
11 Soderköping Dd
18 Soest, Ger. Hc
18 Soest, Neth. Eb
75 Sofala Eb
13 Sofia Dd
51 Sogndal Bd
11 Sognfjord Bc
38 Sohag Cc
19 Soignies Dd
14 Soissons Ec
27 Söke Cb
32 Sokol Hd
23 Sokólka Gb
71 Sokoto Gf
33 Sol-Iletsk Le
70 Solanşverket Db
32 Solikamsk Ld
18 Solingen, Gc
51 Solleftea Dc
26 Söller Cb
56 Solomon Is. Dd
62 Solomon S. Hh
13 Solothurn, &
cant. Ba
26 Soltau Ja
11 Silvesborg Cd
8 Solway Firth Ep
21 Soma Gb
66 Somali Rep. Ge
30 Sombor Bc
30 Sombrerete Dc
91 Sombrero, I. Fc
7 Somerset, co.,
England Df
88 Somerset,
Mass. Bb
74 Somerset East Dd
74 Somerset West Bd
14 Somme, dept. &
R. Db
51 Songkhla Bc
72 Songo Ca
32 Sonkovo Gd
46 Sonmiani Bc
80 Sonora, R. Bb
31 Sonthofen Jb
51 Soochow Gc
52 Sopot Ea
30 Sopron Ab
50 Sör Kvalöy Db
29 Sora Dd

81 Sorel Bb
29 Sorgono Bd
20 Sorgues Ce
12 Soró & co. Ed
95 Sorocaba Fd
49 Sorong Ef
73 Soroti Ec
10 Sortöya Ea
60 Sorrento,
7 Sorrento, Italy Ed
22 Sosnowiec Ec
80 Souris Dc
70 Sousse Ha
69 South Africa,
 Rep. of Eh
2 South America Df
36 South Arabia Hh
93 South Atlantic
 Ocean Ef
59 South Australia,
 st. Fd
88 South Bend Bd
83 South Carolina,
 st. Fc
3 South China S. Ne
61 South Coast Da
49 South Daja Is. Ed
2 South Dakota,
 st. Cb
8 South Downs Gg
2 South Georgia,
 I. Fh
88 South Haven Bc
67 South
 Invercargill Bg
88 South
 Milwaukee Bc
7 South Molton Df
96 South Orkney
 Is. Rd
48 South Pagai, I. Bd
84 South Platte, R. Fc
96 South Pole Ea
8 South Ronaldsay,
 I. Fb
2 South Sandwich
 Group Fh
96 South Shetland
 Is. Rd
6 South Shields Fc
8 South Uist, I. Ac
69 South West Africa,
 mandate Dh
7 Southampton Fg
79 Southampton, I. Db
87 Southbridge De
7 Southend Df
67 Southern Alps,
 mts.
65 Southern Cross Be
2 Southern Ocean Hj
7 Southminster Hf
67 Southport,
 Australia Da
6 Southport, Eng. Ed
75 Soutpansberge,
 mts. Db
35 Sovetskaya
 Gavan Re
24 Soya & C. Da
29 Spaccaforno Ef
4 Spain, Rep. Eg
23 Spala Fc
7 Spalding Ge
84 Spanish Fork Dc
71 Spanish Guinea Gh
63 Spanish Sahara Ac
91 Spanish Town C
8 Sparks Cf
87 Sparti Bb
87 Spartonburg Fd
94 Spencer B. Ac
67 Spenser Mts. De
8 Spey, R. Ec
17 Speyer Cd
18 Spiekeroog, I. Gb
23 Spirding L. Gb
2 Spitsbergen Hb
24 Split (Spalato) Ac
15 Splugen Db
84 Spokane Cb
2 Spoleto Dd
48 Spratly I. Cc
74 Springbok Bc
67 Springburn Ce
86 Springfield, Ill. Cd
87 Springfield,
 Miss. Bd
89 Springfield,
 N.Y. Cc
67 Springfield,
 New Zealand Ce
88 Springfield,
 Ohio De
21 Springhill Cd
75 Springs Dc
62 Springsure Cc
24 Springville Dc
80 Squamish Bc
65 Squires Mt. Ed
35 Sredne Kolymsk Sc

35 Sretensk Od
46 Srikolayabji, see
7 Kolayat De
44 Srinagar Cb
18 Stade Ja
11 Stadlandet Bc
8 Stafta, I. Bd
7 Stafford, & co. Ee
7 Staines Gf
7 Stamford, Eng. Ge
89 Stamford,
 U.S.A. Dd
75 Standerton Dc
80 Stanley, Can. Db
8 Stanley, Scot. Ed
33 Stanovoi Ra.,
 Mts. Pd
61 Stanthorpe Da
28 Stara Gradiška Fb
31 Stara Zagora Ed
33 Starabelsk Gf
32 Staraya Russa Fd
32 Stargard Cb
32 Starogard Eb
7 Start Pt. Dg
89 Staunton Fe
11 Stavanger Ad
33 Stavropol Hf
60 Staweli Bc
23 Stebark Fb
65 Steep Pt. Ad
73 Stefanie, L., (Chew
 Bahir) Fc
13 Stein Ca
18 Steinhuder Meer Jb
74 Steinkopf Bc
74 Stellenbosch Bd
16 Stendal Db
23 Stepanokert Jh
33 Stepok R. Bb
33 Sterlitamak Le
27 Stettler Cb
74 Steubenville Ed
86 Stevens Pt. Cc
80 Stewart Bb
67 Stewart I. Ag
17 Steyr Fd
86 Stillwater,
 Minn. Bb
85 Stillwater,
 Okla. Gc
31 Stip De
8 Stirling & co. Dd
65 Stirling Ra. Be
10 Stjordalshalsen Cc
17 Stockerau Gd
11 Stockholm Dd
8 Stockport Ed
84 Stockton Bd
6 Stockton-on-
 Tees Fc
6 Stoke-on-Trent Ed
28 Stolac Fc
18 Stolberg Fd
8 Stonehaven Fd
80 Stonewald Ee
35 Stony Tunguska,
 R. Mc
10 Stora Lule-
 vatten Db
10 Stören Cc
74 Stormberge,
 Mt. Dd
8 Stornoway Bb
32 Storozhevsk Kc
10 Storsjön Cc
18 Storuman Db
7 Stour, R. Eg
7 Stourbridge Ee
7 Stow-on-the-
 Wold Ff
9 Strabane Db
16 Stralsund Ea
8 Strath, C. Prov. Bd
11 Strand, Nor. Bd
62 Strangeways Fd
9 Strangford & L. Fb
8 Strancaer Cf
14 Strasbourg Gc
11 Stratford, Can. Ab
66 Stratford, N.Z. Ec
7 Stratford-on-
 Avon Fe
30 Strathalbyn Ad
8 Strathdon Ec
8 Strathmore Ed
8 Strathpeffer Dc
8 Strathy Db
65 Streaky Bay Ee
86 Streator Cc
62 Strickland R. Fb
8 Stromness Eb
10 Ströms
 Vattudal Cd
11 Stromstad Cd
8 Stronsay Fa
7 Stroud Ef
22 Struer Bc
31 Struma R. De
7 Strumble Hd. Bf
31 Strúmica Ed
88 Struthers Ed
12 Stubbeköbing Fe

13 Stuben Ea
48 Stung Treng Bb
88 Sturgeon Bay Bb
88 Sturgeon Falls Fa
75 Stutterheim Dd
17 Stuttgart, Ger. Cd
87 Stuttgart,
 U.S.A. Be
39 Suakin Cd
51 Suanhwa Fb
30 Subotica Bb
30 Suceava Fb
73 Suchow Fc
94 Sucre Bc
68 Sudan, st. Fd
81 Sudbury, Can. Ab
7 Sudbury, Eng. He
34 Sudzhensk Ld
41 Suez (El Suweis) Dg
41 Suez Canal Cb
7 Suffolk, co.,
 England He
89 Suffolk, U.S.A. Gf
51 Suihwa Fb
55 Suita Cd
48 Sukabun Bd
49 Sukarnapura Gf
32 Sukhona Hc
94 Sukumi Hg
46 Sukkur Be
49 Sula Is., Dd
43 Sulaiyil Fe
49 Sulawesi I. Dd
43 Sulaymaniyah Fb
67 Sulphur Ca
80 Sulphur Cb
92 Sultana Ac
28 Sulmona Dc
49 Sulu Arch. & S. Dc
48 Suluq Ed
19 Sulzbach Ge
48 Sumatra, I. Ac
43 Sumba, I. Dd
49 Sumbawa, I. Cd
73 Sumhawanga Ee
54 Sumisu, I. Cd
81 Summerside Cb
87 Sumter De
55 Sumy Fe
48 Sunda Str. Bd
48 Sundarbans Mg
6 Sunderland Fc
11 Sundsvall Dc
33 Sungari, R. Fb
27 Sungurlu Da
10 Sunndalsora Bc
55 Suo, B. Bd
84 Superior, Neb. Gc
88 Superior, Wis. Bb
86 Superior, L. Cb
40 Sur (Tyre) Bc
33 Sura Jc
48 Surabaja Cd
48 Surakarta Cd
44 Surat Dh
48 Surat Thani Ac
62 Surendranagar Cg
92 Surinam, Neth.
 terr. Fc
7 Surrey, co. Gf
54 Suruyga, B. Cd
28 Sušak Eb
13 Susten P. Cb
8 Sutherland, co. Db
48 Sutlej, R. Dd
55 Suwa & I. Cc
23 Suwalki Ga
48 Suzzara Jd
43 Svalbard I. Db
33 Svatovo Gf
63 Svendborg & co. Dd
34 Sverdlovsk Jd
34 Sverdrup Is. Ga
30 Svishtov Ed
62 Svitavy Dd
62 Swain Reefs Dc
74 Swakop, R. Ab
74 Swakopmund Ab
80 Swan Hill Bc
80 Swan River Db
7 Swanage Fg
7 Swanscombe Hf
44 Swat, Dist. Cb
75 Swatow Fd
4 Sweden, King. Jc
85 Sweet Water F
8 Sweet Water
 Canal Cf
74 Swellendam Cd
62 Swindnica Dc
62 Swiebodzin Cb
80 Swift Current Db
9 Swilly, L. Da
7 Swindon F
13 Switzerland, st. Cb
9 Swords Ec
61 Sydney,
 Australia Db
81 Sydney, Can. Cb
45 Sylhet Gd

34 Syr Darya R. Je
89 Syracuse Gc
36 Syria, st. Gf
43 Syrian Des. Dc
33 Syrian He
20 Sárvas Cb
22 Szczecin
 (Stettin) Cb
22 Szczecinek Db
75 Szczwan, prov. Ec
30 Szeged Cb
73 Szekesfehervar Bb
34 Szekszárd Bb
52 Szeman Ed
30 Szentes Cb
51 Szeping Gb
30 Szolnok Cb
90 Szombathely Ab
23 Szydlowiec Fc

70 Tabarka Ga
43 Tabas Hc
73 Tabora Ee
43 Tabriz Fb
52 Tacloban Db
94 Tacna Ac
94 Taco Pozo Ce
84 Tacoma Bb
84 Tacuarembó Df
73 Tademait, plat. Fc
67 Tadmor Dd
81 Tadoussac Bb
43 Tadzhikistan Kf
52 Taegu Bb
52 Taegu Bb
70 Tafassasset,
 Wadi Cc
71 Tafjord Bc
43 Taga-Dzong Me
33 Taganrog Gf
60 Tagish Aa
55 Taguatinga Fb
62 Tagula I. Hj
26 Tagus, see Tajo, R.
57 Tahakopa Bg
48 Tahan mt. Bc
70 Tahat, mt. Gd
50 Tahcheng Cb
43 Taheri Gd
43 Tahiti Fd
51 Taichung Gd
66 Taihape Ec
66 Tailem Bend Ac
21 Tailfingen Ga
35 Taimyr, L. Nb
53 Tainan Gd
27 Tainaron, C.
 (Matapan) Bb
51 Taipei Gd
51 Taiping Dc
35 Taiset Md
51 Taitung Gd
10 Taivalkoski Fb
51 Taiwan (Formosa)
 I. Gd
51 Taiyuan Fc
26 Tajo (Tagus) R. Ab
48 Tak Ab
55 Takada Cc
55 Takada Cc
55 Takamatsu Bd
55 Takaoka Cc
66 Takapuna Eb
55 Takasaki Cc
55 Takaungu Fc
55 Takayama Cc
55 Takefu Cc
50 Takla Makan,
 des. Cc
66 Talaud Is. Dc
49 Talaud Is. Dc
93 Talca Bf
93 Talcahuano Bf
51 Tali Ec
81 Tall Kalakh Cb
87 Tallahassee De
52 Tallinn Ed
94 Talltal Af
71 Tamale Eg
55 Tamano Bd
70 Tamanrasset (Ft.
 Laperrine) Gd
69 Tamatave Gg
59 Tambey He
33 Tamboy Hg
72 Tambura Db
71 Tamchakett Ce
71 Tamgak Mts. Gf
52 Tamsag Bulak Fb
61 Tamworth Db
61 Tamworth Db
39 Tana, L. Cd
73 Tana, R.,
71 Tana & Fd.,
 Norway Ef
49 Tanahgrogot Cd
23 Tanalitskata Le
82a Tanana Cb

69 Tananarive Gg
21 Tanaro, R. Fe
9 Tanderagee Eb
93 Tandil Df
48 Tandjung
 Pandan Bd
48 Tandjung Selor Cc
46 Tando Adam Bf
66 Taneatua Fc
55 Tanega Shima Bd
70 Tanerouft Fd
73 Tanga Fc
73 Tanganyika, L. De
70 Tanger
 (Tangier) Da
51 Tangshan Fc
46 Tanimbar Is. Ed
46 Tank Cb
12 Tannis Bay Cb
71 Tanout Gf
38 Tanta Cb
40 Tantura (Dor) Bb
68 Tanzania Ff
51 Taonan Gb
26 Taoudenni Ee
70 Taourirt Eb
67 Tapanui Bf
49 Tapuruquara Cb
49 Tarabulus
 (Tripoli) Bb
49 Tarakan Cc
76 Taranaki, dist. Ec
26 Tarancon Bb
72 Taranga Hill Dg
29 Taranto, & G. Fd
51 Tarare Cd
66 Tarawera Fc
28 Tarazona Ba
8 Tarbert Bc
15 Tarbes Df
65 Tarcoola Ee
52 Tardin Dc
26 Tarentaise, dist. Ed
70 Tarfaya Cc
33 Targoviste Ec
33 Targu-Jiu Dc
30 Targu Mures Eb
52 Targu Neamt Fb
94 Tarija Cd
51 Tarim Cb
43 Tarkhankut, C. Ff
48 Tarkwa Eg
23 Tarnobrzeg Fc
23 Tarnów Fc
23 Tarnowskie
 Góry Ec
43 Taroom Cd
24 Tarragona Ca
26 Tarragona Ca
40 Tarsus Db
57 Tartary, G. of Re
32 Tartu Ed
30 Tartus Bb
52 Tashchereau Bb
50 Tashigong Bc
24 Tashkent Je
24 Taskhurgan Bc
65 Tasikmalaja Bd
67 Tasman Bay Gd
3 Tasman Sea Pg
59 Tasmania, st. Hg
52 Tatabanya Bb
34 Tatarsk Kd
55 Tateyama Cc
50 Tatsaitan Dc
55 Tatta Af
51 Tatung Fb
55 Taumarunul Ec
45 Taunggyi Hd
67 Taunton Df
66 Taupo Fc
66 Tauranga Fb
27 Taurus Mts. Db
30 Tauz Jg
93 Taveta Fd
85 Taveuni, I. Hk
26 Tavira Ab
44 Tavoy & I. Hf
27 Tavsanli Cb
88 Tawas City Db
85 Taylor Ge
62 Tayma Dd
81 Tayport Fd
76 Tayulehsze Jd
58 Taz R. Lc
12 Taza Eb
10 Tbilisi Jg
52 Tczew Ea
66 Te Aroha Eb
66 Te Awamutu Ec
66 Te Hora Ed
66 Te Kuiti Ec
66 Te Puke Fb
29 Teano Ed
10 Tebessa Ga
35 Tecuci Fc
48 Tegal Bd
91 Tegucigalpa Gd
43 Tehran Gb
43 Tehtsin
 (Atuntze) Dd
90 Tehuantepec Dd
7 Teignmouth Dg

72 Teixeira de Sousa Cf
26 Tejo, R. Ab
27 Tekirdağ Ec
40 Tel Aviv-Jaffa Bc
91 Tela Ac
48 Telanaipura Bd
33 Telavi Jg
80 Telegraph Creek Ab
44 Tellicherry Df
48 Telok Anson Bc
48 Teluk Betung Bd
48 Telukdalum Ac
91 Tema Eg
90 Temax Gd
26 Temora Cb
29 Tempio Bd
85 Temple Ge
9 Tempiemore Dd
93 Temuco Bf
67 Temuka Cf
45 Ten Degree Chan. Gg
45 Tenasserim, & Dist. Hf
7 Tenby Cf
21 Tenda, Col di, P. Fe
68 Tenerife, I. Ac
90 Tengchung Dd
72 Tenke Df
24 Tennant Creek Eb
87 Tennessee, R. Ce
8 Tennessee, st. Cc
55 Tenryu, R. Cc
7 Tenterden Hf
61 Tenterfield Da
75 Teófilo-Otoni Gc
90 Tepic Dc
62 Teplice Bc
62 Teramo Dc
62 Terang Bc
33 Terek Jg
92 Teresina Ec
70 Terhazza Jf
24 Termez Jf
62 Termini Df
85 Terminos, Laguna de Fd
49 Ternate Cc
28 Terneuzen Cc
28 Terni Dc
33 Ternopol Ef
29 Terracina Dd
21 Terralba Bc
8 Terre Haute Bc
87 Terrell Ae
73 Terschelling, I. Ea
26 Teruel Ba
28 Tešanj, Fb
73 Tessalit Fd
33 Tessenei Cd
7 Tetbury Ef
75 Tete Ea
70 Tetuan Da
16 Teutoburger W., mts. Cb
7 Tewkesbury Ef
87 Texarkana Be
82 Texas, st. Cc
73 Texel, I. Da
45 Tezpur Gc
75 Thabana Ntlenyana, mt. Dc
48 Thailand (Siam) Bb
7 Thame Gf
66 Thames Eb
7 Thames, R. Hf
46 Thana Dj
44 Thar Desert, see Gt. Indian Des.
46 Tharad Cf
60 Thargomindah Ba
17 Thasos, I. Ba
45 Thaton He
45 Thazi Hd
84 The Dalles Bb
7 The Fens Ge
18 The Hague ('sGravenhague) Db
80 The Pas Db
17 The Skaw Db
12 The Sound Hd
38 Thebes Cc
63 Theodore Dc
27 Thérmaikos, G. of Ba
27 Thermopylai, pass. Bb
27 Thessaloniki Ba
27 Thessaly, dist. Ba
27 Thetford Mines Bb
65 Thevenard Ee
14 Thianville Gc
62 Thiers Bd
71 Thiès Bf
73 Thika Fd
27 Thionville Fe
27 Thíra, I. Cb
12 Thisted & Co. Bc

73 Thomson's Falls Fc
62 Thomson R. Bc
20 Thonon Ec
47 Thor Ke
10 Thórshöfn Ba
27 Thrace, dist. Ca
81 Three Rivers Bb
21 Thun Bb
13 Thurgau, cant. Da
9 Thurles Dd
62 Thursday I. Ba
8 Thurso Eb
22 Thysville Ae
70 Tiaret Ea
72 Tibati Ab
40 Tiberias Bc
40 Tiberias, L. (S. of Galilee) Bc
50 Tibet, Aut. Reg. Cc
90 Tiburon, I. Bb
71 Tichit De
13 Ticino, R. & cant. Cb
18 Tielt Cd
50 Tien Shan, mts. Cb
51 Tienen Dd
51 Tienshui Dc
51 Tientsin Fc
21 Tierra del Fuego Ch
88 Tiflin Dd
81 Tignish Cb
43 Tigris, R. Fc
50 Tijuana Aa
23 Tikhoretsk Hf
35 Tiksi Pb
18 Tilburg Ec
71 Tillabéry Ff
88 Tillsonburg Cc
27 Tílos, I. Cb
67 Timaru Cf
71 Timbédra Df
70 Timiris, C. Be
55 Timmis Ab
17 Timor, I. & S. Dd
70 Tindouf Dc
81 Tingha Da
27 Tinos Cb
49 Tintinara Bc
9 Tipperary & co. Cd
31 Tirane Be
33 Tiraspol Ef
40 Tirat Karmel Bc
8 Tiree, I. Bd
13 Tirol, prov. Ea
29 Tirso Bd
44 Tiruchchirappalli Df
44 Tirunelveli Dg
44 Tiruvannamali Df
80 Tisdale Db
94 Titicaca, L. Bc
31 Titograd Bd
31 Titov Veles Ce
30 Titovo Uzice Bd
72 Titule Dc
7 Tiverton Dg
28 Tivoli Dd
20 Tizi-Ouzou Fa
48 Tjilatjap Bd
48 Tjirebon Bd
90 Tlaxcala Ed
50 Tlaxiaco Ed
70 Tlemcen Eb
48 Toba L. Ac
91 Tobago, I. Fd
83 Tobermory Eb
31 Tobol R. Jd
34 Tobolsk Jd
62 Tobriand Is. Hh
28 Tobruk Db
55 Tochigi & pref. Cc
94 Tocco Bd
94 Tocopilla Ad
60 Tocumwal Cc
62 Todcaster Fd
50 Togtral Combo Cc
49 Togian Is. Dd
61 Togo, rep. Ce
54 Tōhoku, dist. Dc
73 Toinya Db
30 Tokaj Ca
67 Tokanul Bg
39 Tokar Cd
55 Tokara Str. Ad
67 Tokarahi Cf
28 Tokat Ea
55 Tokelau Is. Ed
66 Tokoroa Ec
55 Tokushima & pref. Bd
55 Tokuyama Bd
87 Tokyo & pref. Cc
66 Tolaga Gc
29 Tolbukhin Fd
6 Toledo & Sa. de, Spain Bb
88 Toledo, U.S.A. Dd
78 Tolo Bd
49 Tolo, G. of Dd
54 Toluca Ed
54 Tomakomai Db

26 Tomar Ab
23 Tomaszów Ec
71 Tombouctou (Timbuktu) Ee
85 Tombstone Ee
49 Tomini, G. of Dd
34 Tomsk Ld
90 Tonala Fd
7 Tonbridge Hf
12 Tönder & co. Be
66 Tonga (Friendly) Is. Hk
66 Tongatabu, I. Hk
18 Tongeren Ed
94 Tongoy Af
48 Tonkin, G. of Ba
48 Tonle Sap L. Bb
55 Tonopah Cd
11 Tönsberg Cd
61 Toowong Da
61 Toowoomba Da
32 Top L. Fb
86 Topeka Ad
90 Topolobampo Cb
16 Torgau Ec
18 Torhout Cc
90 Tori Shima (Mitsugo) I. Cd
21 Torino (Turin) Fd
89 Troy, U.S.A. Jc
28 Torokina Jh
27 Toronaios, G. Ba
61 Toronto, Australia Da
81 Toronto, Can. Bd
32 Toropets Fd
81 Truro, Canada Cb
71 Torori Ec
7 Torquay Dg
29 Torre Annunziata Ed
26 Torrelavega Ba
90 Torreon Db
95 Torres, Brazil Fe
90 Torres, Mexico Bb
21 Torres Novas Ab
26 Torres Vedras Ab
89 Torrington Jd
60 Torrowangee Bb
28 Tortoli Bc
21 Tortona Ge
26 Tortosa & C. Ca
22 Tortum Eb
55 Tosa, B. Bd
28 Toscana, reg. Cc
27 Tosya Da
74 Toteng Cb
32 Totma Hd
7 Tottenham Gf
95 Tottori & pref. Bc
70 Toubkal, Dj., mt. Db
70 Touggourt Gb
71 Tougué Cf
19 Toul Ef
15 Toulon Df
19 Toulouse Df
43 Toungoo He
49 Tournai Cd
13 Tournal Cd
13 Tours Dd
54 Towada, L. Db
7 Towcester Gf
62 Townshend C. Dc
62 Townsville Cb
89 Towson Ge
55 Toyama, & pref. Cc
55 Toyama, B. Cc
55 Toyohashi Cd
55 Toyooka Cc
70 Tozeur Gb
42 Trabzon Da
50 Tradam Cc
26 Trafalgar, C. Ab
80 Trail Cc
9 Tralee Cd
61 Trangie Cb
21 Trani Fd
75 Transkei Dd
75 Transvaal, prov. c
30 Transylvania, dist. Db
30 Transylvanian Alps Dc
29 Trapani Cf
90 Traralgon Cc
88 Traverse City Cb
28 Travnik Fb
21 Trebbia, R. He
22 Trebic Cd
28 Trebinje Cc
28 Trebon Cd
7 Tregar Df
11 Trelleborg Cd
95 Tres Lagôas Ed
21 Treviglio Hd
28 Treviso Db

19 Trier Fe
28 Trieste Db
27 Trikkala Bb
9 Trim Ec
44 Trincomalee Dg
7 Tring Gf
94 Trinidad Cb
85 Trinidad, I. Fd
81 Trinity B. Db
68 Tripoli, Libya Db
40 Tripoli(Tarabulus), Syria Bb
27 Tripolis Bb
45 Tripura, St. Gd
2 Tristan da Cunha, I. Fg
44 Trivandrum Dg
22 Tmava Dd
22 Troia Ed
32 Troitsko-Fechorsk Lc
13 Trollforsen Db
13 Trombudo Fe
10 Tromsö Db
10 Trondheim Cc
27 Troodos, Mt. Dc
8 Troon De
7 Trowbridge Ef
27 Troy, Turkey Cb
94 Troyes Ca
36 Trucial Oman, st. Jg
91 Trujillo, Hond. Ac
92 Trujillo, Peru Bc
81 Truro, England Cg
22 Turnov Cc
22 Truyere, R. Be
71 Tsamkong Fd
74 Tsane Cb
74 Tsane Cb
44 Tselinograd Kd
51 Tsetserleg Eb
33 Tshkinali Hg
51 Tsiaotso Fc
51 Tsinan Fc
51 Tsinghai, prov. Dc
51 Tsingshih Fd
51 Tsingtao Gc
51 Tsinghai Cb
51 Tsitsihar Gb
51 Tsu Cd
51 Tsu Shima Ad
55 Tsuchiura Dc
55 Tsugaru Str. Db
54 Tsumeb Ba
51 Tsunyi Ed
54 Tsuruga Cc
54 Tsuruoka Cc
68 Tsushima, & Str. Bb
72 Tuamotu Arch. Gd
55 Tuapse Gg
67 Tuatapere Ag
48 Tuban Gd
91 Tubarão Fe
19 Tübingen Jf
57 Tubuai Is. (Austral. Is.) Fe
94 Tucacaba Dc
85 Tucson Dc
94 Tucumán Be
85 Tucumcari Fd
92 Tufi Gh
75 Tugela, R. Ec
49 Tukangbesi Is. Dd
50 Tul Karm Bc
90 Tula, Mexico Cc
55 Tula, U.S.S.R. Ge
50 Tulan Dc
90 Tulancingo Ec
50 Tulcan Cd
30 Tulcea Gc
69 Tulear Gh
9 Tulia Cd
9 Tulla Cd
9 Tullamore Dc
8 Tulloch Dd
7 Tullow Ed
87 Tulsa Ad
54 Tulun Nd
48 Tulungogung Cd
92 Tumaco Bb
72 T., mba, L. Bd
61 Tumbarumba Cc
65 Tumby Bay Fe
70 Tumkur Cf
71 Tumut Cc
44 Tunbridge Wells Hf
51 Tunghsan Fc
51 Tungchuan Ec
51 Tunghwa Gb
51 Tungkiang Hb
51 Tungliao Gb
44 Tunis Ca
48 Tunisia, king. Cb
51 Tunki Fd
92 Tunja Cb
94 Tupiza Bd
47 Tura Nf

42 Turaba Ed
30 Turda Db
22 Turek Eb
50 Turfan Cb
31 Turgovishte Cb
22 Turgutlu Cb
21 Turin, see Torino
36 Turkey, rep. Gf
34 Turkmenistan Hf
91 Turks, Is. Db
90 Turku (Åbo) Ec
90 Turnefie, I. Gd
18 Turnhout Dc
32 Turnovo Ed
30 Turnu Magurele Ed
30 Turnu Severin Dc
49 Turtle Is. Cc
32 Turya Kc
24 Tuscaloosa Ce
44 Tuticorin Dg
21 Tutrakan Gb
66 Tutuila, I. Dj
51 Tuxtla Fd
52 Tuymazy Ke
51 Tuyun Ed
27 Tuz, L. Db
31 Tuzla Bc
30 Tuzla Db
6 Tweed, R. Ee
83 Twillingate Db
86 Two Harbors Bb
88 Two Rivers Bb
87 Tyler Ae
6 Tynemouth Fd
40 Tyre (Sur) Bc
17 Tyrol, mts. Dc
81 Tyrone, co. Db
74 Tyrrhenian Sea De
34 Tyumen Jd
51 Tzekung Ed
51 Tzepo Fc

95 Uba Gd
46 Ubauro Bd
55 Ube Bd
95 Uberaba Fc
95 Uberlandia Fc
34 Ubon Bb
54 Uchiura B. Db
6 Uddaipur Df
10 Uddjaur Db
46 Udhampur Cb
21 Udine Da
75 Udot Mts. Ea
18 Eala Cc
75 Uelen Db
72 Uere, R. Ld
6 Ufa & R. Ld
73 Ugalla, R. Ee
68 Uganda, st. Fe
9 Uig Bc
72 Uige Be
75 Uitenhage Dd
70 Ujda Eb
70 Ujiji Dd
46 Ujjain Eg
73 Ukerewe Ed
Kc Ukhta Kc
33 Ukraine Ef
90 Ulan Bator Eb
55 Ulan Ude Nd
51 Ulanhot Gb
46 Ulhasnagar Dj
61 Ulladulla Dc
55 Ulung Do, I. Dc
21 Ulm Ha
31 Ulmarra Da
9 Ulster, prov. Eb
22 Ultava, R. Cd
60 Ultima Bc
27 Uluksia Db
61 Ulverstone Cd
33 Ulyanovsk Je
9 Uman Ef
46 Umarkot Bf
75 Umata Db
22 Umbol I., Gh
24 Umbria, reg. Dc
10 Ume, R. Dc
10 Umeå Dc
44 Umm Lajj De
66 Umm Ruwaba Ea
44 Umm Said Ge
44 Umtali Ea
75 Umvuma Ea
75 Umzimvubu Dd
75 Umzinto Ed
83 Unalaska, I. Fe
94 Uncha Bc
33 Uncha Bc
79 Ungava B. Lc
30 Ungeni Ga
95 União da Vitoria Ee
83 Unimak, I. Eb
24 Union of Soviet Socialist Reps. Pd
88 Uniontown Fe
68 United Arab Rep. (Egypt) Fb
7 United Kingdom Ee
77 United States of America He

47 Unnao He
8 Unst, I. Inset
13 Unter Walden, cant. Cb
32 Unzha Hd
72 Upemba, L. De
78 Upernavik Ma
74 Upington Cc
66 Upolu, I. Dj
67 Upper Hutt Ed
73 Upper Nile, prov. Eb
68 Upper Volta, rep. Bd
11 Uppsala Dd
32 Ural Mts. Lc
31 Ural, R. Hd
34 Uralsk Hd
80 Uranium City Db
55 Urawa Cc
88 Urbana Bd
28 Urbino Dc
90 Ures Bb
42 Urfa Db
13 Uri, cant. Cb
43 Urmia, L. Fb
31 Urosevac Cd
94 Uruguaiana De
93 Uruguay, rep., & R. Df
32 Urumchi Cb
33 Uryupinsk He
32 Usa R. Lb
27 Usak Cb
74 Usakos Bb
75 Useko Ee
42 Usfan De
14 Ushant, I. Ac
27 Uskdar (Scutari) Ca
33 Usman Ge
32 Ust-Izhma Kb
75 Ust Kamchatsk Td
34 Ust Port Lb
32 Ust-Shchugar Lc
32 Ust Tsilma Kb
34 Ust-Usa Lb
34 Ust Urt Plat. He
32 Usti Cb
22 Ustka Da
34 Ustyug Jc
55 Usuki Bd
84 Utah, L. Dc
82 Utah, st. Bc
73 Utete Fe
94 Utiariti Db
93 Utica Hc
75 Utrecht, Nat. Ec
18 Utrecht & prov., Netherlands Eb
55 Utsunomiya Cc
47 Uttar Pradesh, st. He
48 Uttaradit Bb
10 Uusikaariepy Ec
85 Uvalde Gf
73 Uvinza Ee
55 Uwajima Bd
94 Uyuni Bd
32 Uzbekistan Je

75 Vaal, R. Dc
10 Vaasa Ec
30 Vac Bb
10 Vadso Ga
21 Vaduz Hb
96 Vahsel Bay Rb
14 Val-d'Oise, dept. Ec
34 Valgach L. Hb
13 Valais, cant. Bb
93 Valcheta Cg
25 Valdepeñas Bb
82a Valdez Db
93 Valdivia Bf
24 Valenca Aa
20 Valence Cf
25 Valencia & G. of, Spain Bb
92 Valencia, Ven. Ca
9 Valentia I. Ae
21 Valenza Gd
23 Valga Ed
31 Valjevo Bc
18 Valkenswaard Ec
24 Valladolid Gd
24 Valladolid Ba
21 Valle d'Aosta, prov. Fd
94 Vallejo Bd
94 Vallenar Ae
14 Valley City Gb
28 Vallombrosa Cc
13 Valorbe Ab
93 Valparaiso, Chile Bf
94 Valparaiso, U.S.A. Bd
21 Valtellina, dist. Hc
71 Valverde Dc
42 Van, L. Eb
87 Van Buren Bd
64 Van Diemen C., & G. Ea

20 Vancluse, dept. Df
80 Vancouver, Can. Bc
84 Vancouver, U.S.A. Bb
80 Vancouver I. Bc
11 Vänern, L. Cd
14 Vanersborg Cd
73 Vanga Fd
62 Vanimo Fg
10 Vännäs Dc
55 Vannes Bd
10 Vannöy Da
66 Vanua Levu, I. Gk
47 Varanasi (Banaras) Jf
10 Varangeren Ga
10 Varanger Pen. Fa
28 Varazdin Fa
21 Varazze Ge
32 Vardar, R. De
12 Varde & R. Bd
12 Vardingborg Be
10 Vardo Ga
18 Varel Ha
21 Varese Gd
31 Varna (Stalin) Gd
12 Varnamo Cd
10 Vaslui Fb
10 Vatna Jökull Bb
30 Vatra-Dornei Eb
11 Vättern, L. Cd
21 Vaud, cant. Ab
18 Vechte, R. Fb
10 Vega, L. Cb
30 Vegreville Cb
12 Vejle & co. Cd
20 Velay, Mts. du, Be
28 Velebit Planina, mts. Eb
29 Velletri Dd
26 Vélez Málaga Bb
32 Veliki Hc
32 Velikie Luki Fd
12 Velizh Fd
44 Vellore Df
18 Velsen Db
32 Velsk Hc
12 Vendsyssel, dist. Db
28 Veneto, reg. Db
92 Venezuela, rep. Cb
28 Venice, Gulf of Db
19 Venice (Venezia) Db
20 Vénissieux Cd
18 Venlo Fc
21 Ventimiglia Ff
7 Ventnor Fg
20 Ventoux, mt. Df
32 Ventspils Dd
20 Vera Ca
90 Veracruz Ed
46 Veraval Ch
21 Vercelli Gd
10 Verdalsöra Cc
90 Verde, R. Kd
16 Verden Cb
16 Verdun Fc
20 Verdun, R. Ef
16 Vereeniging Dc
71 Verga, C. Cf
35 Verkhoyansk, & Ra. Qc

32 Vermilion, R. Fb
83 Vermont, st. Fb
74 Verneukpan, L. Cd
90 Vernon, Can. Bc
84 Vernon, U.S.A. Ge
28 Verona Jd
14 Versailles Dc
18 Verviers Ed
15 Vesoul Gd
10 Vesterålen, I. Cb
10 Vestfjorden Cb
10 Vestmannaeyjar, I. Ab
29 Vesuvius, vol. Ed
10 Veszprem Ab
32 Vetluga, & R. Jd
13 Vevey Ab
10 Viana do Castelo Aa
28 Viareggio Cc
22 Viborg & co. Cc
28 Vicenza Cb
20 Vichy Bc
87 Vicksburg Be
80 Victor Harbor Ac
80 Victoria, Can. Bc
55 Victoria, Guin. Cf
85 Victoria, U.S.A. Gf
75 Victoria Beach Eb
75 Victoria Falls Da
73 Victoria, L. Ed
46 Victoria Land Kb
19 Victoria Pt. Hg
64 Victoria River Downs Eb
59 Victoria, st. Gf

74 Victoria West Cd
89 Victoriaville Ac
30 Vidin Dd
18 Viedma Cg
17 Vienna (Wien) Gd
20 Vienne Cd
48 Vientiane Bb
18 Viersen Fc
13 Vierwaldstatter See, L. Ca
48 Vietnam, st. Bb
21 Vigevano Gd
90 Vigia Chico Gd
26 Vigo Aa
45 Vijayavada Ee
10 Vikna I. Cc
73 Vila Cabral Ff
72 Vila de Cangamba Bf
75 Vila de Manica Ea
75 Vila Fontes Ea
72 Vila Henrique de Carvalho Ce
75 Vila João Belo Ec
72 Vila Luso Bf
75 Vila Machado Ea
75 Vila Mariano Machado Af
26 Vila Nova de Gáia Aa
72 Vila Salazar Af
94 Vila Vila Bc
75 Vilanculos Fb
94 Vilhena Cb
90 Villa Ahumada Ca
92 Villa Bella Cd
68 Villa Cisneros Ac
14 Villaich Cf
93 Villa Mercedes Cf
94 Villa Montes Cd
17 Villach Ee
21 Villafranca di Verona Jd
90 Villahermosa Fd
26 Villanueva y Geltru Ca
28 Vilaputzu Bg
30 Villarosa Ef
94 Villarrica De
20 Villefranche Cd
26 Villena Bb
17 Villeneuve Bf
19 Villerupt Ee
23 Villingen Ga
32 Vilnius Ec
75 Vilo del Mar Bf
20 Vinaroz Ca
88 Vincennes Be
48 Vinh Bb
33 Vinnitsa Ef
60 Virden Dc
91 Virgin Is. Fc
86 Virginia Bb
83 Virginia, st. Fc
89 Virginia Beach Hf
28 Vis, I. Fc
71 Visby Dd
78 Viscount Melville Sd. Ga
73 Vishakhapat-nam Ee
32 Vishera Kc
48 Visoko Gc
20 Visp Bb
22 Vistula (Wisła) Ec
66 Viti Levu, I. Gk
28 Vitoria, Braz. Ee
26 Vitoria, Spain Ba
94 Vitoria da Conquista Ed
20 Vitry le François Ef
20 Vitteaux Cb
28 Vittorio Db
29 Vittoria Ef
47 Vizianagaram Jj
18 Vlaardingen Dc
32 Vladimir Hd
35 Vladivostok Qe
18 Vlieland, I. Da
18 Vlissingen (Flushing) Cc
31 Vlone Be
99 Vogelkop, mts. Ff
24 Voges, mts. Ge
21 Voghera Ge
73 Voi Fd
10 Volron Ed
21 Volda Bc
21 Voldagno Kd
33 Volga R. Jf
33 Volgograd Hf
21 Voltefjell Ec
19 Völklingen Fe
75 Volksrust Ec
32 Vologda Hd
27 Vólos Bb

33 Volovo Ge
33 Volsk Je
71 Volta L. Eg
68 Volta, rep. see Upper Volta Bd
71 Volta, R. Eg
28 Volteri Cc
18 Voorburg Db
10 Vopnafjördur Ca
10 Vopnajökull Bb
21 Voralberg, prov. Hb
13 Vorderrhein, R. Cb
72 Voriai Sporades, Is. Bb
32 Vorkuta Mb
20 Vosges, mts. & dept. Ea
11 Voss Bc
96 Vostok Sb
32 Votkinsk Kd
32 Voznesene Gc
33 Voznesensk Ff
31 Vranje Cd
31 Vratsa Dd
74 Vredenburg Bd
30 Vrsac Cc
75 Vryburg Cc
75 Vryheid Ec
30 Vukovar Bc
77 Vuolvo, L. Db
32 Vyatka Kd
52 Vyazma Fd
32 Vyborg Ec
33 Vychegda Kc
32 Vyshni Ec
32 Vystegra Gc

71 Wa Ef
18 Waal, R. Ec
88 Wabash Cd
22 Wabrzezno Eb
23 Wachock Fc
85 Waco Ge
39 Wad Medani Cd
48 Wadden Zee Ea
80 Waddington, Mt. Bb
44 Wadi De
42 Wadi ar Rima Dd
42 Wadi as Subai, R. Ee
42 Wadi Dawasir, R. Ee
42 Wadi Hauran, R. Ec
43 Wadi Sabha, R. Fe
42 Wadi Sirhan, R. Dc
16 Wageningen Ec
78 Wager B. Hb
55 Wagin Be
66 Wagga Wagga Cc
86 Wahpeton Ab
57 Waiau Sb
48 Waigeo, I. Ed
69 Waihi Eb
67 Waikaia Bf
67 Waikato, R. Eb
54 Waikerie Ab
66 Waikokopu Fc
57 Waikouaiti Cf
80 Waimarino Ec
67 Waimate Cf
49 Waingapu Dd
80 Wainwright Cb
66 Waiouru Ec
62 Waipara De
66 Waipawa Fc
66 Waipu Ea
55 Waipukurau Fd
66 Wairoa Fc
66 Waitara Ec
66 Waiuku Eb
55 Wajima Cc
54 Wakasa, B. Cc
55 Wakayama & pref. Cc
56 Wake I. Dc
67 Wakefield Dd
68 Wakeham Bay Kb
54 Wakkanai Da
22 Walbrzych Dc
41 Walcha Db
18 Walcheren, I. Cc
64 Walcott Pt. Bc
7 Wales De
61 Walgett Cb
88 Walkerton Eb
94 Walla Walla Cb
84 Wallace Dc
55 Wallaceburg Dc
74 Wallachia, dist. Ec
30 Wallsend, Dc
61 Walsall Fe
85 Walsenburg Fd
54 Walvis & B. Af
39 Walwal De
80 Wama Bb
60 Wanaaring Ba
67 Wanaka Bf
61 Wandoan Cd
66 Wanganui Ec

60 Wangaratta Cc
13 Wangen Da
18 Wangerooge, I. Ga
51 Wanhsien Ec
75 Wankie Da
94 Wanks, R. Bd
7 Wantage Ff
73 Warandab Gb
46 Warangal Gd
61 Waratah Cd
21 Warburton Cc
63 Warburton R. Ad
67 Ward Bd
46 Wardha Gh
7 Wareham Eg
18 Warendorf Gc
74 Warkworth Ec
74 Warmbad, S.W. Afr. Bc
75 Warmbad, Trans. Dc
7 Warminster Ef
60 Warragul Cc
60 Warrego R. Ca
61 Warren, Australia Cb
85 Warren, U.S.A. Ed
9 Warrenpoint Eb
75 Warrenton Dc
60 Warri Warri Ba
65 Warrina Fd
6 Warrington Ed
60 Warrnambool Bc
23 Warsaw (Warszawa), Poland Fb
88 Warsaw, U.S.A. Cd
22 Warta, R. Cb
61 Warwick, Australia Da
7 Warwick & co., England Fe
85 Wasatch, Mts. Dd
6 Wash, The He
89 Washington, D.C. Ge
88 Washington, Ind. Be
88 Washington, Ohio De
88 Washington, Pa. Ed
82 Washington, st. Ab
18 Wassenaar Db
87 Water Valley Ce
74 Waterberg Bb
89 Waterbury Jd
9 Waterford, & co. Dd
89 Waterford Hr. Dd
86 Waterloo, Can. Ec
86 Waterloo, Iowa Bc
71 Waterloo, Sierra Leone Cg
89 Watertown, N.Y. Hc
86 Watertown, Wis. Cc
32 Waterways Cb
7 Watford Gf
89 Watling I. S. Salvador I.) Db
80 Watson Lake Bb
8 Watten Eb
18 Watten Eb
7 Watton Ha
74 Wattrvil Da
72 Wau, Australia Gh
73 Wau, Sudan Db
58 Waukegan Bc
84 Wauwatosa Bc
64 Wave Hill Eb
66 Waverley Ec
45 Waw Fe
87 Waycross De
88 Waynesboro Fe
46 Wazirabad, West Pakistan Eb
38 Wazirabad, Afghanistan Fb
7 Weald, The Gf
86 Webster City Bc
2 Weddell Sea Ej
61 Wee Waa Cc
18 Weert Ec
55 Weesen Da
13 Weggis Ca
55 Weifang Fc
21 Weilheim Kb
77 Weimar Dc
13 Weinfelden Ca
21 Weingarten Hb
16 Weinheim He
24 Wejh Dd
66 Weiherowoo Ea
65 Weld Spring Cd
18 Welland Fc
62 Welkesley Is. Ab
74 Wellingborough Fe
74 Wellington, Cape Province Bd
7 Wellington, England Ee
7 Wellington, N.S.W. Cb

67 Wellington, New Zealand Ed
66 Wellington, dist., New Zealand Ed
85 Wellington, U.S.A. Gd
93 Wellington I. Bg
7 Wells Ef
88 Wellsville, Ohio Ed
89 Wellsville, N.Y. Gc
17 Wels Fd
7 Welshpool De
51 Wenchow Gd
13 Wengen Bb
60 Wentworth Bb
18 Werne Gc
61 Werris Creek Db
16 Wesel Bc
18 Weser, R. Ha
22 West Bedskids, mts. Ed
88 West Bend Bc
47 West Bengal, st. Lg
7 West Bromwich Fe
49 West Daja Is. Dd
32 West Dvina, R. Ed
18 West Frisian Is. Ea
7 West Ham Hf
51 West Harbour Cf
6 West Hartlepool Fc
49 West Irian, prov. Ff
8 West Lothian, co. Ee
75 West Nicholson Db
36 West Pakistan Kg
87 West Palm Beach Df
18 West Schelde, R. Cc
83 West Virginia, st. Ec
61 West Wyalong Cb
89 Westbrook Kc
51 Westbury Cd
58 Western Australia, st. Cc
44 Western Ghats, mts. Ce
66 Western Samoa, Is. Ch
67 Westland Bight Be
67 Westland, dist. Ce
9 Westmeath, co. Dc
6 Westmorland, co. Ec
49 Weston, Sabah Ec
88 Weston, U.S.A. Ee
7 Weston-super-Mare Ef
9 Westport, Ire. Bc
67 Westport, N.Z. Cd
8 Westray, I. Fa
18 Wetar, I. Dd
18 Wetteren Cc
19 Wetzlar Hd
7 Wewak Fg
9 Wexford, & co. Ed
80 Weyburn Dc
81 Weymont Bb
7 Weymouth Eg
66 Whakatane Fb
6 Whanga-momona Ed
66 Whangarei Ea
65 Wheeling Ed
65 Whidbey Pt. Fe
6 Whitby Gc
7 Whitchurch Ff
22 White Mts. Dd
39 White Nile (Bahr el Abiad) R. Gd
33 White Russia De
32 White Sea Gb
47 Whitecliffs Ce
86 Whitefish B. Db
6 Whitehaven Dc
78 Whitehorse Db
8 Whithorn Df
66 Whitianga Eb
7 Whitstable Hf
82a Whittier Db
60 Whitton Cb
88 Wharton Eb
85 Wichita Gd
85 Wichita Falls Ge
8 Wick Eb

9 Wicklow, & co. Ed
9 Wicklow, mts. Ed
22 Wielun Ec
17 Wiener Neustadt Ge
19 Wiesbaden Hd
23 Wierzbnik Fc
6 Wigan Ed
8 Wigtown, co. Df
13 Wil Da
60 Wilcannia Bb
21 Wildspitze, mt. Jc
18 Wilhelmshaven Ga
18 Wilhelmsburg Ja
80 Wilkie Da
89 Wilkes Barre Hd
96 Wilkes Land Hc
91 Willemstad Ed
65 William Mt. Be
89 William sburg Gf
88 William son Df
89 Williamsport Gd
60 Williamstown Bc
84 Williston Fb
86 Willmar Bb
74 Willowmore Cd
18 Wilmette Bc
60 Wilmington, Australia Ab
87 Wilmington, N.C. Ee
89 Wilmington, N.J. He
7 Wimborne Fg
89 Wilson Gg
7 Wilton Ff
7 Wiltshire, co. Ff
65 Wiluna Cd
75 Winburg Dc
7 Winchester, England Ff
88 Winchester, Ind. Cd
89 Winchester, Wash. Fe
6 Windermere Ec
74 Windhoek Bb
63 Windorah Bd
81 Windsor, Can. Ab
7 Windsor, Eng. Gf
91 Windward Is. Fd
91 Windward Passage Dc
61 Wingham Db
81 Winisk Aa
73 Winisk Fb
65 Winnemucca Cc
87 Winnfield Be
80 Winnipeg & L. Dc
80 Winnipegosis, L. Db
86 Winona Bb
85 Winslow Dd
88 Winston-Salem Ef
18 Winterswijk Fc
13 Winterthur Ca
7 Winton Fg
65 Winton, Australia Bc
67 Winton, N.Z. Bg
7 Wisbech He
86 Wisconsin Rapids Bb
83 Wisconsin, st. Db
8 Wishaw Ee
18 Wismar Db
22 Wista (Vistula) R. Eb
7 Witney Ff
18 Witten Gc
16 Wittenberge Db
89 Witwatersrand Dc
22 Wloclawek Eb
23 Wlodawa Gc
23 Wloszczowa Ec
17 Wolfsberg Fe
22 Wolin, R. Cb
80 Wollaston L. Db
7 Wollaston Pen. Fb
61 Wollongong Db
75 Wolmaransstad Dc
22 Wolomin Fb
7 Wolverhampton Ee
52 Wonsan Bb
60 Wonthaggi Cc
7 Woodbridge Je
65 Woodlark I. Hh
65 Woodroffe Mt. Ed

80 Woods, L. of the Ec
81 Woodstock, Canada Cb
7 Woodstock, England Ff
66 Woodville Ed
85 Woodward Gd
62 Woolgar Bb
65 Woomera Fe
74 Woonsocket Kd
65 Wooramel & R. Ad
60 Woorooroka Ca
88 Wooster Dd
7 Wootton Bassett Ff
74 Worcester, Cape Province Bd
7 Worcester, & co., England Ee
89 Worcester, U.S.A. Kc
17 Wörgl De
6 Workington Dc
19 Worms He
7 Worthing Gg
33 Wrangel I. Vb
49 Wrexham Ed
78 Wrigley Eb
22 Wroclaw (Breslau) Dc
51 Wuchang Ec
51 Wuchow Fd
51 Wuhan Fc
51 Wuhu Fc
18 Wuppertal Gc
16 Wurzen Ec
51 Wusih Gc
51 Wusu Cb
48 Wyandotte Dc
63 Wyandra Cd
7 Wye, R. De
64 Wyndham, Australia Db
67 Wyndham, N.Z. Bg
61 Wynnum Da
61 Wynyard Cd
82 Wyoming, st. Cb

40 Yarmuk, wadi Bc
32 Yaroslavl Gd
8 Yarrow Ee
61 Yass Cb
94 Yati Cc
35 Yatsushiro Bd
68 Yaunde De
55 Yawatahama Bd
43 Yazd Gc
87 Yazoo R. Be
51 Yehsien Fc
3 Yelets Ge
38 Yell, I. Inset
52 Yellow Sea Bb
80 Yellowhead P. Cb
80 Yellowknife Ca
84 Yellowstone, R. Eb
36 Yemen, st. Hh
45 Yenangyaung Gd
42 Yenba De
35 Yenisei, R. Lc
35 Yeniseisk Md
50 Yenki Cb
33 Yenotayevsk Jf
46 Yeotmal Gh
7 Yeovil Eg
35 Yerevan Hg
33 Yershov Je
27 Yesil, R. Ea
15 Yeu, Ile de Bd
35 Yeviakh Jg
33 Yevpatoriya Ff
33 Yeysk Gf
51 Yilan Gb
51 Yinchwan Ec
51 Yingkow Gb
51 Yiyang Fd
10 Yli Kitka Fb
10 Yliveska Ec
55 Yoakum Gf
71 Yobe, R. Hf
55 Yokkaichi Cd
55 Yokohama Cc
55 Yokosuka Cc
54 Yokote Dc
55 Yonago Bc
54 Yonezawa Dc
89 Yonkers Jd
20 Yonne, R. & dept. Cc
65 York, Austral. Be
6 York, England Fd
89 York, U.S.A. Gd
62 York C. Ba
50 York Factory Eb
65 York Moors Fc
64 York Sd. Ca
6 Yorkshire, co. Fc
60 Yorkton Db
33 Yoronezh Ge
5 Yosemite National Park Cd
54 Yoshiwara Cc
9 Youghal Ce
13 Young Cb
88 Youngstown Ed
77 Yozgat Db
18 Ypres Bd
11 Ystad Cd
50 Yuanyang Ed
54 Yubari Db
54 Yubetsu Db
90 Yucatan, reg. Gd
91 Yucatan Str. Ab
4 Yugoslavia Jg
78 Yukon Bb
50 Yumen Db
44 Yungas reg. Bc
60 Yungera Bb
51 Yungtsi Fc
50 Yunnan, prov. Ed
54 Yuri Cd
13 Yverdon Ab

22 Zabrze Ec
90 Zacapa Gd
76 Zacatecas Dc
90 Zacoalco Dc
28 Zadar Eb
40 Zafed Bc
42 Zagan Cc
20 Zagharta Bb
28 Zagreb Eb
43 Zagros, mts. Fc
43 Zahedan Jd
30 Zaječar Cd
27 Zakinthos Bb
28 Zaklikow Gc
40 Zalau Db
69 Zambesi, R. Ec
69 Zambia Eg
12 Zambrunga Dc
30 Zamegerzeg Ab
90 Zamora, Mex. Dd
26 Zamora, Spain Aa
35 Zamosc Gc
22 Zanaga Ad
18 Zandvoort Db
23 Zanesville Ee
43 Zanjan Fc
65 Zanthus Ce
73 Zanzibar & I. Fe
70 Zaouiet Reggane Ec
93 Zapala Cf
33 Zaporozhye Gf
62 Zaragoza Ba
68 Zaria Gf
40 Zarqa, wadl Bc
22 Zary Cc
75 Zastron Dd
63 Zawada Gc
23 Zawichost Fc
33 Zawiercie Ec
12 Zdunska Wola Ec
18 Zeebrugge Cc
61 Zeehan Cd
75 Zeerust Cc
30 Zella Dd
18 Zeist Eb
26 Zeitz Ec
5 Zelechów Fc
32 Zelenodolsk Jd
68 Zella Dc
30 Zemun Cc
28 Zepce Gb
16 Zerbst Ec
13 Zermatt Bb
69 Zetland, co. Inset
22 Zgorzelec Cc
33 Zhdanov Gf
28 Zilagnak Fc
33 Zhitomir Ee
44 Zhob R. Bb
27 Zile Ea
75 Zimane Eb
75 Zimbabwe Eb
30 Zimmicea Ed
33 Zimovniki Hf
71 Zinder Gf
43 Zira Gd
27 Zivarik Db
52 Ziatoust Ld
22 Zlin (Gott-waldov) Dd
33 Znamenka Ff
23 Znojmo Db
13 Zofingen Ba
69 Zomba Fg
27 Zonguldak Da
36 Zrenjan Cc
18 Zuid Holland, prov. Dc
13 Zug Ca
33 Zugdidi Hg
73 Zululand, dist. Cc
71 Zungeru Gd
13 Zürich, & cant. Ca
13 Zürichsee, L. Ca
18 Zutphen Fb
25 Zwai, L. Gc
19 Zweibrücken Ge
13 Zweisimmen Bb
17 Zwettl Fd
17 Zwickau Ec
18 Zwischenahn Ga
18 Zwolle Fb
23 Zyrardów Fb
23 Zyrzyn Gc